MASTER OF LOVE AND MERCY

Dharma Master Cheng Yen, Master of Love and Mercy

"By reaching out I was given the gentle hands of the Bodhisattvas who guided my way through the pages of this book."

Yu-ing Ching

MASTER OF LOVE AND MERCY: CHENG YEN

by

Yu-ing Ching

Blue Dolphin Publishing
1995

Published by Blue Dolphin Publishing, Inc.
P.O. Box 1920, Nevada City, CA 95959
Phone: 916-265-6925
Orders: 1-800-643-0765

ISBN: 0-931892-27-9

    Library of Congress Cataloging-in-Publication Data

Ching, Yu-ing.
    Master of love and mercy / by Yu-ing Ching ; photography
by Bai Shang.
        p.   cm.
    ISBN 0-931892-27-9
    1. Cheng-yen, Shih.   2. Women Buddhist priests—Taiwan—
Biography. I. Title.
    BQ946.E547C55 1995
    294.3'092—dc20
    [B]   95-1191
                                                               CIP

Photos on front and back cover: Si Chi Ko
Photo of author, Yu-ing Ching: John LaPorte
Photo on page ii: Courtesy of the Tzu-chi Foundation
All other photos: Courtesy of Frank Bezine (Bai Shang)

Printed in the United States of America

10   9   8   7   6   5   4   3   2   1

TABLE OF CONTENTS

PROLOGUE

"Love and Mercy transcend races,
nationalities and geographical distance."

— Master Cheng Yen —

September 15

The phone rang, breaking the silence in a study shared by Shang—my husband—and I.

"Someone wants to speak to you," Shang said, handing me the receiver. "She says that she is Chinese."

I was surprised. We were in Bark River, Michigan, a peaceful small town where I was the only Chinese among a population of less than two thousand.

"She asked for Yu-ing Ching," Shang added.

"Wei," I took the receiver, using the Chinese term for "hello." "This is Yu-ing Ching."

"Ms. Yu-ing," the female voice was young and polite. "I'm sorry to trouble you. My name is Mary Yao and I'm calling from California. I'm a member of a . . . well, you can call us a Concerned Group. We've been trying to find you for quite some time."

The voice, filled with enthusiasm, continued, "We are concerned about a very important matter . . . we would like to know if you would be interested in writing a book."

"What kind of book?" I asked.

"The biography of Master Cheng Yen, to be written in English."

I nearly dropped the phone.

vi

Master Cheng Yen was the mother superior of Buddhism. I had just heard that she had been nominated for the Nobel Prize for Peace. She had millions of followers and was well-known by people in various regions throughout the globe.

* * *

December 15

With our suitcases packed, Shang and I sat across a low table from each other, sipped tea and looked out the window, watching the bare willow branches bending and shaking in a strong wind.

"Do you think your mother's spirit is responsible for your being contacted by this Concerned Group?" Shang suddenly asked.

I didn't answer. Turning from the window, I gazed toward a display case.

A silver chalice, a little less than a foot in height, stood behind glass doors. The strong rays from the winter sun pierced through the glass, reflecting off the brilliant surface with a golden inner light.

My mother had been a Buddhist all her ninety years of life. This chalice had become her incense burner when the Yu-ing family still lived in Ching-dau. In 1937, the Japanese invaded China, and my family was forced to escape on foot. There had been thirteen of us—my parents and nine children, plus my mother's older sister and my wet nurse; I was only twenty days old. The nurse carried me on her back. My father carried the youngest of my seven sisters who was two at the time. My mother, aunt, and the older children strained under the weight of what they had strapped on their backs and were holding in their arms: clothes, food, silver and gold, small antique pieces, and jewelry. The only item not essential to our survival had been Mother's silver chalice.

Keeping my eyes on the glowing chalice, I mumbled, "Shang, you may be right. Mother always wanted me to write a book centered around someone who teaches love and mercy. . . ."

The past reappeared in my mind. My vision was clouded by tears and the chalice became a small blur of yellow.

At the long journey's end, we had arrived in Nanjing after losing six of my sisters, some due to illness and the lack of medicine, the others a result of the Japanese soldiers' bullets. We lived in two rooms upstairs in an old farm house; the landlord and his five children lived downstairs. The only beautiful thing we had was the silver chalice, and Mother used to kneel with her hands in front of her and palms together, her face uplifted and her eyes following a thread of rising smoke. At that moment, all her sorrows seemed to have disappeared, and her lips were curved into a peaceful smile.

Shang reached across the table to take my hand. The warmth of his touch created a strength in me, enabling me to climb out of the gutter of grief. Blinking away the tears, I jumped up, grabbed the silver chalice and said, "Mother carried it from Nanjing to Shanghai and then to Taiwan. She took very few things with her when emigrating to America, but the chalice was in her suitcase. She used it to burn incense every day for the rest of her life, then gave it to me when realizing that her days on earth had become numbered. . . ."

I swallowed the lump in my throat and went on. "I would like to see the chalice returned to my homeland, be placed in a site where it can be appreciated far more than in our home here."

Without uttering a word, Shang began to help me wrap the chalice in layers of paper, then place it in my large purse.

❊ ❊ ❊

"I'm scared!" I said to Shang as our commuter plane with its eighteen passengers cut through the night air away from Michigan.

Shang looked at me questioningly.

I continued uneasily, "In the past three months, Mary Yao has mailed numerous books to me, and I have acquired more knowledge in both Buddhism and the life of Master Cheng Yen. But how can I write a book about a person who is known to be protected zealously by her followers and never willing to give an interview?" I asked.

The Concerned Group had the noble intention of seeing this book written for the pure sake of letting a great person like Master Cheng Yen be recognized by the world. But even with such a worthy goal, they had to leave the rest to the Master's own decision. I had learned from Mary Yao that no one could guarantee if the Master would make an exception for me: she was unenthusiastic about becoming the subject of any article or book; she had allowed reporters and writers to observe while she worked, but had never changed her busy schedule to sit down and answer the questions of any interviewer.

"Don't worry. Everything will work out just fine," Shang answered reassuringly, patting my hand.

We continued to fly, journeying towards Chicago where a jet plane would take us to Taiwan. Outside the oval window, a crescent moon shone brightly in the wintry sky, accompanied by a hundred million twinkling stars.

I stared out at the heavenly sight. When we were somewhere near Chicago and still more than five thousand feet above the ground, suddenly, in the silver beams of the moon and the glimmering light of the stars, I saw a woman.

Her face was porcelain smooth but her hair silver white. She had a long robe that was a part of the clouds and covering her, except her head. She nodded at me, and the next moment parted her lips slightly. She did not make any tangible sound; however, I could hear her uttering my childhood name.

"Ching-ching," she called, then continued soundlessly to relate a message I alone could receive, "There is no need to fear or worry."

The next moment she paused, tilting her head to one side, gesturing towards my purse and reminding me of its content.

I reached for my purse and touched the bulky bundle, feeling the silver chalice inside.

Outside the window and among the clouds, my mother's image resumed speaking in a voice that was meant for the comprehension of no one but her daughter. "Offer the chalice to the Master, and see if she will accept it. . . . Perhaps there is a place in the Master's temple for the chalice, and perhaps everything will go smoothly for you. . . ."

The vision of my mother smiled, and the next instant it began to fade. I leaned tightly against the window, gluing my forehead to the icy glass. Don't go, Mama! Please stay with me a while longer!

"Ching-ching, my silly child, dry your tears!" Mother's voice continued to echo in my soul as the view of her started to melt into the moonbeams and the starlight. "I am with you and in you, just like Buddha is in us and with us all the time. You and I are not truly parted, and of course I'll help you to write this book!"

PART ONE

THE PURE ABODE
OF
STILL THOUGHTS

The Tzu-chi Foundation Building in Taipei, Taiwan

CHAPTER ONE

*"All lives deserve to be respected, and all beings need to be loved.
It ought to be easy for us to feel the pain experienced by
the bodies other than our own and grant happiness
to those who are but strangers."*

— *Master Cheng Yen* —

A SMALL BLACK CAR picked us up in front of the Lai Lai Sheraton Hotel in Taipei. After driving on the busy main road for a while, our pace slowed to a crawl. The driver weaved his way through the narrow street where cars were parked on both sides, leaving only enough room for a single car at a time. There were places where we had to back up and edge into a wider space in order to let a car coming from the opposite direction get through. At times we passed so closely to another vehicle that the driver had to retract the mirrors on either side, a feature that seems to come as a standard on all cars in Taiwan. After traveling for a long time in this concrete gorge of tall buildings, we stopped at a large white structure several stories high.

"This is the Taipei Hall of Buddhist Compassion Relief Tzu-chi Foundation, a charity organization established by Master Cheng Yen in 1966," said Alex Chow, a young man fluent in several languages and flawless in English, our escort arranged by the Concerned Group. "The Master is here today, and it's a good way for you to meet her."

I looked at the Tzu-chi Hall in awe. All the Buddhist temples that I knew were fashioned in gold, red, and green. This gleaming white hall was stunning and yet so different from what I had imagined.

We were greeted by a sea of blue—there were numerous men in navy suits and women in dark blue dresses. With hands in front of them, palms touching and fingers pointing skyward, they smiled at us warmly and greeted us with easy bows.

We returned their bows and copied their gesture. Alex led us through the crowd and up a flight of stone steps. We entered a large, sparklingly clean room that looked like a library, with shelves packed with books and long tables displaying pamphlets.

"Take anything you want," a young lady in dark blue smiled at us and said, "This literature is free. If you are willing to read them, we'll be extremely grateful for your interest in Tzu-chi."

After climbing several more flights of concrete steps, we moved down a long corridor and reached the assembly hall where we were asked to remove our shoes before entering.

The hall was immense, the ceiling breathtakingly high. The wooden floor was polished to a mirror shine, and there were tall windows to let in the morning light. The light, reflecting from the floor, gave the entire place a golden glow. Every inch of the floor was occupied by people sitting cross-legged on large gray pillows, their stocking feet covered by small gray blankets. I estimated the number to be at least four hundred. Glancing up, I discovered a balcony extending on three sides with more men and women in dark blue peering down.

"All the men and women of the Tzu-chi Foundation wear the same color," Alex explained. "It is said that Master Cheng Yen designed the uniform, choosing dark blue as a color of humbleness and patience."

We were given a spot against the wall near the front of the room, then offered pillows and blankets. Sitting on my pillow, and with my feet modestly concealed by the blanket, I looked at the raised platform a few yards away.

A massive carved Buddha stood in a recess, reaching towards the high ceiling. On the altar a few candles were burning near a large display of fresh flowers, their fragrance filling the hall. I could hear myself breathing, the place so quiet that I could detect the sound of the wind blowing through a row of ancient pine trees standing outside the open windows.

I was amazed by the simple elegance of this room. There were no gaudy colors nor flashy ornaments, no incense to fill the place with smoke nor the burning of paper money to create an unpleasant odor.

"It's not like any of the Buddhist temples I ever saw. . . ," I whispered to Shang, then stopped in mid-sentence.

A deeper hush had suddenly fallen over the hall, as if all the people in this massive room had stopped breathing. The next moment the entire congregation rose to their feet without a sound. Shang and I got up clumsily and almost tripped over the blankets tangled around our feet. Everyone was looking at a door beside the altar. Following their eyes, we had our first sight of Master Cheng Yen.

Gliding gracefully and soundlessly, her fragile body appeared to be floating on air. She was wearing a wide-sleeved, soft gray robe, long enough to allow me only a glimpse of her feet covered in white, high socks. Guided by a disciple on either side, she stepped up onto the platform and approached the podium. Stopping at stage center, she turned slowly and faced the audience.

Her round face had a celestial glow as she looked around. Her large penetrating eyes shone with not only wisdom and authority, but also gentleness and compassion. The assembly brought their hands up, palms together, bowed deeply. She returned the greeting. After everyone sat back down, she cleared her throat and moved closer to the microphone. After explaining that she could not speak loudly because of her cold, she began to lecture without reading from any paper.

It was a speech to thank a group of followers who had gone to various places in mainland China to help the victims of a recent flood. Her voice was soft as a whisper, her tone gentle as a breeze, her words unhurried like a comforting hand, and yet her sermon had enough power to shake the earth. She used the simplest words to convey deep thoughts, and the most understandable examples to interpret complicated theories.

Her audience was captivated. She started to describe the suffering of the homeless in China, and men and women alike reached for their handkerchiefs. ". . . All lives deserve to be respected, and all beings need to be loved. It ought to be easy for us to feel the pain experienced by the bodies other than our own and grant happiness to those who are but strangers . . . ," she went on.

Observing from a distance, my admiration for the Master was born. It had never been so easy for me to admire anyone. Surprised at myself, I turned to Shang, who had been busy watching everything and listening to Alex's translation of the Master's words. I asked under my breath, "What do you think of the Master?"

"Impressive and amazing!" Shang murmured his answer, his face the face of a boy in wonderland. "Not only the Master, but also everyone else! We've been to churches before, but no place is like this! I can feel a strong sense of love and peace. And I've also noticed something extraordinary: the Master and her followers never voiced their requests to Buddha—'Grant us this, oh God!' 'Give us that, oh Lord!'—those are the most frequently used sentences in all church services that you and I have ever attended."

Shang paused to listen to more of Alex's translation, then continued in greater disbelief, "The Master is talking about nothing but how to help others. You can search the audience, and not find one face that looks bored or impatient. How can the Master make her followers forget to be self-centered? It seems that by this time a congregation would be saying with their weary eyes: Come on, let's forget the others! How about me and all the things that I want?"

Up on the podium, the Master continued with her sermon. "The act of asking for things from others can cause disappointment and distress, while the deed of giving can only result in happiness and satisfaction. It is a privilege to extend our helping hands to people regardless of who or what or where they are . . . love and mercy transcends races, nationalities and geographical distance. And we owe our hearty thanks to our receivers, because it is their unfortunate condition that makes it possible for us to know the joy of giving. . . ."

Shang and I looked at each other, our bewilderment written in our eyes, but we were lost for words.

*"We are all human beings, the best of us a saint, but never a god.
We can follow a saint's conduct and imitate his behavior,
but it is unnecessary to worship him."*

— *Master Cheng Yen* —

When I entered the room, my eyes were immediately drawn to Master Cheng Yen.

Long wooden tables formed an open square in the middle of the room, and the Master was sitting at one end. Hanging on the wall behind her was a framed picture of her standing in the assembly hall in front of Buddha. There were glass-door cabinets on every wall, and behind the glass could be seen volume after volume of what were apparently books on Buddhism and the Master's accomplishment, and Tzu-chi information.

We were apprehensive about approaching her. We took two chairs off to one side and watched as she talked to one of the followers. After a while, my right shoulder began to ache from the large purse hanging from it—the pressure was caused by the weight of the silver chalice in it.

I had wanted very badly to offer the chalice to the Master, but was now too shy to take action. I looked at Shang, and whispered to him that he should present the chalice.

He took the chalice reluctantly. When the Master was free, he approached her and presented the chalice to her. People watched and stopped talking. The room was very quiet as everyone waited for the Master's reaction.

The Master took the chalice from Shang and held it in her small hands to examine it closely. Then she put the chalice on the table and took out her glasses to look at it more carefully.

The three-legged chalice was about eleven inches high. At the base of each leg was the face of an animal. The legs were attached to a round-bodied base with several inscriptions; they were in ancient Chinese and not even I could tell what their meanings were. There was a smaller rounded section above the base and another smaller section with a carved opening to allow air in and the smoke

The author and her husband, Bai Shang,
offer the silver chalice to the Master

The author, Mrs. S. J. Wen, and the Master

of the incense to escape. A lid fit snugly on top. The carved workmanship of vines and leaves was exquisite.

The Master removed her glasses, lifted her head and looked toward me, smiled and beckoned me to join her.

I had been told that it was almost impossible for anyone to persuade the Master to accept anything. Afraid that she would turn down my gift, I said defensively as quickly as I reached her, "Master Cheng Yen, it's all right if you don't want it. It is my mother's treasure and sort of a family heirloom, but I'll understand if you don't like it."

Glancing at the tables that were piled high with things donated by others for the upcoming charity auction, I hurried on, "If you wish, Master, you can sell it at the auction."

At that very instant, my heart ached. Mother would cry in heaven if her cherished chalice should fall into some unappreciative hands.

With her eyes on my face, the Master shook her head slowly. Her understanding smile gave me the impression that she had read my mind. "Your mother's chalice is not going to the auction. Our memorial hall is at its last stage of construction. Upon its opening, the chalice will have a permanent place there."

My heart beat fast and a large lump rose in my throat. I bowed my head to hide the sudden tears in my eyes, and was able to recapture the image of my mother that had appeared among the clouds outside the airplane window.

I called soundlessly: Mama, the Master has found a perfect home for your precious chalice, and I am ready to start on that book.

The Master and I talked for a few minutes more. I had many questions to ask, but restrained myself from asking, for I felt that this was not the time. More people arrived. Shang and I moved to give them room. Withdrawing to a remote corner, we watched some of them approaching the Master with their eyes filled with tears and dropping to their knees. The Master tried to get them to rise and appeared to be somewhat uncomfortable with their gesture of supreme respect.

Her reaction to people's kowtowing reminded me of what she had written in one of her many books:

*The Master and the Tzu-chi members
from all parts of Taiwan and also overseas*

"We are all human beings, the best of us a saint, but never a god. We can follow a saint's conduct and imitate his behavior, but it is unnecessary to worship him."

As the people began to talk, the Master's brows were gathered in concentration, absorbing every word and action of the speaker. Her lips were parted a little, ready to encourage and comfort. It was at this moment that I noticed, although her head was shaved and she wore no worldly adornment, her beauty was divine and eternal, her presence commanding and irresistible.

"The Master is running a fever and has been sick for several days . . . ," someone nearby whispered.

Watching the Master closely, I could not see any sign of illness. At one point, however, there was a lull and she relaxed. The exhaustion she must have been feeling all this time suddenly appeared on her face; her shoulders dropped and my heart reached out to her. The next instant a young woman approached. By the time the Master turned toward the woman, all signs of the weariness vanished and once again the Master's radiance filled the room.

Witnessing this, my admiration for her quickly flowered into a strong affection, and to write about her turned into a pleasure.

Mr. and Mrs. C. C. Lee, Honorary Members
of the Tzu-chi Foundation

"Shang," I turned to my husband, "We must start to interview as many of the Tzu-chi members as we can. If you think of the Master as the moon and each of the followers as a lake reflecting her image, then it is imperative that we look into the many reflections in order to better understand the Master."

CHAPTER TWO

"Life is a journey;
we board an express train at birth
and head for the unavoidable destination of death.
The scenery drifts by, and the only meaningful thing we can do
is to be good and kind to our fellow passengers."

— *Master Cheng Yen* —

Mr. Chung Chi Lee was a large man. From looking at him today, you could not help but think that in his youth he must have had the body of an athlete. His shoulders were wide and he was barrel-chested, but age had given him an ample mid-section. His kind face was broad, with intelligent eyes set far apart, and a straight aquiline nose. He wore a dark two-piece suit and, because Taiwan was having a cold wave, a wool cardigan sweater. His shirt was white and his tie blue with white diagonal stripes. The pointed edge of a white handkerchief was neatly tucked into his breast pocket.

We were in the Tzu-chi Hall, in one of the many small rooms. In the center of the room was a long table on which were cups of hot tea for everyone. Mr. Lee sat with his big hands together and fingers interlocked. On his left wrist he wore prayer beads made of yellow stone—an item that could be seen on all Tzu-chi members.

"We of the Tzu-chi Foundation believe in Truth, Virtue, and Beauty. We try to be selfless and most sincere in whatever we say and do. We don't believe in burning incense or in similar rituals, since good deeds mean much more than creating smoke." He spoke in a soft, gentle voice.

"The Tzu-chi Foundation's full name is Buddhist Compassion Relief Tzu-chi Foundation. It was established in 1966 by our Master, along with five disciples and thirty devoted followers. All shared her dream: to help the needy. It was financed with no more than fifty cents of daily savings from each of thirty housewives, plus what each disciple earned from sewing one additional pair of baby shoes per day. From this humble beginning the Foundation today, in Taiwan alone, has a membership of over three million, and of this number there are three thousand commissioners."

He went on to explain the difference between a member and a commissioner. Both were followers of the Master; the commissioners, however, were the central figures of the Foundation responsible for collecting the monthly donations, and making family visits and case reports on the afflicted and poor.

I listened intently as he continued. "The Foundation's four major projects are charity, medicine, education and culture. All of us members work as one, pursuing the realization of our Master's goal, which is: 'one eye observing as one thousand eyes, and one hand functioning as one thousand hands.' I am in my seventies now, and my shipping fleet no longer requires my full attention. It gives me great pleasure to participate in the Foundation, and I am proud to be a Commissioner."

The Tzu-chi members are subdivided into eleven groups. Mr. Lee belonged to the group of Honorary Board Members, who gave most generously in both time and money—an Honorary Board Member's donation started at the amount of NT$1,000,000, equivalent to $40,000 U.S.

Mr. Lee was the chairman of Kee Yeh Maritime Corporation but was known in Taiwan as a self-made man. Once upon a time, nylon stockings were a rarity, and if runs appeared, women would find ways to mend them. Mr. Lee had been so destitute that Mrs. Lee had helped put food on the table by taking in stockings that needed mending.

Mrs. Lee, although dressed simply without any jewelry or makeup, still gave people the impression that she was a lady of refinement. Throughout the interview she sat quietly next to her husband and only occasionally interrupted to whisper a few words to remind him of something he might have overlooked. According to the lunar calendar, it was the first day of winter. Carrying out the role of a considerate hostess, she asked the kitchen workers to bring us bowls of sweet dumplings, made from powdered glutinous rice, floating in a thin soup.

"Eat while the soup is still steaming," she said with a friendly smile, nodding to Shang and me. "It's good for your health to eat something sweet and hot at the beginning of winter . . . it will give your body the strength to face the coming cold weather."

Her words stirred in her husband a reminder, and he said with a sigh, "No matter what we eat, our body will perish eventually, and our duration on earth is but a short one. Our Master realized this when she was still a young girl, but I didn't see it until I was already an old man.

"I had a stroke a few years ago, almost died. When recovered, I realized the impermanence of my body and my wealth and everything else, and started to search for the truth of life. I talked to many ministers and priests, and also monks of all denominations. They couldn't satisfy my searching, nor could they help me make life more meaningful. I finally had the chance to meet Master Cheng Yen. After listening to her for only an hour, my view of life changed. So, life is not empty when you spend it on helping others and benefiting mankind! I made an appointment to see the Master, and soon after that became one of her devoted followers.

"The Master believes that life is a journey; we board an express train at birth and head for the unavoidable destination of death. The scenery drifts by, and the only meaningful thing we can do is to be good and kind to our fellow passengers. . . ."

Mr. Lee stopped when someone knocked on the door.

A young lady entered. She was beautiful with an oval face and white clear skin. She wore her lustrous black hair shoulder length and in soft waves, and not a trace of makeup. She smiled at us, and there appeared two dimples creating a vision of innocence.

"Yee-hui, our daughter," Mr. Lee introduced proudly. "We have three girls, each just as good, if not better, than any boy. They are also my business associates, helping me to run the company. Yee-hui is also a Tzu-chi Commissioner, and her other name is Josephine . . . she can speak English very well."

Shang's interpreter, Alex Chow, had to go somewhere. All this while, the conversation was taking place in Chinese. Shang could understand only a fragment of what was being said. Besides taking pictures and keeping the recorder going, he had been staring at us and was obviously bored.

"Mr. and Mrs. Lee, may I have your permission to allow my husband to interview your daughter in another room?" I asked eagerly.

The Lee couple nodded, and Shang left with Miss Lee.

Mr. Lee resumed.

"In the summer of 1991, there was this great flood in eastern China. More than 220 million people were affected. The Master instructed us to give relief to the most devastated areas.

"Since 1949, the people in mainland China and those in Taiwan have been living under the rule of two different governments. But the Master's teaching is that all beings are but members of one family, that we should love, trust, and forgive all living creatures under heaven . . . by the way, have you heard of our song?"

Without waiting for my answer, taking a deep breath, Mr. Lee started to sing. It was a simple but captivating song, the lyrics composed by the Master herself:

Under heaven, there is no one that I don't love.
Under heaven, there is no one that I don't trust.
Under heaven, there is no one that I don't forgive.
Therefore there is no anger, regret, or sorrow in my heart.

Mr. Lee proceeded to describe his experience in mainland China:

"The first group of us Tzu-chi members consisted of only six people, and our mission was to persuade the mainland Chinese government to grant us permission to help the flood victims. After conquering numerous obstacles, we succeeded and found over five thousand families living in twenty-two different towns who needed help desperately.

"We returned home to report what we saw to the Master. Starting August, 1991, the Tzu-chi members began to work hard in raising funds. Prominent businessmen not only donated large amounts but also went to street corners to collect money from those passing by. Wealthy ladies also stood in public places, selling jasmine flowers grown by themselves.

"By February of 1992, after only six months, the Foundation had already collected, in Taiwan money, four hundred and twelve million dollars, equivalent to about sixteen million dollars in American money. And after that, more trips were made by a great many Tzu-chi members, heading for mainland China and carrying with them not only monetary assistance but also love and mercy.

"We did all this with Master Cheng Yen's teaching in mind: 'The only meaningful thing we can do is to be good and kind to our fellow passengers on this express train!'"

*"A happy person creates a happy home,
and from that is able to contribute to his country
and finally the world."*

— *Master Cheng Yen and Confucius* —

"Josephine Lee, or Mrs. Chen, became a Tzu-chi Foundation member by following her parents' example," Shang said.

Shang and I were still in the Tzu-chi Hall, but alone and on a patio overlooking the city of Taipei. Glancing down, we could see the traffic darting in every direction, like small toy cars riding on an electric track and, at any moment, one of them could take flight and crash into any of the tall buildings. In front of us on a low table a dwarfed maple, probably several decades old, was trimmed into a bonsai. Facing the modern city and at the same moment an ancient form of art, Shang continued to talk.

"The Foundation's home base is in Hwalien, a quiet city southeast of Taipei and more than three hours by train from Josephine's home. There are always people interested in visiting the Master who spends most of her time in Hwalien, and Josephine frequently volunteers to be their escort," he went on.

Four years ago, Josephine still had no idea what a lucky woman she was. Her parents' difficult days were over when she was born. Raised in luxury, she had taken everything for granted, including her husband.

He was a good man, absolutely dependable. When she really needed him, he was always there. Honest, hard-working and stable, he was not a dreamer. He had given her his complete devotion and undivided loyalty, but showed few romantic gestures. He was a practical man who seldom thought of surprising her with flowers.

Living an elegant life, she was not totally happy. She felt that whatever her husband had already given her was but what he owed her, and that he should give her much more.

During one of her trips to Hwalien, while showing people the Master's temple of residence, the Pure Abode of Still Thoughts, Josephine had found herself face-to-face with the Master.

"So, you are here again," the Master commented and then asked, "Doesn't your husband mind?"

"No," Josephine answered in bewilderment. "Why should he?"

The Master looked at her deeply and said calmly, "You have a very good husband. You should be very grateful and appreciate him more."

The Master's words continued to linger in Josephine's mind. During the long ride on the train, she started to count the things that were in her husband's favor: he never drinks or gambles, and he always comes directly home after work. . . .

His good points continued to grow, and by the time she reached home, he appeared to be different from the person she had seen before.

Josephine had told Shang, "He was sitting on the sofa, reading his evening paper as he always did. But one look at him and I found him more lovable than ever. I suddenly realized just how much he has been giving me, and how lucky I have been all this time. It was then that I decided, even if he is not a romantic man, I can still be a romantic woman. It was foolish of me to wait for him to say 'I love you' first. Well . . ." Josephine had smiled with true happiness glowing in her eyes, "I never waited from then on."

Shang paused to pick a brown leaf off the bonsai, and I murmured, "The Master must be watching and observing her followers closely, and has the ability to perceive their personal life. Among all things, she has to be the best marriage counselor. Without any of the long sessions on a leather coach, she has changed Josephine into a better wife and a happier woman."

Nodding in agreement, Shang said, "And the Master's teaching seems to reinforce Confucius' philosophy: a happy person creates a happy home, and from that is able to contribute to his country and finally the world.

"After becoming a better wife and a happier woman, Josephine was able to give much more of herself to people less fortunate than she."

*"To study Buddhism under me is to adopt
a new way of life."*

— *Master Cheng Yen* —

We were in an office complex owned by Mr. and Mrs. Ming Der Wang. There was a low table. Across the room was a large desk, and behind it, recessed in the wall, were an illuminated altar with a white statue of Kwan-yin and two vases containing fresh flowers.

Mrs. Wang said, "I was with a group of women, each an affluent lady, arranging flowers as a hobby. My girlfriend and I were quiet as we listened to the others talking. They were describing the fine clothes and extravagant jewelry that they had recently acquired, comparing, competing, and showing off."

She had a youthful, round face framed by short, wavy hair that was exquisitely coifed. Her chin came delicately to a rounded point, her narrow mouth the shape of a miniature bow curving upward. Her most striking feature was her sparkling eyes, resembling pools that contained black water while burning with a mesmerizing fire. She reminded me of the waves that embraced the Hawaiian islands—soft and lovely, at the same time with an energy that was lashing and forceful. Unlike the other Tzu-chi Commissioners, she was wearing a pale green suit instead of dark blue dress. She had on only a faint touch of makeup, her only jewel the prayer beads on her left wrist.

"All of a sudden, something inside me stirred. The women's voices began to fade, and their words turned meaningless," Mrs. Wang continued. "My girlfriend must have felt the same way. She and I exchanged looks and read each other's mind: There has to be more to life than this!"

While talking, Mrs. Wang busily shelled chestnuts. She watched me devour the first chestnut she had offered and saw how much I liked them. Insisting that I was too busy taking notes to shell them myself, she had been feeding me. Her unpretentious manner and easy-going personality made it difficult for me to believe that she was the wife of a most successful business tycoon.

Mr. Ming Der Wang was the president of the Der Jey Affiliated Organizations that owned at least five large companies. Real estate development was one of the main enterprises, urban construction another, and, on top of everything, the Ming Der Department Stores. The building we were in was designed and constructed by him.

"I went home and waited with a strong feeling that something was about to happen . . . something that would change my life by showing me the way to life's true meaning. A few days later, a woman knocked on my door. When shown in, she introduced herself as a Tzu-chi Commissioner," Mrs. Wang said, pushing towards me a white napkin containing more shelled chestnuts. "She asked me to make a small donation and I did. It was such an insignificant amount that when she wanted to give me a receipt, I told her that it was unnecessary. But the woman insisted that she must write me the receipt, saying that the Tzu-chi Foundation believed in doing things in a proper manner. And then this woman said something that I had never heard before. . . ."

Mrs. Wang paused, leaned closer to her husband who was sitting next to her and placed a hand on his shoulder. "The woman told me that to the Tzu-chi Foundation there is no such thing as an 'insignificant amount of contribution,' and that fifty cents and fifty million are equal in value as long as both the givers are truly sincere. When she told me that she was quoting Master Cheng Yen's words, I knew I must meet the Master.

"I met the Master in 1982, in Taipei, and immediately felt that my soul belonged to her. Without hesitation, I was determined to become her follower, but the Master didn't accept me right away. She said that all her followers must participate in the Tzu-chi Foundation, that to study Buddhism under her is to adopt a new way of life carried out in the Foundation's daily function. She also told me that if I really wanted to become a part of the Foundation, I must vow to devote myself, to give generously, and to do relief work to help the needy. She made certain that I understood that a half-hearted member is not what the Foundation needed or wanted."

Mrs. Wang squared her shoulders and lifted her head, her commitment to the Foundation disclosed in both her firm voice and her gleaming eyes. "The Master's words did not discourage me.

Soon after that I paid my first visit to the Tzu-chi Hall in Hwalien—the Pure Abode of Still Thoughts. That place was magical, and it grabbed my soul as did the Master. As a result of that trip, I became even more dedicated in my commitment. I've been a part of the Tzu-chi Foundation for over ten years now—first as a member, a year later, after proving my worthiness in every way, I became a Commissioner—and my life in the past decade has been more wonderful than it had ever been."

A warm glow appeared from within Mrs. Wang, intensifying her radiance and giving her a breathtaking appearance. Her voice was filled with emotion as she continued, "While loving my husband and a son and a daughter and friends and relatives, there is also room in my heart to love those who are but strangers. For years I had been searching for a way to deliver my love, and finally the Tzu-chi Foundation showed me the way.

"It is because of Master Cheng Yen that my lifestyle was completely changed. Instead of doing useless things, I've been participating in much of the relief work and donating money, strengthening the Foundation's ability to give to the needy, to build schools and hospitals, and to carry out a variety of other good deeds."

"A person's power is as strong as his wish.
Therefore a man should be self-reliant instead of depending
on anyone . . . not even Buddha."

— *Master Cheng Yen* —

"I have always been a Buddhist," said Mr. Wang, "but did not become an Honorary Board Member of the Tzu-chi Foundation until much later. Actually, it was because of my wife. She was donating money to the Foundation, and I was afraid that someone was taking advantage of her. So I followed her to one of their meetings to inspect the situation.

"As soon as I met the Master, I knew that I must follow her, like a sunflower must look up towards the sun and a hummingbird must fly towards a flower. And it didn't take me long to see that the Tzu-chi Foundation is a great organization and my wife was doing the most wonderful thing she could possibly do under heaven.

"My wife and I have been participating side-by-side for almost ten years now, and we will continue to do so for the rest of our days on earth," Mr. Ming Der Wang said in a low melodic voice, sitting back and looking extremely relaxed.

He was tall and slim, with an oblong face and pleasant features. He was immaculately dressed in a tailored light gray suit, a pale lavender shirt, and a darker lavender tie with a surrealistic design. The way he carried himself gave one the immediate impression of a brilliant man, sure of himself and knowing how to get what he wanted out of life. However, he could not be further from what was fixed in my mind by the image of a tycoon: loud-mouthed, self-important, and reluctant to give up his valuable time to a mere writer. With his gentle manner and warm smile, he quickly put me at ease in this elegant room that was only one corner of his empire.

Sipping his tea, Mr. Wang said, "The Master's words affected me in ways more than I can count. For instance, the Master says, 'A person's power is as strong as his wish. Therefore a man should be self-reliant instead of depending on anyone . . . not even Buddha.' And it helped me to realize that my being a Buddhist doesn't give me the right to pray to Buddha and expect Buddha to perform miracles for me. Buddha is a man. But since his wisdom, courage and perseverance are superior to those of all men, he is also a saint. Only a greedy and foolish man will think of Buddha as a wish-granting God, and then offer Buddha a promise, or the light of a few candles, or the fragrance of some incense, therefore expecting Buddha to give him whatever he wants in return.

"A good Buddhist must try his best to bring out the Buddha within himself, to strengthen his own courage, perseverance and wisdom, and be able to acquire the life he yearns for through his own hard work."

After a pause, Mr. Wang frowned as he continued, "However, it is not easy for a man to be courageous, persistent and clever at all times . . . especially when facing misfortune or devastation. I had lost my composure a short time ago, when I was about to lose a large tract of land, for such loss just might lead to bankruptcy."

The recollection of this almost catastrophic experience darkened Mr. Wang's face. He turned towards his wife. She smiled at him with love and comfort. The next moment the bad memory was swept away and there no longer appeared the dark shadow in his eyes.

Mr. Wang went on with his usual peacefulness, "I went to the Master, had a long talk with her. She calmed me down and told me that things will be all right. She also instructed me to go to the opposing party who was trying to take the land from me, to confront him peacefully but unbendingly.

"I followed the Master's instruction. Because of her reassurance, during the meeting I was unafraid, confident, and determined. The outcome of the meeting was much better than what I had been fearing. I still ended up losing some of my land, but only about one fourth of what my opponent wished to take. The incident was far from a crushing blow. I recovered quickly and now no longer feel the loss.

"The Master saved me, that is true. But the Master did not tell me to do this or that for the temple and then wait for my problems to be solved by some mysterious power. Instead, the Master brought out the best in me, which enabled me to solve the problem as successfully as I did. Well, that's enough of that incident!"

Mr. Wang shook his head, as if shaking off the past. "Our Master also says that the past has to be forgotten, or one will never be able to progress into the future—a man cannot move forward if his right foot takes a new step but his left foot still clings to the old ground.

"My future plan is also based on the Master's teaching: to walk carefully and speak with caution, while carrying my ambition on my left shoulder and my devotion on my right," Mr. Wang said with a confident smile, his eyes lingering on his wife and filled with enthusiasm. "For the rest of my life, I'll proceed to be a good husband and father, a productive businessman, a devout Buddhist, and a hard-working member of the Tzu-chi Foundation."

CHAPTER THREE

*"Most of the disasters and calamities in this world
are created by people who have complete body and limbs
but incomplete mind and spirit."*

— *Master Cheng Yen* —

A T 7 AM Shang and I entered the restaurant located in the hotel lobby. We were surrounded by Christmas trees, each beautifully decorated, the colorful lights reflecting in our crystal glass and silverware. Jingle Bells was followed by Silent Night, both translated into Chinese and sung by a man with a soft voice.

"I'm homesick," I sighed. "I miss our own tree!"

"No matter how great this hotel is, it's just not the same," Shang agreed. "I, too, miss Christmas at home."

My heart was heavy as we walked out of the hotel, thinking we should have waited until after Christmas to come to Taipei. The air was cold and damp and there was a light rain. We were met by Mrs. Su Jen Wen, a Commissioner of the Tzu-chi Foundation who had been most helpful and always had the loveliest smile. She introduced a group of ladies to us, all Commissioners of the Foundation and wearing the same dark blue uniform. We entered a mini bus, and Mrs. Wen began to prepare us for the journey:

"The Foundation receives money from contributors and gives it to the poor. We'll take you to one of our contributors and also one of our receivers."

The brighter side of Taipei began to diminish and the darker side came into view. As if a page had been turned on a picture album, the glorious image was replaced by an image of despair. When we reached the entrance of a narrow alley, the van could go no further.

Walking through the back streets, we passed many stands, each cooking their special variety of finger-food. Deep puddles appeared like small lakes in the potholes that were everywhere. Also along this alley men, women and children were standing or squatting in front of their homes, washing or cooking or doing other chores in the rain. There was a foul smell, and the noise was ear-shattering. Mrs. Wen stopped at one of the buildings and we began to climb the wet concrete steps to the second floor. She knocked on the door. It opened slowly, the rusty hinges grinding in protest.

We were greeted by a neatly dressed young woman who introduced herself as a government social worker. We walked through a narrow hallway, and Mrs. Wen guided us into a room no larger than eight by eight feet.

A woman was lying on a cotton mat. She smiled up at us, displaying a few yellow teeth. Rolling her head from side to side, she squealed out a series of sounds. I could not understand her, but the Tzu-chi Commissioners could; they had been visiting her so often that they had learned to make sense of the noises that were unintelligible to my ears.

Mrs. Wen interpreted for me, "Lin-mei Chai says that she is very happy to see us, and that she always looks forward to our twice-a-month visit."

Mrs. Wen introduced me to Lin-mei, and I forced out a cheerful greeting as I studied the woman. Her black hair was cut short, showing a few strands of gray. She was dressed in black slacks, a gray cotton blouse and a blue sweater.

"Lin-mei is fifty-three-years-old," Mrs. Wen said. "At the age of two she had polio. At age thirty-five her parents died and she began to live with her younger brother and his wife. At the age of forty-three she suffered from rheumatic fever. The fever raged for days. Her brother and his wife ignored her condition, resenting having to take care of her. As a result of the burning fever, she lost her ability to speak intelligibly. But she can continue to think clearly, and always knows what is going on."

Once again, Lin-mei started to roll her head, her mouth working, and she squealed out something.

Mrs. Wen translated for me again, "She is trying to say that she missed the days when she could speak well, but does not hold any bad feelings towards her brother and his wife . . . who had not been by to see her for a long time."

I had no doubt that Chai Lin-mei was a charity case and a receiver of aid, and I asked, "How long has the Tzu-chi Foundation been supporting this poor woman?"

"No," Mrs. Wen answered quickly, "We are not supporting Lin-mei at all!"

Mrs. Wen began to tell us that when the Foundation first discovered Lin-mei in 1986, she was deserted by her brother and left to die in a shack. The Foundation Members helped her in many ways including teaching her Buddhism. When they showed her a picture of Master Cheng Yen, tears poured out of her eyes and her whole body shook. She then reached with both hands to bring the picture to her heart. She held the picture there for a long time, and when finally letting go of the picture there was a beautiful peaceful smile on her face.

The government was unaware of her existence at the time. The Foundation brought her to this rooming house, and started to provide for her at the cost of NT$3,600 per month, an equivalent of about $150 U.S.

It wasn't until 1989 that the government was able to put Lin-mei on the list of the needy. Ever since then, Lin-mei has been receiving a monthly allowance and daily visits by a social worker who cooks for her and takes care of the rest of her needs. The young woman who opened the door for us was her current social worker.

"This may surprise you," Mrs. Wen said with her gentle smile. "As soon as Lin-mei started to receive governmental help, she informed us that she no longer needed our money."

Waving an arm around the spartan room, Mrs. Wen sighed, "Of course, if willing to accept help from both the government and us,

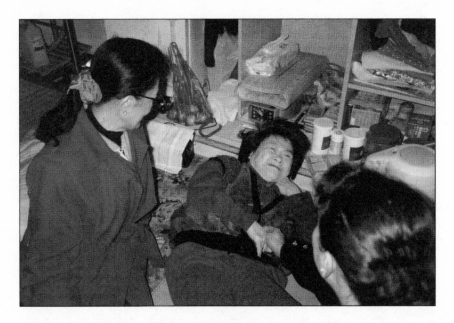

Ms. Lin-mei Chai

Lin-mei would be able to live much better. We are still willing to help her, but she is adamant in her conviction and insists that her share of the Foundation fund should be used on others who are in worse shape than she."

From her thin cotton mat, Lin-mei shouted out something else. Mrs. Wen said, "Lin-mei says that the government gives her more than NT$3,600 a month, and she does not need all that money to live on. All she needs is rice, vegetables and a few strips of meat now and then. She already has everything else, so it is only right that she should give the rest of the money to the ones who are not as rich as she."

Mrs. Wen continued proudly, "Yes, Lin-mei Chai is one of the contributors and also a member of the Tzu-chi Foundation. She donates all that she can spare monthly, and wants us to collet it at the end of each month."

Rolling her head from side to side, a large grin appeared on Lin-mei's face. I had grown somewhat accustomed to her way of speaking, and was now able to make out what she was saying. "You see . . . I don't . . . date much anymore. So I . . . don't have to

spend a lot of money on clothes . . . high-heel shoes . . . perfume
. . . or at the . . . beauty parlor."

She began to laugh. I was astonished by her sense of humor.
Staring at her, I asked, "You have been lying like this for ten years,
and yet you can joke about things. Has it always been easy for you
to laugh?"

"No. . . !" Lin-mei struggled to answer. ". . . it is much . . . much
easier to cry. . . !"

Gathering all the strength that she had, she made a motion
towards a shelf in back of her.

Following her gesture, I saw a small television and resting on
top of it was an unframed picture of Master Cheng Yen.

". . . I look at the picture of the . . . Master. . . ! And I . . . listen
to her tapes. . . ! And it . . . becomes . . . e . . . easier!" she said. "But
. . . before I learned that the . . . Master is in my heart and . . . Buddha
and Kwan-yin are also with me . . . I . . . cried all the time!"

The room was not heated. But beads of sweat appeared on her
forehead as she labored to get more words out, the effort taking its
toll. "The M. . . Master says . . . Having a . . . deformed body is . . .
is not real suffering. Real . . . suffering is . . . being deformed in
mind and . . . character. . . ! Most of the di . . . disasters and . . .
calamities in this world . . . are created by . . . pe . . . people who
. . . who have complete body and limbs but . . . incomplete mind
and spirit. . . ! I am . . . not a . . . cripple when . . . compared to
the . . . true cripples of . . . this world. . . !"

Swallowing hard, I leaned closer to Lin-mei and asked, "Do you
wish that your days on this world could be shortened?"

She tried to nod, but only managed to roll her head from side
to side. "Yes . . . yes! I do . . . do wish that . . . very . . . very much!"

There was another question on my mind, and I had to ask it.
"All Buddhists believe in reincarnation. Lin-mei, when your suffering in this world is over, do you think you'll be interested in coming
back?"

Lin-mei smiled, and at that moment I no longer could see her
affliction. My heart went out to her by the gleam in her eyes and
the look of joy on her face. She said, "Defini . . . tely! I . . . I want
. . . to return a . . . as a . . . strong and . . . healthy human being
. . . so that . . . I may . . . become a part . . . o. . .of the Tzu-chi

Foun . . . dation and s . . . spend a lifetime . . . helping . . . o . . . others!"

Up to now, I had been successful in swallowing the lump in my throat and holding back my tears. But now the lump was rising again and my tears were welling up beyond control.

I turned my head, looked away from Lin-mei. Through the haze I saw a small sink next to the only window in the room, and next to the sink was a hot plate. On the ground, there was also an area of concrete with a drain where Lin-mei could lie down and be bathed. Under close observation, I discovered that the toilet facility was under Lin-mei, where a board could be removed to reveal a small pot.

I gazed back at Lin-mei, saw that she had noticed my tears. She shrieked again, and this time it was for the sake of comforting me, "Don't . . . fe . . . feel sorry fo . . . for me! I am ra. . . rather ha. . . happy! Giving i . . . is a. . . joyful th . . . thing! Knowing that I . . . can give at th . . . the month's end and . . . that makes me feel s . . . strong the rest of the . . . the time!"

The wall of self-control crumbled and I started to sob. Mrs. Wen put her hand on my shoulder and I stood up.

The rain was coming down in torrents when we left the building. We were walking back to the van when I realized that Shang had not uttered a word all this time, although one of the ladies had been translating for him and making certain that he understood everything. I looked at him with a silent question.

"How ridiculous of us to complain about spending Christmas away from home!" Shang's voice was unusually shaky and low. "The meaning of Christmas is giving, and the lesson we received in giving is a Christmas gift that will last us a lifetime!"

"All lives are equal,
and therefore deserve to be loved and respected equally.
And Buddha exists in all the living beings, whether the being
takes the physical form of a person, a fish, a cat or a dog.
And the spirit of a dog can be just as noble
as the spirit of a human, or even more admirable!"

— *Master Cheng Yen* —

We climbed into the van and drove to another section of the
city that appeared to be a new business district. The buildings were
modern, and signs of prosperity were all around. The van was
parked on the main street, and we walked towards an alley. Turning
into it, we suddenly came upon several old structures that resembled piles of used lumber and building material.

"How can this be possible? How can heaven and hell be only
a few steps apart. . . ?" I asked, then stopped.

In between two battered low houses, a cat was in the middle
of a crater created by garbage, eating something. Upon the sound
of our footsteps it looked up, and in its eyes I saw panic that had
to be the result of brutal abuse.

I shivered. It was thin and dirty. But I could still tell that it was
solid white.

"No!" A scream rushed out of my throat and escaped my mouth
when I saw that it had a deep cut on the back of its neck; the flesh
was raw and the wound obviously infected.

I didn't mean to frighten it by my scream. But, conditioned by
years of neglect and mistreatment, it dashed away, obviously in fear
that without doing so it would receive further abuse. The last glance
it gave me contained a soundless accusation: I am not bothering
you, why won't you let me fill my aching stomach?

"No!" I screamed again, crying hard. I felt unbearably guilty for
forcing the cat to part from its food, which I could now see as the
remains of a bloody rat.

Shang, Mrs. Wen and the other ladies were waiting for me. But
I stayed motionless, staring at the other end of the alley where the
cat had disappeared.

Shang and I have one dog and four cats. We love them as much as we do each other. When there was only a limited amount of grocery money, we never needed to discuss with each other as to whether we should head for the pet-food section before buying any human food. We don't believe in wasting money on our own medical needs, but always see to it that our dog and cats have all the shots that are required. Before leaving home we had asked two of our friends to look after our babies—a lady came twice a day to feed them, and a gentleman made sure they were all right.

Crystal, our magnificent white cat, is our treasure. She was acquired from an animal shelter, but has the air of a princess. She means everything to us, and we are especially fond of white cats because of her—and now this cat with a gash on the neck just happened to be white!

"I can't stand this any more!" I said, trembling and clutching my hands into fists. "I know there are many people in Taiwan who are nice to cats and dogs . . . but where are they?"

My statement was caused by the homeless dogs and cats sighted by us during the previous days in back alleys and narrow lanes.

Suffering from mange or hunger or both, crippled or wounded or incurably ill, or all of the above—these were the causes of their horrible appearance. But that was not as heartbreaking as the way they behaved and the expressions that they wore.

They had run with their tails between their legs as soon as they had seen us, and were apparently conditioned to view the two-legged beings as the inducers of pain and misery. The look they had given us just before running away was wide-eyed and distrusting and filled with great fear, and it was nothing like the looks we received from the dogs and cats in the USA who seemed to be asking with a trusting pout, 'Well, don't you think I'm cute and aren't you going to take me home and feed me and be nice to me and then be stuck with me for the rest of your days?'

"This is too sad to be true! Why isn't there an animal shelter?" I continued to moan, looking at Mrs. Wen accusingly, "When will your Tzu-chi Foundation get around to doing something for the stray dogs and cats?"

"We will be able to start that project in the near future," Mrs. Wen said calmly.

Shang put an arm around me as we proceeded to walk through the alley. After turning at its end and going a few more yards, we came to a shack with a make-shift door on one side.

There was no doorknob or lock, but still an old faded cutout of the character *Good-luck* pasted on to the weathered wood. Mrs. Wen knocked, and immediately we heard the loud barking of what seemed to be more than one dog.

The door swung open. We were greeted by a frail woman. Her spine was crooked and her neck bent forward. She had to turn her head to one side then look up, so that she could see our faces. She recognized the Tzu-chi Commissioners and beckoned us in. Then she gestured the dogs to stop barking.

The room was less than ten feet by eight feet, and so crowded that there was not enough room for all of us. Shang and a few of the ladies had to remain outside. Standing next to the door, I looked around and could not find a single square inch of floor that was unoccupied. There were dishes stacked everywhere, clothes lying around, an old bureau, cardboard boxes, pots and pans. A single

Ms. Quai Li

light bulb was hanging from a wire. Up on one wall was a shelf
displaying a small statue of Buddha. However, the place was very
clean, just like the old woman herself.

"Mrs. Quai Li," Mrs. Wen greeted her in a pleasant voice. "How
have you and the boys been in the past weeks?"

"We've been just fine," the old woman answered. Her wrinkled
face was covered with age spots. Her remaining gray hair was held
in place by a hair-net. She was wearing a threadbare green sweater
over a brown shirt.

At the word "we" she had waved an arm around, her claw-like
fingers pointing at a large mattress placed on a platform constructed
with boards and bricks.

Two medium-sized dogs, one black the other brown, appeared
to be rather old; they were sitting beside a cotton quilt and several
pillows, glaring at us with doubt. They were not fat nor of a special
breed, but they seemed healthy and showed no sign of hunger.
There was a musty smell of age in the room, but no offensive
stench—the dogs were as clean as their owner.

"Have they been good boys?" Mrs. Wen asked, pointing at the
dogs.

"As always, they have been perfect," Mrs. Li said, her voice the
voice of a loving mother bragging about her marvelous children.
Reaching out to pat the black dog that was nearer to her, she
crooned while smiling at both of them, "Haven't you, my babies?
Oh, yes, you certainly have! But that was a silly question, wasn't it?
Because you don't even know how to be otherwise. . . ."

Mrs. Wen interrupted the crooning, "Mrs. Li, have you changed
your mind?"

The old woman glanced at Mrs. Wen from the corner of her
eye. Still patting the black dog, she answered in an innocent tone
of voice, "I don't know what you're talking about!"

"Oh, yes, you do, Mrs. Li." Smiling, Mrs. Wen continued as if
speaking to a naughty child, "I'm talking about your moving out of
this place and into a nice, clean and warm home for the old folks."

Like a balloon suddenly losing its air, all the strength began to
disappear from Mrs. Li's flimsy body. She sank gradually to her
knees, eventually collapsed on the mattress. Kneeling between the
two dogs, she spread her arms and touched both of them. "Moving
away from here and into a home for the old folks . . ." she repeated

the words she had just heard, then added, ". . . where no dogs are allowed!"

Shaking her head, she continued to mumble in a hoarse voice, "Leaving my babies! Turning them out to the streets! There'll be no home for them, nor a mother to feed them! No! I won't be able to stand that! There is no way! They are such nice babies . . . why, they are MY babies!"

She went on; I studied the place more carefully and soon discovered that the room was attached to an old structure which was tumbling down. There was a small window high on the wall, presenting a view of new office buildings and apartment complexes like giants towering above us.

"Mrs. Quai Li is seventy-seven," Mrs. Wen said as the old woman continued to serenade her dogs. "And she has been living here since she was three. At one time this was a nice house, but now the years have taken its toll.

"Fate has been unkind to Mrs. Li. After suffering a hard life all these decades, she is now all alone except for her dogs. The main section of this house no longer belongs to her, and its owner has agreed to sell it to the government. The road is to be widened, and this building stands in the way. The government can't demolish the building without touching this little room. Mrs. Li's unwillingness to move is creating a problem for many people.

"Mrs. Li is not qualified for governmental aid, for reasons that we don't understand. She has been one of our Foundation's recipients. We are here twice a month to give her food and money, to clean the place and bathe her when she can't do it herself. We do all sorts of things for her, including trying our best to convince her that before long she will have to move."

Mrs. Wen's last word reached the old woman's ears. She stopped chanting. Glancing at us sideways, she raised her voice, "Move? I'll never move!"

She pointed first to one dog and then another while shouting, "They are descendants of the first dog I ever owned and also the only family I have . . . except maybe for people from the Tzu-chi Foundation!"

Her voice softened a little as she went on, "Well, if it were not for the money and food from the Foundation, I would have lost my babies a long time ago!"

She looked towards the far corner of the mattress. I didn't notice until now a low table on the other side of the pillows and leaning against the wall. A large, old-fashioned radio stood on the table, topped by a framed picture of Master Cheng Yen and a flower vase and a candlestick. The plastic flowers were pink and the unlit candle red, giving the dreary room a touch of life.

"I have always been a Buddhist, but did not know true Buddhism until one day when I heard Master Cheng Yen speaking on the radio. It was a few years back. Now I listen to the Master's voice every day. I'm glad that they broadcast her sermons often. I can recite almost everything said by her, and the most touching thing to me is what she said about all the living beings other than human.

"Well, with all her wisdom, Master Cheng Yen believes that all lives are equal, and therefore deserve to be loved and respected equally. The Master also said that Buddha exists in all the living beings, whether the being takes the physical form of a person, a fish, a cat or a dog. She is absolutely right! It is Karma that decides what form we deserve to take in each of our lifetimes. And it is also our mission in life that determines in what form we should house our spirit to better serve the purpose. Therefore the spirit of a dog can be just as noble as the spirit of a human, or even more admirable!"

Mrs. Li smiled at the Master's picture, as if the Master was right in this room and as close to her as a dear old friend. "The Master understands my feelings towards my babies, I'm sure. Actually, dogs are better than babies . . . sons, anyway."

I wondered about the reason for her statement, but didn't ask, for fear of opening an old wound.

Mrs. Wen put a hand on the old woman's bony shoulder and said softly, "But Mrs. Li, the Master wouldn't want you to stay in a place like this indefinitely because of your babies. The Master would want you to take care of yourself first. . . ."

With a firm shake of her head, the old woman interrupted Mrs. Wen, "It's only natural for a mother to treat her babies better than she does herself. My babies eat three times a day; I eat only once. In their eyes I can see that they know my love for them, that they love me too and are grateful to me. Why, if someone comes here to harm me, my babies would give their lives to protect me, and I have no doubt about that at all. Oh, yes. Take my words for it, the spirit of dogs are exactly the same as the spirit of humans . . . if not better!"

The Tzu-chi Commissioners began to talk to her, checking her medicine supplies and giving her money and food. When they started to straighten the place, I knew I was in their way. I walked out the door and saw Shang standing at the other end of the alley, taking pictures of a potted orchid blooming on the balcony of another building almost as old and crumbling as Mrs. Li's home. He saw me and rushed over with a worried look.

"Are you all right?" he asked, looking at my eyes that were still red from crying over the dogs and cats.

"Yes," I smiled, answering in a voice that was no longer sad or angry, "I'm perfectly all right now. I've learned that Master Cheng Yen preaches love and mercy, and her teachings have reached people of all phases of life. With her and Buddha in their hearts, many people in Taiwan are kind to all living beings, and the dogs and cats on this island will be just fine."

CHAPTER FOUR

"Buddha is a person who is awake,
and Buddhism is the philosophy of awakening.
The Buddhists are not god-worshipers, but people
determined to enlighten themselves and become wide awake."

— *Master Cheng Yen* —

MASTER CHENG YEN traveled often between Taipei, the capital city of Taiwan, and her home base in Hwalein, a smaller city located near the sea coast on the east central part of the island. She always traveled by train, because of a heart condition that precluded any flying.

She was once again on her way to Hwalien soon after Shang and I had met her in Taipei. Knowing that there was only a slim chance of getting an interview, we still decided to follow, thinking that if nothing else we might at least get to know her better through closer observation.

"Ching, I noticed you shivering yesterday, so I brought you these," Mrs. Wen Su Jen said as soon as she met us at the train station late in the afternoon of December 21.

It was a black cashmere sweater and a heavy wool coat of dark blue with large gold buttons. Her keen observation and consideration touched me. The cold wave was lingering on, and both Shang and I had left our warm clothing in Michigan. I put the clothes on without hesitation. Smiling at Shang, Mrs. Wen handed him something also navy in color, "A sweater for you, too. It may still be warm with body heat. I didn't have anything to bring you, so I took it off a man who is also a Tzu-chi member . . . he has enough on and can survive without this."

The clothing warmed not only our bodies but also our hearts, and a sense of belonging was born since we were now dressed in the Tzu-chi color. Numerous dots of dark blue created a mighty wave and began to flow into the Taipei Railway Station, a huge structure taking up an entire city block. The wave cascaded down a flight of steps leading to the lower level. Ahead of us Master Cheng Yen and her ever-present disciples were moving in their long gray robes, like light foam in a dark sea upheld by the wave and protected from the jostling crowd.

"Does the Master always travel with such a huge number of followers?" I asked curiously.

"No," Mrs. Wen answered, pointing at those carrying and pulling a mountain of luggage. "Those Tzu-chi men and women have just returned from mainland China this morning, helping victims of a most recent flood. They have started their progress reports in the Tzu-chi Hall of Taipei and are now going to Hwalien to complete their reports."

We reached the lower level and walked along a concrete median with tracks running on both sides. Lines, formed by people with luggage, appeared everywhere. As a long sleek-looking train came into sight, the lines broke and the crowd began to shove and push their way towards the door.

At the door, Shang gave me a helping hand and we boarded the train. The Master and her disciples and the Foundation members had reserved-seat tickets, and Alex Chow, our constant companion and Shang's translator, had purchased the same tickets for us. Our seats were cushioned and comfortable and surrounded by luggage piled in the aisle in front of our feet and in racks above our heads. Around us people were standing. There were no straps for them to hold on; they had to lean against the arms or backs of seats, but seemed quite at home—most of them were reading and some soon closed their eyes and drifted into sleep.

The train went through a long tunnel. When it finally came out into the open air, it was dark outside. Both Shang and I had trouble keeping our eyes open. Just when I was about to doze off, one of the ladies in dark blue walked towards us from the front of the car and tapped me on the shoulder.

"Shuen Sheh-fu, who has a seat next to mine, would like to speak to you," she said with a nod and a smile. "It was also suggested that since I can speak English that I might join your husband and answer a few questions for him."

I became fully awake. Sheh-fu is a respectable title applied to monks and nuns, meaning a Mentor or a Teacher. Shuen Sheh-fu was one of Master Cheng Yen's senior disciples; wherever the Master was, Shuen Sheh-fu could always be found nearby. Standing up to give my seat to the young lady, I said to Shang, "If our chance of interviewing the Master stays beyond reach, talking to Shuen Sheh-fu will be our greatest compensation!"

✳ ✳ ✳

"The Master has nothing against interviews," Shuen Sheh-fu said. "It's just that she has so much to do and so little time to spare, and there are always interviewers coming from all regions of the world . . . not only from Asia, but also Europe and America, the latest being the National Geographic crew. Granting everyone's wish would mean that she should have no time left for anything else."

A deep concern shadowed her round, peaceful face as she continued, "And the Master is not in the greatest health. We must try our best to preserve her energy, and I'm sure you can understand. By the way, why are you writing this book?"

I described my being contacted by the Concerned Group, then said, "But after meeting the Master I'm no longer writing this book for them. I'm writing it for the Master, the Tzu-chi members, the Buddhists of the world, and all others who need to know the true meanings of life. I'm writing it for those who are not yet familiar with Buddhism but should be and could be in the future. And I'm writing it for my mother, my husband, and myself—this is going to be the most important book of my life."

As I talked, Shuen Sheh-fu's guarded expression softened. The next moment her face lit up with a broad smile, sending out a loving warmth.

I reached into my briefcase, produced a notebook containing the questions that I had carefully prepared while still in Michigan and after reading several books about Master Cheng Yen. I handed my notebook to Shuen Sheh-fu.

"They are not the usual questions!" Shuen sheh-fu said after reading them, looking at me with a surprised look in her intelligent eyes.

"No," I said, somewhat uneasy because I didn't know whether she approved of what she had read. "I don't want to ask the Master questions about her life. Those are the questions she had already been asked over and over again. It's not that I'm uninterested in the story of her life; from what I've read, it's a miraculous story and absolutely fascinating. . . ."

Shuen Sheh-fu interrupted me with a bright smile and the wave of a hand. "I like your philosophical questions, although some of them repeat themselves. We won't reach Hwalien for a while yet . . . it's a three-and-a-half-hour journey . . . and we'll have plenty of time to combine some of the questions."

She moved quickly to copy the questions and stack the sheets, her movements confident and certain. And at the same time she said, "I can insert software into my computer and turn it into a Chinese word-processor. I'll type these questions and give a copy to the Master. If possible, she'll read your questions before talking to you . . . why do you look so shocked?"

I stared at her, "Did you say that the Master will talk to me?"

Shuen Sheh-fu nodded, "I think so."

She opened a large appointment book. After turning the pages and moving a finger down the lines, she said, "On the 25th of December she has some free time in the morning, around nine o'clock." She closed the book and started to work with me on combining my questions.

It was difficult for me to concentrate. I couldn't wait to go back to Shang and tell him that we now had an appointment with Master Cheng Yen.

✻ ✻ ✻

The Pure Abode of Still Thoughts in Hwalien, Taiwan

Shang and I left our hotel at 4 AM. A taxi took us through a sleeping town, brought us to the base of the Central Mountain Range and stopped at a tree-lined path.

"No vehicles are allowed beyond this point," the driver said, letting us out.

We stood in the morning mist, breathing in deeply the clean air scented by a sweet fragrance. Other than the crowing of roosters, the only sound was the melodic ringing of a chime—it rode on the soft breeze, traveling from a distance before reaching our ears. Following the beckoning call, we walked as the pearl-gray sky gradually turned pink. After a while we could see the mountains that seemed within our reach, green at the base, but as our eyes traveled towards the summit, they took on a purple hue. And then we saw the Pure Abode of Still Thoughts standing in the dawn's glow.

It was a white temple with four round pillars supporting a curved roof that covered the entrance, a relatively small structure with simple lines and no adornments. A short-cropped hedge and several shrubs were the only accents against the stark white of the building, and yet this place appeared to have a captivating magic.

In front of the temple, about a hundred men and women were already lining up. Most of the women were ordained nuns with their heads shaved; some were novice nuns, their heads still unshaven; others were followers like Mrs. Wen, with their hair confined in hair-nets. Their attire varied from dark blue to black robes, and a few had on brown outer robes draped over one shoulder. There were no monks in this place. All men were the Master's visiting followers; other than dark blue, the only other colors that they wore were black and white. Shang and I joined the lines, he with the men and I the women.

A pair of screen doors led into the interior of the temple. Three altars, carved out of wood, faced the room from the front wall, displaying candles, flowers and a small receptacle for incense. A carved, gleaming white figure was centered on each altar; they were

The white statue of Buddha in the Pure Abode of Still Thoughts:
candles represent the light of knowledge,
flowers remind people to capture the fleeting beauty.

Morning service

the statues of Sakyamuni Buddha, Kwan-yin the Goddess of Mercy, and Ti-tsang the Guardian of Earth. A carved round hollow wooden fish sat on a pillow to the right of the central altar. A large black gong and a large red drum, both adorned with gold writing, were suspended from the ceiling. Framed calligraphy embellished the walls, with messages reminding people to lead a moral life and be useful to the world.

The men headed for the left front side of the room; the women followed and filled the rest of the space. We all knelt on large white pillows and began the morning chanting by reading the scrolling characters on two television monitors at either side of the central altar.

". . . When there is no dream or desire, then there is no agony or pain . . ."—it was the Hymn of Lotus.

The wooden fish was struck at intervals; the gong sounded softly. There was no obvious leader of this ceremony, and yet all voices had become the voice of one. No one stirred except a nun who stood up a few times in the right front of the room, each time carrying a few items with special meanings beyond my understanding, such as a brass plate centered with a small cup. She walked to the back of the room, then to the front, and placed the items on the central altar. As she did so, the chanting increased in speed for a while, then slowed down.

An hour had passed, and the chanting never stopped; the rhythmic refrain went on and on. I turned to look at Shang, thinking that he had to be bored. To my surprise, I found him comfortable and content. Looking away from him, my eyes met the eyes of the silver-haired lady kneeling next to me. She smiled at me, and the lines on her thin face deepened. She whispered, "You are new here, I know. If you have any questions, I'll be happy to help, if I can."

I glanced back at the altars, and a question suddenly rose to my mind. "There are three large statues. And I thought that the Master does not believe in worshiping idols."

The ancient lady's voice was low but clear, "The definition of "idol" is: an image or statue worshiped as a god. We Buddhists here do not believe that Sakyamuni, Kwan-yin, and Ti-tsang are gods."

She paused, coughed softly, then went on, "According to Master Cheng Yen's teaching, the word Buddha comes from the word Budhi, which means 'to wake up.' Thus Buddha is a person who is awake, and Buddhism is the philosophy of awakening. Even in a more sophisticated sense, Buddha still means either The Saint or The Enlightened One, but never God. The Buddhists are not god-worshipers, but people determined to enlighten themselves and become wide awake."

She looked at me, as if trying to find out whether I was still listening. Seeing that she had captured my full attention, she continued, "Sakyamuni was an Indian prince. He realized the insignificance of our mundane existence and the constant round of reincarnations. He sat in contemplation for many years until he discovered that by living a moral and useful life one can erase his negative Karma and reach nirvana where all sufferings are extinct and all beings are transported across the bitter sea of mortality.

"Sakyamuni advised people to wake up from the worldly dreams in which they were dwelling but never asked his followers to accept any of his preaching by blind faith. To true Buddhists, a theory must make sense, or it is not worth believing.

"And also to the true Buddhists, Kwan-yin was the daughter of a king. She has done many good deeds and is known as either the Goddess of Mercy or the Protector of All in Distress. Ti-tsang was a Korean monk who came to China and helped the suffering people, and he is referred to as the Guardian of Earth. There are all sorts of mythological tales about Sakyamuni, Kwan-yin and Ti-tsang, but those tales are not rooted in the hearts of the true Buddhists.

"Only a true Buddhist can understand that Sakyamuni, Kwan-yin and Ti-tsang were but three of the physical forms that housed the true nature of selfless love, mercy, compassion, justice, kindness and wisdom. All of us can strive for enlightenment. Once enlightened, you and I can also be just like Sakyamuni, Kwan-yin, and Ti-tsang.

"And I'm sure you can see now that we are definitely not idol-worshipers."

I looked away from the old lady's wise face and glanced at the tranquil faces of the statues. The next moment I turned to study the peaceful faces of those around us, and the resemblance amazed me. A person's inner feeling is responsible for his appearance. When greedy or sad or angry, looking good is impossible. While at peace with oneself, beauty is born. No one in this room was glaring at these statues and asking for favors; everyone was striving to perfect themselves by following the examples of the ancient ones. And because of this, these people were as beautiful as the three statues on the altars.

At this moment I realized that the morning chanting was not a routine prayer listing the things we earthlings wished to be done by those high above, but a daily meditation to help develop the awareness and the energy needed to transform us into better and more awake individuals.

I had studied diligently all the books I had on Buddhism. As I combed my brains to recapture the messages in these books, the room began to look different in my eyes. The flowers, incense and candles were not placed on the altars to please any superior beings, but for the sake of all of us in this room—the perfume of incense resembled the pervading influence of virtue, the candlelight a symbol of the light of knowledge, and the flowers which would soon fade and die were a reminder of impermanence. The sounding of gong and drum were for the sake of keeping awake those whose hearts might fall asleep and go into daydreams, and also for creating an atmosphere where troubled minds could be purified and complicated thoughts simplified.

*"It is necessary that I and my ordained and novice nuns
earn our daily morsel with a full day's work."*

— *Master Cheng Yen* —

The ceremony lasted for an hour and a half and ended at 6 AM. It was a beautiful experience. We filed out and walked into a bright day with a golden sun shining in the eastern sky.

We made our way to the large dining area. There were many tables with lazy-susans, and placed around them were stools. We sat down to eat. Mrs. Su Jen Wen sat next to us. The rice gruel was steaming hot. There were also a variety of vegetables cooked in different ways.

After the meal, a small kettle of hot water was placed on each table. Except for Shang and me, everyone knew what to do. They poured a small amount of water in their bowls, sloshed around with their chop sticks, then poured the water into their dish where it was again sloshed around and poured back into the original bowl. My eyes widened as I watched them drink the water.

"We don't believe in wasting anything, not even the oil that was left in our bowls and dishes," Mrs. Wen explained.

Shang and I followed her example. We then left the dining room, walked around and saw the nuns and followers begin their morning activities. The grounds were swept, the shrubs trimmed, the lawn manicured, the many bonsai watered, and back in the rear of the temple a large vegetable garden was tended.

"As the Master's followers, we come from all walks of life. But while visiting here, we all work hard," a graceful lady said as she looked up from under a coolie hat. She then pointed at the nuns working around her, "They work much harder. It is the Master's teaching that she and her ordained or novice nuns must earn their daily morsel with a full day's work."

Shang nodded after I translated her words for him. He and I soon noticed that as the plants were weeded, no pesticides were used. Even the weeding was done carefully in order not to kill any of the insects that lived underground. And in spite of the lack of insecticides, the plants were thriving.

"According to the Master's words, all lives must be loved and respected," the lady reminded us. We walked towards the kitchen, saw a large stack of wood piled next to the door.

"We cut down the dead trees in the mountain," a young and fragile nun said as she gathered an armful of the wood to bring to the kitchen, "and then we'll use them to heat the cooking stoves."

There were many buildings scattered around the temple grounds. We entered one, saw people working on computers, transcribing information about the Tzu-chi Foundation, answering correspondence, sending out brochures, keeping accounting records, and a multitude of other business-related tasks. The workers were either nuns or followers, speaking, typing or writing in not only Chinese but also Japanese, English and several other languages.

We walked into another room, saw four women, two children, and an old man. Their bodies were protected by aprons, and they wore kerchiefs over their heads. One woman was busy melting chunks of white wax in a large pot, then adding color to turn the wax red. Another woman was helping her pour the hot liquid into a machine with openings, each about two inches across and three inches deep. A fan was blowing on the machine to cool the surface. A young girl, about twelve, was scrapping off the excess wax carefully and skillfully, without disturbing the wax in the holes.

"Hi, are you from America?" the girl greeted us in perfect English when she saw Shang.

We nodded yes and she went on, "My mother, younger brother and I are from California." She pointed at a middle-aged lady and a boy of about ten. "My parents are Honorary Board Members of the Tzu-chi Foundation, my brother and I just members. While visiting, we always make ourselves useful." She giggled. "And it's fun, too, to play with the wax and turn them into candles."

The girl's mother, whose fine clothes could be seen underneath the apron, was cutting a special kind of incense into short sticks. She attached each stick to a thin metal ring, then passed them to another lady. The lady inserted these incense-sticks into the candles, then put them onto a tray; the metal rings became bases for the candles and the incense the wicks. When the tray was filled, the young boy carried it to the old man, who seemed to be in his late seventies, and he wrapped cellophane around each candle.

Overseas Chinese return to the Abode to help make candles

The girl continued while working, "These candles symbolize the Tzu-chi Foundation. The followers are like the lighted candles, giving out brightness and heat to a dark and cold world. While burning, these candles will create an aroma, because in the candles' hearts their wicks are made of incense. And while giving, we utter only sweet, comforting words, because in our hearts we have but sincerity and compassion."

The girl's mother did not stop cutting the incense into wicks, but joined in to speak in a soft voice and in English. "When the Master was young, she used to read by candlelight. Watching a candle burn, she discovered that when a drop of tear fell down the candle, it was stopped quickly by a layer of thin membrane. She compared the candle tear to the tears that all beings must shed when suffering the unavoidable pains in life. She realized that in our life, the only membrane that can prevent the tears from falling is love and mercy."

The girl waited for her mother to finish, then said with a smile, "But these candles are tearless, and each of these Chandana incense-wicks can burn for ten hours. When finished burning, it doesn't leave a trace of having shed a single tear. These candles are selling very well. And it's a good thing too. Because although the Tzu-chi Foundation has many generous contributors, the Foundation money is used for charity alone."

The girl worked faster and continued with pride: "Everyone here including the Master leads a very simple life. The vegetables that they eat come from the garden, but still that's not enough to sustain them. Our candle-making is very important. From selling these candles and the popped rice and the Dol-yuan powder, enough money can be brought in to put food on the tables for the Master and her disciples and the nuns and visiting followers."

After leaving the candle-making room, Shang and I were eager to find out what was popped rice and the Dol-yuan powder. We asked around, and a novice nun showed us to a two-story building. The upper floor was lodgings for the nuns and female visitors, the bottom floor for various other activities. Passing one of the doors, we heard a loud noise resembling the sound of popping corn. We knocked on the door and a young nun appeared, wearing a mask over her face and a kerchief over her head. She let us in, and we saw a room with several machines, each a giant-sized corn-popper. The floor was stacked with large bags, containing grains that we could not identify.

"We make popped rice out of a special kind of rice," the nun pointed at some of the grains and said in accented English. "It is high in protein and vitamins and minerals. Once it is heated up in the machine over there and then tumbled in this large wire cage over here, before long it will expand and start to pop."

The popped rice looked like white cashews, only twice as large. They were bagged and gathered onto a table. The nun told us that, except for a small portion which would be consumed by themselves, the rest would be sold.

And then she pointed at the other bags of grains and said, "Those are beans and seeds and nuts for making Dol-yuan powder. Dol-yuan means Basically Beans. There are lotus seeds, almonds, soy beans, red beans, broad beans, black beans . . . a total of ten different kinds of grains. We dry them in the sun, then grind them into powder. We mix the powder with sugar then bag them. With one cup of boiling water and half a cup of powder, a delicious drink can be made. We sell them, too, and people really like them for the taste and nutritious value."

We thanked her and left the room. The next room we entered was a large sewing room. We saw three nuns working among piles of gray material, and we stopped to observe.

"Don't you need a pattern?" I asked the first nun who was drawing directly onto the material the lines to be cut.

"No," she answered. "We make all of our robes, and I've been doing this for years. Besides, there is only one size for everybody." She stopped, thought, then laughed. "Well, when it goes to a small person, she will have to tie the rope around her firmly, and when it goes to a big one, she will feel it a little tight on her. But it will fit perfectly on the one whose body is sized just right."

The second nun was cutting out the material according to the drawn lines. The third was working on an old black Singer sewing machine updated with a small motor attached to the belt, and not far from the old machine was a six-thread serger which looked like one of the original prototypes.

The author and Mrs. Ming Der Wang join all others to wash dishes after lunch in the Pure Abode of Still Thoughts

There were many other rooms, where people were busy making things such as prayer beads and macrame ornaments. We were about to take a closer look when a bell started to chime softly, telling everyone it was time for lunch.

CHAPTER FIVE

"There is a great difference
between what we need and what we want.
There are the needs that
are essential and fundamental;
they can and should be obtained with hard work.
Desires beyond what we need are our wants;
they are endless, ought to be modified and lessened."

— *Master Cheng Yen* —

S HANG AND I left the dining room accompanied by two of the Master's disciples, Shuen Sheh-fu and Ming Sheh-fu; both of them could speak English very well; the former had talked to me on the train and promised me an appointment with the Master; the latter was a petite girl with an angelic face.

The sun, shining brightly, had made it warm enough that we no longer needed to wear the borrowed clothes. Shuen Sheh-fu and Ming Sheh-fu had changed from the long gray robes that they wore when going out into knee-length gray robes and long gray pants. They also had on light gray leggings and flat black sandals.

As soon as we left the temple grounds, I noticed the road was now bordered by a grove of papaya trees. "Do these trees belong to the temple?" I asked.

"No, but the papayas you had for lunch were donated by the farmer who owns them," Shuen Sheh-fu answered, then continued: "These trees, as soon as the ripe fruit is harvested, are cut down and a new crop will be planted. This way the farmer can get more and larger fruit."

Continuing on, we came upon a grove of tall, thin coconut palms and in the top, hanging among the fan-like branches, were clusters of nuts each about the size of an acorn. Shang pointed up and asked if they were young coconuts.

Ming Sheh-fu shook her head vigorously, "That is a curse to many of the people on this island! It is called Bean-long, and is chewed very much like tobacco. But it is a much stronger drug, and many are dependent on it, although they know it is the major cause of mouth cancer. We are doing our best to help people stop using it."

Staring at the treetop, Shang studied the nuts carefully and then exclaimed, "They are beetle-nuts! We've seen Bean-longs being sold everywhere in Taiwan, but didn't know what they are and how they grow!"

Beetle-nut stands could be found all over the island, sometimes more than a dozen stands within one city block, displaying nuts piled into the shape of a pyramid. Chewing them for a while, then spitting them out, the users' teeth were dyed permanently black and the sidewalk was stained red.

We continued walking and passed a small wood shack. On one of the walls was a faded painting of an aborigine man done in black ink with fine detail; Shang and I couldn't help stopping to admire it.

Shuen Sheh-fu said, "The artist came here several years ago, built himself a shack and lived in it to paint and carve. A pretty young girl, who was working in the temple at the time, fell in love with him. She married him and moved into this shack, where there was no electricity or water. They have two children now. The artist is still the same . . . totally uninterested in monetary things. Now they have water and electricity, but very little of anything else. She takes the children to our temple to eat now and then as he continues to bury himself in his art."

"Was it the influence of Buddhism that caused this artist to stop chasing after fame and wealth?" I asked.

Shuen Sheh-fu shook her head and said with a smile, "No, the artist in this shack is not a Buddhist, nor is he a follower of our Master. According to our Master's teaching, there is a great difference between what we need and what we want. There are the needs that are essential and fundamental; they can and should be obtained with hard work. Desires beyond what we need are our wants; they are endless, ought to be modified and lessened."

Shuen Sheh-fu paused, then added slowly, "Obtainable goals are to be respected. It is only the extravagant and endless desires that we discourage—our Master has many noble goals, each aimed at helping mankind."

Before long we came to a small white temple with two large maroon plaques above the entrance. The gold-raised letters on the higher one indicated the name of the temple, the Temple of Prevailing Light, and the writings on the lower one stated Ti-tsang, the Guardian of Earth.

Shuen Sheh-fu said, "The Temple of Prevailing Light is Master Cheng Yen's starting point. It was in the early 1960s; the Master was barely in her twenties and had only a handful of disciples. They were here learning Buddhism and chanting Buddhist Sutras, while supporting themselves by taking any job they could find, from knitting sweaters to making chicken-feed bags and sewing baby shoes. They never went out to beg for alms, nor did they ever take money for performing any religious services."

I noticed inside the Temple of Prevailing Light the brightly colored trim and the gold statue of Ti-tsang, flanked on one side by a dark-faced figure and on the other side a red-faced one. There was also a large urn outside the temple for the burning of paper money, paper clothes, paper furniture, etc., and whatever they considered needed by the dead. It had all the characteristics of the majority of temples but on a much smaller scale, and it was totally different from the Pure Abode of Still Thoughts.

I asked Shuen Sheh-fu and Ming Sheh-fu why the difference.

Shuen Sheh-fu said, "There are over four thousand Buddhist temples in Taiwan, built to suit various types of Buddhism. The Temple of Prevailing Light was built in the early 1960s by several people. One of them was Mr. Hsu, a devout Buddhist who believed that all Buddhas were either human beings or saints.

The Temple of Prevailing Light and an interior view

"Mr. Hsu has since departed this earth and gone to nirvana. The temple's current owners believe that Ti-tsang is an overlord and a savior who has supreme power over the various hells. They also believe in the existence of many more divine beings, such as the red-faced and black-faced deities.

"Our Master thinks differently. Even in the very early days, she denied the existence of supernatural power, divine revelations, messengers or prophets.

"However, different sects of Buddhism have never gone to war with or expressed hostility towards each other. Regardless of their different ideas, they still go to each other's temples and help each other as best they can.

"Many years ago, our Master was a close friend to Mr. Hsu . . . almost like a granddaughter to the old gentleman. Mr. Hsu built a hut for our Master right over there on a hilltop, only a short distance behind this temple."

We walked around to the back of the Temple of Prevailing Light, and looked out to where the hut had been. But we could not find much—the hut was long gone.

"The hut was removed from its original site and placed next to the Temple of Prevailing Light, and there it stood for quite some time. But I'm not familiar with the details, because I've been with the Master only since 1981," Shuen Sheh-fu said as we headed back towards the Pure Abode of Still Thoughts. "You must talk to Tze Sheh-fu. She is Master Cheng Yen's First Disciple and has been with the Master for over thirty years. Besides our Master's little hut, she also shared the Master's most difficult days."

*"While cultivating Buddhism, a person must be
patient like a camel and brave like a lion."*

— *Master Cheng Yen* —

*"Legend goes that the Goddess of Mercy has a thousand eyes
watching over those in need of help
and a thousand hands reaching out with love and mercy.
We will become her watchful eyes and useful hands,
and the world can never call us Buddhists
a passive group again!"*

— *Master Cheng Yen* —

"I am known as the Master's First Disciple, not because I am the best, but the first of them all," Tze Sheh-fu said, smiling humbly, sitting next to me relaxed, her right hand resting in the palm of her left.

She had an oval face, full lips, and bright eyes set far apart. Her earlobes were long and thick. According to the old sayings of China, large ears are a symbol of longevity; I had no doubt that Tze Sheh-fu would live for many years to come.

"I am in my sixties now. I have always lived in the city of Hwalien. I paid my very first visit to a Buddhist temple when I was fourteen years old. As I looked at the statue of Buddha, something happened to me. I just stood there staring at the statue's peaceful face and didn't want to go home." She paused, laughed softly, and raised a hand to cover her mouth.

We were in a room where handicrafts were being made. Shang was at the other end of the room watching two ladies make wall ornaments: they were interweaving colorful threads, then tying the tassels onto painted sections of bamboo.

"I wanted so badly to stay in the temple. Since I couldn't do that, I acquired some books from the temple and brought them home, then started to read about Buddhism. At the time I had just graduated from elementary school, and I could not understand many of the things that were translated into Chinese from ancient Hindu. But what I did understand made me decide to become a Buddhist nun," Tze Sheh-fu said. "When I told my mother what I wanted to do, she was furious. She told me that it was impossible!"

Tze Sheh-fu frowned slightly, thinking of the past. But after a while she smiled again, and her voice was soft when she resumed talking. "Mother and I continued to argue, as the days turned into months and then years. She wanted me to marry and lead the life of a 'normal' woman; I wanted to 'chu-ja,' which means to 'leave home and become a monk or a nun.'

"I have only one sibling, a brother a few years younger than I. Finally, my mother promised me that she would let me leave home when my brother could find a wife to take over the chores that I had been doing."

Laughing from behind her palm, Tze Sheh-fu said, "I waited and waited, but my brother still could not find a wife. He was rather slow at it. When he finally found one, I was already thirty. But still he was only engaged to the girl but not married. I had been waiting for sixteen years already, and could not wait any longer. So I ran away."

Tze Sheh-fu continued with a twinkle in her eyes, "Once out of my mother's reach, I cut my long hair shorter and shorter, and eventually shaved my head. Then I went home to show them what I had done. I'll never forget my mother's and brother's faces! It took my brother eight more months to get married. I stayed home during those eight months, but never let my hair grow back. Once the wedding was over and the bride learned to do the household chores, I left home for good."

She went on to say that, according to religious tradition, shaving her head by her own hands could not make her a Buddhist nun. In order to become a true nun, her head had to be shaved by a teacher-monk or teacher-nun, and then she had to be ordained officially by a senior monk or senior nun.

"I stayed in a temple in the city of Hwalien, searching for a teacher-monk or teacher-nun. I searched until the tenth month of 1963, when Master Cheng Yen, a newly ordained nun several years younger than I, came to the temple to teach the Words of Ti-tsang."

Tze Sheh-fu's eyes sparkled at the fond memory, and she continued with enthusiasm, "I was captivated by her even before she opened her mouth, for reasons beyond my ability to describe. I then listened to her teaching, and suddenly everything became clear to me. She used today's terms to interpret the words that were written over two thousand years ago and applied Chinese phrases to the Indian thoughts. She made the most complicated philosophy simple and the most hard-to-understand ideas down-to-earth.

"We have a term, 'den-po,' which means 'to punch a hole in a large balloon.' All the doubts I had about Buddhism had ballooned up inside of me. With only one word or two the Master punched a hole in this balloon. My doubts were dissolved, and it didn't take me long to decide that she is the Master I'd been looking for, that I must follow her wherever she goes and stay with her for the rest of my life."

Narrowing her eyes, Tze Sheh-fu looked towards the other end of the room. I followed her gaze, saw only a blank wall. But I knew that her reminiscing thoughts were seeing on the wall the days of yesteryear.

She went on softly, "I was not the only one determined to follow the Master after meeting her and listening to her. Many others were also deeply impressed, seeing in her their Master for at least one lifetime. However, when the Master left the city of Hwalien, she left with only me. There were four others who joined us, but that was not until a few months later.

"After that, for several years, the six of us stayed in a little hut on a hilltop behind the Temple of Prevailing Light. The room was six by six feet, and the six of us had to crowd in, sharing two cotton quilts at night."

Shaking her head, Tze Sheh-fu continued, "The Master's teaching was that we must work for our keep. And when she said work, she didn't mean going out to beg for offerings or performing religious services for money. We supported ourselves by working with our hands—growing peanuts and vegetables, making chicken-feed bags out of cement sacks, knitting sweaters and making baby shoes . . . we did all kinds of work to feed ourselves.

"Hard as we worked, we could only earn enough money to buy a few cakes of tofu and coarse rice for all of us for the entire month. We salted the tofu to make it last. Frequently we ran out of oil and rice and were forced to ask the owners of the Temple of Prevailing Light to loan us some. We always paid back what we borrowed.

"The Master told us then that we must be patient like a camel and brave like a lion while we continued our cultivation of Buddhism. After a full day's hard work, she always made sure that we studied at night. In the early days, before the temple provided us with electricity, we shared a candle to read not only books on Buddhism, but also the *Four Classics* (Confucius) and many other books. The Master also instructed us to improve our penmanship by copying various canonical literature and Sutras."

Tze Sheh-fu withdrew her gaze from the wall. In her eyes, I saw tears glistening, and as she resumed talking, I realized that they were tears of gratitude.

"I had only a grade-school education but became a well-learned person through the years while living beside the Master. My family was far from being poor. While at home, I never needed to worry about lacking for anything. But I was never so rich as I am now after becoming a disciple to the Master. Rich and poor are such relative terms. As a disciple to the Master, I feel rich because we are always accomplishing things, and therefore our quality of life has always been great. But as far as money is concerned, we never had any. We still don't.

"In the old days, night after night I would force myself to read or write, while my mind kept flying towards the same question: how can I earn a little more money? Besides the daily necessities, there were always bills waiting to be paid, and among them the doctor's bills.

"We couldn't help becoming sick, especially in winter months. The Master herself, in order to save money, never went to the doctor. But when one of us was sick, she always forced us to go. I still remember one day, I was so ill that I stopped working and had to lie down to rest. The Master saw me lying there and knew immediately that something was wrong. She ordered me to go to the hospital, saying that even if we must borrow money, I still had to take care of myself and value my life.

"The Master values not only human life and the lives of all other beings, but also the lives of things that no one else would consider alive—to the Master, even a cup, a piece of paper, or a wrist watch has its own life. She takes care of everything, so that it will last a long time and thus have a long life."

Tze Sheh-fu paused, tilted her head to one side and smiled the mischievous smile of a young girl. "Who can say that a wrist watch does not have life? Isn't the ticking its heartbeat? When it stops ticking, isn't the watch-repairman a heart surgeon? Well, there are so many things in this world that are beyond people's ability to understand. But we cannot say they do not exist only because we are unable to explain."

She went on to say that as the young Master and her five followers were staying in that simple hut, for reasons unknown the Hwalien police department suddenly decided to clear the hilltop area and demolish their home.

The electricity was cut off, and the wrecking crew began to dig up the ground. Then, as the wreckers continued working, the weather changed unexpectedly. Dark ominous clouds rolled across the sky, blotting out the sun; it was as if night had come. A strong wind rose, shattering the stillness with its howling through the valley. No one could open their eyes; they could barely breathe in such a powerful gale. The villagers screamed; the children cried; the beasts shrieked and wailed.

The wreckers were frightened. They ran from the site and approached their foreman. The stubborn man yelled at the crew but to no avail, so he led a new crew up to the hilltop, driving a truck. But while driving on the mountain road he suddenly lost control of the steering wheel; it simply refused to turn regardless of his effort. The brake would not work either. The truck rolled off the road and was totally smashed, but as if protected by a giant hand, no one was seriously hurt.

Tze Sheh-fu covered her mouth with her hand once again and giggled. "The demolishing crew and the men in the police department believed that both the change of weather and the car wreck were warnings from heaven, and decided to leave our hut alone. Then the villagers began to observe our hut at night. They swore that even with the electricity cut off, they could still see bright light that seemed to radiate around and over the top of our hut. The light kept shining over our hut, and the Master and we, her five disciples, were considered divine beings for quite a while.

"Eventually, after an elaborate ceremony to plead forgiveness from the warning forces in heaven, the hut was carefully lifted and placed next to the Temple of Prevailing Light. But the Master didn't want to live that close to the Temple of Prevailing Light. It was a noisy place with a lot of celebrations, and the sound of firecrackers was a threat to her congenital heart condition. We had to find a new home. It wasn't easy. We explored for possibilities and searched long and hard."

She shook her head and sighed, then continued softly, telling me that finally, in 1967, the Master's mother came to their aid and gave them some money to buy a piece of land.

"We found the land . . . you and I are on it right now. . . but the money from the Master's mother was not enough to pay for the land; we were thirty-one-thousand Taiwan dollars short. So we borrowed money from a bank. We had worked hard and lived on a tight budget all this while, and now we had to work even harder and be more frugal. Besides paying back the loan, there were also the tax and an interest to be paid. So we took on more work, including planting rice and knitting gloves. But we never touched the charity fund of the Tzu-chi Foundation."

I looked at her questioningly, and she said, "Oh, I'm sorry. Did I not tell you that the Foundation was established in 1966, a year before the buying of the land?"

I shook my head and she went on. "In the beginning of 1966, when we still lived in the straw hut, the Master went to a private hospital in Fon-ling, a small town near Hwalien, to visit someone she knew who had just been operated on. Like most of the hospitals along the east coast and far from the capital city, this hospital was poorly equipped and insufficiently staffed. The way the patients were treated saddened the Master, and she began to wish that she could do something to help those who were poor and sick.

"On her way out of the hospital, the Master's eyes were caught by a puddle of blood in the entrance hall. The Master asked, and learned that there had been an aborigine woman suffering from miscarriage, who was carried to the hospital on a stretcher by her family and neighbors all the way from the faraway Fun-bin Mountain. It had taken them eight hours to reach the hospital. But because they could not pay the required advance, the hospital had refused to take care of her. The woman was carried away once more, and there was no telling what had happened to her.

"The Master stared at the blood, and she became resolved of the necessity to help the poor and sick. When she discovered that the required advance was eight thousand dollars, a little over three hundred dollars in American currency, her heart ached—to the Master, life ought to be worth much more than money.

"Soon after that, three Catholic nuns came to our hut to pay our Master a visit. They had heard of our Master's commitment, but felt that her devotion was going in the wrong direction. There was a long discussion. The Catholic nuns mentioned that there are all sorts of Catholic hospitals and schools and charity organizations, but never any Buddhist ones. They told the Master that in the eyes of the world, the Buddhists are but a passive group of people contributing nothing to society.

"During that time, the Master was offered a chance to leave Hwalien for a large temple in Jar-yee, a southern city. When people in Hwalien heard that the Master might go away, they petitioned her to stay. At the next gathering, the Master looked at the crowd, met their pleading eyes, and saw their beseeching hands with palms touching. Suddenly she realized that by joining all these eyes and hands a force could be formed—a force with enough eyes to locate the suffering ones and enough hands to grant them help.

"The Master smiled when she thought of Kwan-yin, the Goddess of Mercy and the Protector of All In Distress, who, according to legend, has a thousand observing eyes and a thousand helping hands. The Master then said, 'We will become Kwan-yin's watchful eyes and useful hands, and the world can never call us Buddhists a passive group again!'

"The Master shared her idea with the gathered crowd and received an eager response—as long as the Master was willing to stay in Hwalien, they would do anything for her. But the Master did not ask them to do much; she only asked each of them to donate fifty cents per day.

"She suggested that each of them should put fifty cents worth of coins into a bamboo container, and do the same every day. When asked why not put aside fifteen dollars all at once at the month's beginning or end, the Master answered, 'Because giving is a pleasure and you deserve to enjoy that pleasure every day instead of only once a month!'

"The Master named the newborn organization Buddhist Compassion Relief Tzu-chi Foundation. "Tzu" means Love and Kindness, and "Chi" means Mercy. The Tzu-chi Foundation was established on March 24, 1966, with thirty active members who were housewives. The Master then talked to the five of us who were her only disciples at this time, and told us that all of us, including herself, must make the daily contribution.

"The six of us were still making baby shoes, selling each pair for four Taiwan dollars. We came up with the solution of working harder and making one more pair of shoes per person per day. When the twenty-four extra dollars added up, we would have seven hundred and twenty dollars per month to donate to the Foundation—in a year's time we would be able to have more than eight thousand dollars to save at least one woman from being turned away by the hospital.

"Our Master had decided that she would take in disciples but never accept followers. However, in order to help the Foundation grow, she changed her mind. She made a rule that whoever wishes to be a follower, must also be a Tzu-chi member—not only in name but also in action, giving time or funds or both. The Tzu-chi Foundation's membership increased at unbelievable speed. We were soon able to do many things to help the poor. After a while, we began to expand our work into other fields—such as the building of hospitals and schools and the enrichment of our cultural world.

"However, from the very beginning until this day, the Foundation's funds are always separated from the funds of our temple. As the Foundation prospered, our Master and her disciples continued to be poor."

Tze Sheh-fu paused to drink tea. I looked at my notes and located the place where she backtracked to talk about the beginning of the Tzu-chi Foundation. I asked, "You were saying that in 1967 the Master and her disciples owed the bank thirty-one-thousand for a piece of land. . . ."

"Oh, yes," Tze Sheh-fu put down her teacup and went on. "We were in debt, and our hut was gone. We were living in a room borrowed from the owners of the Temple of Prevailing Light, and paying for the piece of land owned by us and the bank. We planted extra rice on the land, and counted on the harvest. We were going to eat some but sell most of it to pay the bank. It was then that the Master, along with the five of us, had to go away for two weeks. When we returned, we rushed to the rice field, only to find all the stalks drooping and dying. The five of us stood crying beyond control, staring at the field. But the Master stood with her back stiff and lips in a straight line, unwilling to give in to defeat.

"We had no choice but to struggle on, until our Master's mother helped us again—this time she gave us two hundred thousand Taiwan dollars.

"We thought that with this much money, we could not only clear our debt but also build anything we want. We had no idea that the money we had was far from enough to build the temple we had in mind. But the contractor's wife was a Tzu-chi member. He told us to let him know exactly what we want and stop worrying about the cost. We wanted a simple temple in Japanese style, with an assembly hall and altars, a kitchen, a bathroom, and plenty of closets. The construction soon began, and the Pure Abode of Still Thoughts was completed on March 24, 1969, exactly three years after the establishment of the Foundation.

"Our kind-hearted contractor paid a lot of the expenses on his own, but still we owed him two-hundred-forty-thousand dollars. The Master took the two deeds to the bank, one on the land and the other on the temple, and asked for another loan.

"Soon after that the Master's disciples increased. With many hands, we were able to do more work. We continued to live a simple life and work hard—farming, printing, knitting, sewing, carving, crocheting, making toys and plastic flowers and candles—a total of twenty-one different things. We paid the bank on time, and our credit was good. We were able to get more loans, and so we added on to the original building—the offices, workshops, storage rooms, and everything else that you see."

Tze Sheh-fu glanced at the wall-clock and smiled at me apologetically. "I must go back to work now. There are bills to be paid. Besides, I have not forgotten what the Master always said, 'Without a day's work, one doesn't earn a day's food.' I'm old, have grown used to eating, and don't intend to put myself on a diet!"

CHAPTER SIX

"The obligation of a Sramanerika, a novice nun,
is to bend her back and offer it as a stepping stone
for those traveling from darkness to enlightenment.
And once she becomes a Bhiksuni, a nun,
she will stop loving only a few people and start loving
all the living beings, and she will also move from serving
only her family towards serving the entire world."

— *Master Cheng Yen* —

I T WAS MID-AFTERNOON. Shang had gone to a nearby building where
a detailed report was being given by those recently returned
from the flood areas in mainland China. I was in a large upstairs
room looking at photographs of Nepal, where the needy have been
receiving aid from the Tzu-chi Foundation.

I was in the company of Ming Sheh-fu, who, like Shuen Sheh-fu,
could speak Taiwanese, Mandarin, and also English fluently. She
and I were sitting on a sparkling wood floor, with gray cushions
under us for comfort. There were several desks around us,
equipped with typewriters and computers that could be used as
either English or Chinese word-processors. We were not alone.
People came and went, taking papers in and out of the filing
cabinets, using the machines, or checking into the many books of
photos and slides.

The women were of different ages, dressed in either gray or dark blue. Some of them had shaved heads, others either wearing a single long queue or their hair pulled back, then confined into nets. None of them wore any makeup, and yet many were strikingly beautiful. In several of the ordained young nuns I saw a beauty that could not be marred by their lack of hair. I also noticed the exquisite looks of some of the girls who still had their hair but were already wearing gray pants and short gray robes—they were soon to be ordained and have their heads shaved.

I looked from them to Ming Sheh-fu and suddenly realized that none of them was as beautiful as she. Her round face was deeply tanned, her lips naturally red. She had a delicate nose, and her large eyes were surrounded by thick long lashes. However, her features were only partially responsible for her captivating charm—it was her movement and gestures that were enchanting. She moved with the agile grace of a ballerina, but at the same time was straightforward and direct like a tomboy. Although wearing gray, she appeared to be as colorful as a fire-bird that was soaring fearlessly across the sky.

"Ming Sheh-fu," I called hesitantly.

"Yes?" she answered with a brilliant smile, revealing a perfect set of white teeth.

"I have a question, which may be rather rude."

"What is it?"

"I would like to know why women become nuns. Tze Sheh-fu's reason can't be applicable to everyone—I'm sure you didn't all go to a temple at age fourteen and decide not to go home. I've been looking at the older women who were soon to be ordained; it is easier to imagine that they have awakened from worldly dreams after experiencing life's sorrow and pain. But the young girls and especially the beautiful ones! What caused them to walk away from worldly desires and passion? How can they become determined to give up dreaming when they did not even have a chance to dream? Let's suppose that all of you have heard a call of vocation. How did the call penetrate the sounds of the world and reach the young hearts? Well, what I'm asking is, what caused *you* to become a nun?"

Ming Sheh-fu lowered her eyes; her long lashes were like two black butterflies fluttering their wings on her smooth cheeks. She stared at her small hands that were resting on her lap, her slender fingers trembling unnoticeably. Finally, she let out a long sigh, then began to talk without looking up.

"Eight years ago, I was still a secretary in Taipei. I worked in a large company, dealing with many people and functioning in both Chinese and English. I lived with my parents, and I had a sister and a brother. My brother had gone to the United States of America for schooling. My father was planning for me to go and join him.

"I loved art, enjoyed painting. In the winter of 1985, when my yearly vacation was coming up, I looked for a place where I could draw and paint. A friend tried to help me find a vacation spot by showing me photographs of the Pure Abode of Still Thoughts and told me a little about Master Cheng Yen. I listened but didn't give it much thought.

"At first, I was totally uninterested in spending my precious vacation in a temple. I was not a Buddhist, nor did I know much about Buddhism, and I was not eager to involve myself in any religion. But then as I continued to look at the pictures, I became captivated by the scenery—the dream-like mountains that surrounded the Abode would make such a magnificent subject for my next painting!

"I packed my painting gear, arriving at the Abode as a tourist. I settled in the guest quarter, and the next morning I went to the garden and set up my easel. I then noticed many people standing between my canvas and the fog-shrouded mountain. Their age varied from very old to young children. Some of them were in dark blue clothes, and a few women had shaved heads and were in gray robes. They were busy doing something. I laid down my brush, walked over, and asked what were they doing while wishing that they would soon be out of my way.

"They told me that they were getting ready for the Winter Relief that was soon coming, and that they would be working here for at least a few days. I sighed deeply, being greatly disappointed because I couldn't paint in a more serene environment. And then I started to help without knowing what I was doing.

"There were huge piles of donated clothes and shoes and blankets, also food items and toys and medicine. We had to sort them out, then package them and label each parcel. It was a time-consuming task. While working, I listened to the people around me, and learned about the Tzu-chi Foundation and its

Members and Commissioners and Honorary Board Members. I was especially impressed by the fact that the Tzu-chi members were divided into eleven groups, and among them several groups were art-related.

"I observed more closely, then realized that they represented every class in our society—some were very rich, some were middle-class and some rather poor; there were college professors and prominent government officials as well as hairdressers and sanitary workers. I was amazed to see that, regardless of such differences, their devotion was the same. It was obvious that all of them had only one thing in mind: to give their time and effort and money to the less fortunate.

"Among all of these hard-working people one worked harder than all others. She was doing everything, from folding a piece of clothing to tying a knot on the package, with perfection. She was a nun in mid-forties, around five feet tall and couldn't weigh more than ninety pounds. Like the other nuns, she had on a gray robe and white leggings and black sandals. But she was different because of her special glow—as if she had inside her fragile body the energy of the world. As I stared at her, someone told me that she was Master Cheng Yen.

"I stopped working, remained motionless and continued to gaze at the Master. Daylight disappeared, and those who were not nuns began to leave. I didn't go away, but proceeded to stand there as dusk turned into night. Then the Master looked at me, and I suddenly came to my senses and resumed working. However, I was not truly devoted to my work. Although captured by the Master's appearance and manner, I was used to doing things that required knowledge received through formal training and a great deal of reasoning. This manual labor made me feel degraded. I was certain that I was lowering myself, and that I was much better than everyone else except the Master.

"When I looked at the Master again and met her eyes, I knew instantly that she had read my thoughts. When it was time to rest, she never praised me for my sacrifice, nor did she encourage me to stay. But I stayed on just the same."

Ming Sheh-fu looked up. Her lovely eyes were misty, resembling the faraway mountains on a foggy morning. Shaking her head slowly, she gazed at me and continued to talk, her voice merely a whisper. "The next few days were like a dream—only in dreams would a person do things without knowing why. I spent the rest of my vacation in the Pure Abode of Still Thoughts, then called my boss and told her that I must take more days off from work. I worked in the Abode sorting and packaging things for the Winter Relief. In spite of the fact that I had not had a chance to touch my paint brushes, I was rather happy—actually, happier than I had ever been!

"When the work was done, all participants gathered to celebrate. During the celebration Master Cheng Yen announced that she needed people to help distribute the packages to the needy. A few elderly members volunteered their sons and daughters. As if I had stepped out of myself and was in a daze, I watched myself raising a hand.

"The Master did not object my participating in the distribution. As I worked beside her and with the others, I contacted a world I never knew existed.

"I didn't know that, other than the high buildings and luxurious homes, there were also so many small shacks and pathetic huts. I never imagined that being poor was much more than being unable to have the finer things. While giving out packages to the needy, I stared at their thin faces and bony bodies and wondered. Why must they suffer? They seemed to have been captured by a net of misery and were doomed to stay within its confinement for life! My heart ached for the children because their imprisonment had only just begun. I sighed when looking at the young people who were struggling hard but unable to climb out of the walls of agony. When I hugged the old folks after giving them things, I silently prayed for them: may your days of suffering be over soon!

"And while standing among the impoverished, a question rose from the depth of my heart: other than owning a few more earthly possessions, how much better off are the rich? Isn't aging, struggling, illness and death the common doom for all of us?

"And the next moment I shivered, realizing that the circle of reincarnation is hard to escape, that as long as we are being reincarnated, we must suffer from one lifetime to another, regardless of who we are and what we have.

"I moved in slow motion, wondering whether the Buddhist nuns and monks would be spared from further reincarnation. As

Two of the recipients of the monthly relief

the day's work was about to be done, I became positive that they would.

"The next day I continued to work, and at the same time learned more about the Tzu-chi Foundation. The members who serve as the eyes of the Foundation are responsible for locating the needy, the distressed, and report them to the headquarters in every major city in Taiwan. Every case is investigated by an assigned Commissioner. After several visits with the prospective recipient and the neighbors, the Commissioner files a first-hand report to the committee. Before the monthly meeting, the members and Commissioners will present and discuss their cases and eventually determine the ways and means of relief.

"Those giving out relief are the hands of the Foundation. I worked as one of the newest hands and became deeply interested in the task . . . I've never done anything as meaningful as this!

"When the relief work was done, I was long overdue in returning to work. But still I was unwilling to part from the Master and the other nuns. I knew that their work and the work of Tzu-chi Foundation is endless—after relief comes the quarterly reviews to update the conditions and needs of the recipients. The dollar amount will be either increased or decreased as the situation warrants, with a final goal of helping every recipient become self-sufficient.

"I went to the Master and told her that I wanted to continue working in the Pure Abode of Still Thoughts. My attitude was such that I was not asking for her permission but stating my demand. The Master looked at me without giving me an answer—either that I was welcome to stay or that I was recommended to leave.

"I left the Abode and went home and told my parents that I had decided to move into the temple. My mother cried and my father was furious. They asked why I would want to do such a foolish thing, and I told them honestly that I didn't know. And then my father suggested that instead of going to the Abode, I could go to the United States of America at his expense; my brother would take care of me there.

"The land of America has a strong attraction to many people, but to me its attractiveness was far from as strong as that of the Pure Abode of Still Thoughts. I turned down my father's offer, quit my job, said goodbye to all my friends, and came to Hwalien. At this time, I already knew that I wanted to become a nun.

"After learning that I had already cut off all my worldly ties, the Master allowed me to stay, but told me that moving into the Abode was far from becoming a nun. I would be observed closely for the next two years while learning the rules and regulations. After that, if I still wanted to be a nun, and if she should find me suitable, then we would take the next step.

"I changed my daily clothes into gray pants and a short gray robe, plus white leggings and black sandals. But I still wore my hair long and straight although braided into a queue. I didn't find the temple life easy. I had a great deal of adjusting to do. For instance, I felt it torturous to be up at 4 AM.

"I was assigned my share of work, including cleaning every part of the place, making candles, planting vegetables and harvesting them, tending to the flower garden, sewing, cooking, washing dishes, doing laundry by hand . . . and many other chores, except for a chance to paint or use my secretarial skills. And for many months I also toiled in the hospital in Hwalien that was founded by the Tzu-chi Foundation, doing more strenuous manual work. I didn't know until much later that this was a time for me to humble myself, that in the future I would be granted a chance to do the things that were in my trained field.

"According to Buddhist tradition, before becoming a Bhiksuni, a nun, I must first be a Sramanerika, a novice nun. And since I was no longer a girl under eighteen at the time, I had to serve for at least the first two years as a 'Chon-ju,' which means 'permanent member of the temple.' While a novice nun is almost guaranteed to become a nun in the future, the fate of a Chon-ju is unknown. The reason is that when a woman already lived too many years of her life outside the temple, whether she can become adjusted to the life of a nun is questionable.

"The Master told us that like a novice nun, a Chon-ju has to serve all the nuns while learning from them. And a Chon-ju is obligated to bend her back and offer it as a stepping stone for those traveling from darkness into enlightenment. So I kept my back bent and lips sealed, trying not to complain, even to myself.

"At times it was extremely difficult, because I was not as tamed as the other Chon-ju girls and women. I tried to copy their docile attitude and self-control while sinking my teeth into my lip. But still once in a while I almost screamed. There were less than twenty Chon-ju women and girls in the Abode, but the majority of the hard work was on our backs. When there were large groups of visitors, we had to sometimes cook for over three hundred people and then wash the dishes and cooking utensils.

"The strange thing is, although I was free to leave the Abode at any time, the thought of departing never crossed my mind.

"It took me five years to become adjusted to temple life and reach the stage of being accepted by the Master as a nun in the Abode . . . I was finally initiated in 1990."

While talking to me, Ming Sheh-fu seemed to have revisited each stage of the past eight years and relived the joy and sorrow. When the young secretary heard the first call of vocation, her voice was low and hesitant. As the novice nun began to struggle at the starting point of a long sacred road, the narration turned laborious and the voice hoarse. Now, the struggle was over and the road ahead appeared to be smooth, her voice became steady, and a peaceful smile brightened her serene face.

"Ming Sheh-fu," I asked, "Would you mind talking about the initiation ceremony?"

"No, I don't mind," she answered, then looked down at her hands trying to collect her thoughts before going on in her soft voice, "First, the day of the initiation has to be chosen . . . it's usually on Kwan-yin's birthday or the birthday of another of the enlightened ones. Once the day was determined, I had to go home and say goodbye to my family. Until the final initiation I was still considered my parents' daughter and a sister to my siblings. Once I completed my vows, I would no longer belong to my family.

"At the time I returned home, I had already been away for five years and thought that my family had accepted the idea that I was to become a nun. I sat with them, including my brother who had just returned from America, and we talked. I soon detected that they were wishing that I would change my mind. As the conversation continued, it became painfully clear to them that this was my choice and there would be no turning away. Realizing their distress at my insistence, I made my visit brief, but before leaving, I asked if they would come to the ceremony.

"When the day arrived for my initiation, I rose early as usual, and while at the morning chanting, I saw my entire family—father, mother, brother, sister, along with a few more distant relatives. I had not realized until that moment how much their presence meant to me.

"After the chanting my sister came to me, and we went to my room. There I took off my outer garment, then laid newspapers on the floor. Next I freed my long hair from its braid and combed it out. At that moment, my sister began to cry. She reached over and lifted my hair, holding it draped over her hand and began to stroke the strands. Our eyes met and I could see her look of pain knowing that this would be the last time she would ever see me with hair.

"There was a soft knock on the door followed by the entrance of the Master's Third Disciple. She held a pair of scissors and a razor. First she trimmed my hair to shoulder-length, then continued to cut the strands shorter and shorter. The disciple then picked up the razor and began to shave my head until there was only a small tuft of hair left. All this time my sister never stopped crying, and by the time the cutting was finished she was sobbing uncontrollably. Seeing her that way brought tears to my eyes, but they quickly dried.

"I walked into the temple wearing a black robe, black shoes and white leggings. The altar was brightly lit with candles and the room was accented with freshly cut flowers. The ever present smell of incense filled the room along with soft music, the sounding of a chime and the melodic chanting.

"The Master stood at the altar while all others were either sitting or kneeling on pillows filling both sides of the room. I walked slowly up to the Master and kneeled before her.

"The Master first spoke to me, reminding me what is expected of me as a nun. Then she raised her eyes and addressed my parents, thanking them for bringing up a fine daughter. 'From this day forth, your daughter will stop loving only a few people and start loving all living beings, and she will also move from serving only her family towards serving the entire world. . . .'

"The Master continued to enlighten everyone on the importance of this day and then symbolically shaved off my remaining hair. When the final strand fell to the ground, I became Ming Sheh-fu."

It was late afternoon and the sun was shining above the western horizon, sending its dazzling rays through the high window where we sat. The crimson rays fell upon Ming Sheh-fu, adding a glow to her already beautiful features. As I stared into that tranquil face, I had the feeling that regardless of passing time her radiance would never fade but remain a part of her until the day she left the bounds of this earth.

Unable to take my eyes off her, I told her with a voice filled with emotion, "Ming Sheh-fu, I believe that you became a nun because you were too clever to continue to ride on a merry-go-round. You jumped off the painted horse that was going nowhere, and now you are moving forward on a path that will lead to eternal enlightenment."

Ming Sheh-fu brought her hands up with her palms touching, bowed her head, but did not answer. And suddenly I realized what I was thinking: Am I the one on the merry-go-round envying the peace that she has found?

CHAPTER SEVEN

"Patients should never be treated as numbers,
but always as noble human beings."

— *Master Cheng Yen* —

"Illness is one of the many unavoidable sufferings
between birth and death, and we should do all we can
to help the sick feel less miserable."

— *Master Cheng Yen* —

ON THE FOLLOWING MORNING we arrived at the Buddhist Compassion Relief General Hospital, an eleven-story white structure. Mrs. Su Jen Wen was waiting at the entrance wearing her usual dark blue uniform and warm smile.

"This hospital is different from all other hospitals," she said. "No security deposit is needed for admission. Rich or poor, all are treated equally, except that the poor receive free medical care. It is the first hospital in Taiwan that is admission free, and now some other hospitals are following its example."

We walked into the hospital among people of all ages; some seemed prosperous while others were wearing rags. I noticed some old people with tatoos on their faces and remembered there were many aborigines living in Hwalien and its surrounding mountains. Tattooing had been abolished for years, but could still be found among the very old.

We saw to our left a large, colorful, mosaic mural reaching towards the high ceiling. In the foreground stood Buddha tending to a man who was lying down, in the background five more men were standing and looking on.

Mrs. Wen explained, "This mural represents the policy of this hospital. Besides treating the illness, the staff must, as Buddha did in the mural, also show compassion towards the individual. Master Cheng Yen said that patients in this hospital should never be treated as numbers, but always as noble human beings."

As Shang and I admired the mosaic, Mrs. Wen began to tell us the story behind the mural. "The sick person was one of Buddha's disciples known to be intolerant to those who were ill. When the sick asked him to do anything for them, such as to hand them a pitcher of water, he always turned away. He was neither cruel nor mean, but wished to look away from illness. And then he became ill. No one would help him. He suffered not only physical pain but also emotional agony until Buddha came, bringing him food and water. Buddha also bathed him and offered him love and mercy which was needed the most by a sick person."

We left the mural, walked across a crowded entrance hall, and Mrs. Wen went on to tell us that she knew the hospital well because she was one of the volunteer workers. "The Tzu-chi Foundation members formed a team of volunteers in 1986. There are over two thousand of us now, coming from various cities and towns. The hospital can use only sixty of us each day. We have to wait for our turn, which is about once every six months. When my turn comes, I'll work six days in a row, at various places: the information desk, the out-patient clinic, the ward, the emergency room, the medical record library, the kitchen or the sewing room."

We walked on, and I noticed the wide corridors, high ceilings and the bright sunlight coming in through the large windows. Mrs. Wen said, "Master Cheng Yen specified this open construction to allow plenty of light when the Foundation gathered enough money to build this hospital. She reminded us that illness is one of the many unavoidable sufferings between birth and death, and that we should do all we can to help the sick feel less miserable—if it is at all possible."

An elevator brought us to the tenth floor. Mrs. Wen guided the way. We were soon in the office of the hospital's director.

Wen-ping Tseng, M.D., Director of
Tzu-chi Compassionate Buddhist General Hospital

"A Buddhist hospital is a hospital of love, like a temple, curing not only the sick bodies but also the wounded hearts."

— *Master Cheng Yen* —

It was a large, sunny room with a high ceiling, furnished with black sofas and decorated with watercolor paintings and calligraphy. A secretary brought in hot tea, and then Doctor Wen-ping Tseng entered with his wife.

Both of them appeared to be in their early forties, and I was surprised to learn from Mrs. Tseng, a neatly dressed woman with pleasant features, that their son had already graduated from a medical school in America and has been practicing as a brain surgeon for some years. Mrs. Tseng soon left the room, and Dr. Tseng began to talk.

He had an oval face, high forehead, and was wearing glasses. Underneath his white coat he had on a white shirt, dark pants, and a striped tie. He spoke in a low voice, kept his eyes lowered, and seldom looked at me. He was obviously dedicated to his profession, but rather shy.

"I used to work in Taipei, as assistant director in National Taiwan University Hospital. In May, 1979, Master Cheng Yen called me on the phone and told me that she wished to build a hospital in Hwalien and needed my advice. I pictured a woman with a large and strong physique to match her gigantic wish. When she walked into my office, I stared at her in disbelief—such a fragile lady in a thin gray robe who couldn't weigh more than ninety pounds or be taller than five feet!

"Staring at her, I reminded her that a hospital is not easy to build, and that even if it were built, it would only be the easiest part when compared to all the much greater difficulties that will soon follow.

"But the Master answered me calmly in her soft voice, saying that her mind was firmly made up and could not be changed. I shook my head as she walked out of the door, amazed by her courage.

"Soon the Master visited me again, stating the same wish. I repeated my advice, and she listened politely. This time I gazed admiringly after her when she was leaving, and my heart was touched by her dream. I still believed it was an impossible dream, but maybe my belief had become not quite so unshakable.

"The Master paid me the third visit. This time she talked and I listened. At the end of the visit I decided to help her and believed that we just might succeed.

"For the next four years, the Master and the Tzu-chi Foundation members worked untiringly to raise money for the hospital, and I contacted as many people as I possibly could. I told them that a Buddhist Master and her followers would soon build a special hospital, and it would be in their best interest to help. At the end of the fourth year the Foundation collected seven billion in Taiwan dollars or twenty-eight million in American dollars, and I received warm responses and sincere promises from the majority of those contacted.

"In February of 1983 the ground-breaking ceremony was held on a nice piece of land that we had purchased. The construction continued for two months, and in our mind we already visualized the hospital's completion. But then, suddenly, the land was claimed by the military authority for safety and security reasons, and the construction stopped.

"It was such a blow to all of us, and we thought that the hospital would never be built, that we would have to return the donated money to various people. It was evident that the Master was also hurt and troubled. But she kept encouraging us and telling us to hold on to our faith.

"It took us another year to find a new location for the hospital. In April, 1984, another ground-breaking ceremony was held, and in August, 1986, a five-story hospital was opened to the public.

"For the first twelve days, we offered free medical care to all people, including room and board for those in need of hospitalization. Hundreds of patients poured in, most of them from nearby areas, and some were visiting a doctor for the first time in their lives. We had only twenty doctors then, all overworked, putting in hours both day and night. Master Cheng Yen came to the hospital every day to visit the patients. She still visits them when in Hwalien and time permits.

"Soon after its opening, there was a fifteen-year-old girl involved in a car wreck. She was taken to our hospital and received brain surgery. When her recovery was heard by people near and far, we gained a new name: the Brain Repairing Hospital.

"It did not take long before our hospital was not large enough for all those that required treatment. In December, 1987, the second stage of construction started, and this eleven-story building was completed in May, 1990. The current size of our hospital is 640,800 square feet. It has twenty-four departments and a 750-bed capacity.

"For a long time, it was difficult to find doctors willing to leave Taipei for Hwalien. And so Master Cheng Yen visited the National Taiwan University Hospital again. She quickly recruited enough doctors by telling them the ideology of our hospital: 'It is a hospital of love, like a temple, curing not only the sick bodies, but also the wounded hearts.'

"We are fully staffed now, with 142 doctors, almost 500 nurses, and more than 100 paramedics. And I strongly suggest that you should talk to some of the doctors and nurses."

We left Dr. Tseng and went to visit other doctors. Among them, Dr. Hsing E. Chen was the director of the cardiovascular research center and the medical research center. We visited his lab on the eleventh floor and learned that he was also a literary writer; he showed us his book. And we also met Dr. Simon Chan, who was a doctor not only in Western medicine but also traditional Chinese medicine.

From these doctors we learned about the construction of the Tzu-chi Medical College. It started in March, 1992, and was now a grand building of sparkling white, standing on a 41-acre lot. It would be ready for its first class in the summer of 1994. There would be a seven-year program, and the students would come directly from high school. The first two years would be pre-med, and there would be three areas of instruction—the regular physicians, those going into public health, and those going into research.

*"A good school should place equal emphasis
on skills and moral value."*

— *Master Cheng Yen* —

Our first view of the Tzu-chi Junior College of Nursing with its stark, white exterior resting quietly at the foot of the cloud-shrouded Central Mountain Ranges took our breath away.

We walked through several archways held up by round pillars, entered a vast, open courtyard covered in a freshly cut lawn with sidewalks that led to the main part of the building. The students were in class. We caught glimpses of them in pale blue uniform, sitting in spacious classrooms and concentrating on their lessons. Only a few turned to look at us. Their innocent faces were framed in hair of various length. With youth and dreams in their eyes, they were beautiful with or without lovely features.

We were greeted at the main hall by a woman who introduced herself as Dr. Fwu-mei Chang, principal of the college. She then turned and introduced Ms. Su-jan Hon, a writer and a teacher in Chinese literature. Dr. Chang was middle-aged and kind-looking, with a doctoral degree in education and also a degree in nursing. Ms. Hon was young, but had already received a graduate degree in literature from one of the most prominent research institutes in Taiwan.

After climbing a flight of stairs and walking through a wide corridor with large windows on one side to let in the sunlight, Dr. Chang took us through a spacious, high-ceiling room with sofas placed against the walls and bonsai on every tea-table.

"This is the teachers' lounge," Dr. Chang said, leading us into the inner room which was smaller but just as sunny and comfortable. "And this is my office."

"Master Cheng Yen likes white buildings with high ceilings, wide halls, and large windows," Dr. Chang smiled, waving an arm around. "As you can see, we have all that in our school."

"Tzu-chi Junior College of Nursing was founded on September 17, 1989," Dr. Chang said as we sipped at the fragrant tea served by a young girl. "This is the first educational project of the Tzu-chi

Foundation, as nurses stand at the forefront of the hospital-patient relationship. We have two programs: a two-year program for high school graduates, and a five-year program for middle school graduates. Two classes of the first program were accepted in the first year, and two more of the second program in the second year.

"In 1991, we also started a two-year night school; one class for regular students and the other for on-the-job trainees. There are 829 students now. To continue the Tzu-chi Foundation's charitable contributions, our school offers scholarships to many students. We charge the recipients no tuition, give each of them a 3,000 Taiwan dollars spending allowance monthly, and provide free uniform and room and board—four students in each room. The recipients don't need to pay back any of the money, and they are not obligated to work in the Buddhist Compassion Relief General Hospital after graduation.

"Following Master Cheng Yen's teaching, our school places equal emphasis on skills and moral value. The ladies of the Tzu-chi Foundation formed a Mother-and-Sister Association. There are 130 commissioners appointed by Master Cheng Yen. They come to our school regularly to provide guidance to our students on all matters, physical as well as spiritual. We also have a Tzu-chi Culture Room, serving the purpose of furthering the spirit of compassion and deliverance.

"As of now, there are over 300 graduates of our school working in various highly respected hospitals, and about fifty percent of our graduates either teach or work in the Buddhist Compassion Relief General Hospital."

Dr. Chang, whose English was faultless, continued to tell Shang more of the school administration. I excused myself, went to the outer room to interview Ms. Hon, the slender young lady with lovely long hair.

Smiling humbly, Ms. Hon said, "I've been here for five years now, mainly because I admire Master Cheng Yen and want to be near her. I am a Buddhist and thinking about cutting off all worldly ties to free myself for the path of eternal enlightenment. Besides, I love teaching here—I don't feel that I'm in a place where education is being judged for its commercial value.

The author and her husband Bai Shang
with the aborigine ladies. Many of the aborigine girls
are now in the Tzu-chi Nursing College.

"Among the subjects that I teach is composition. While reading the writings of the young girls, I can understand their dreams and happiness, problems and pain.

"The girls are from all over the island, some from single-parent families—yes, divorces have become more common in China in recent years. All my students live here. Did you see the bicycles parked outside? The girls sometimes ride to town. You should hear them singing on their bikes! Their families don't visit them often, but the ladies of the Mother-and-Sister Association do.

"Among the 829 students, about 100 are aborigines—they are now called Original Residents of Hwalien. Our school improved not only their self-value, but also the value of all daughters in the eyes of the fathers . . . the aborigine fathers used to sell their daughters to either childless couples or people who intended to use the girls for a much worse purpose.

"When a father discovers that it won't cost him anything for his daughter to become a nurse, and that she can bring home three thousand Taiwan dollars a month while still in school, and that once graduated she will be in a highly respected and well-paid profession—he begins to have second thoughts about selling her.

"All of the girls know that they will become nurses someday. Their eagerness is revealed in their composition, just like their love for Master Cheng Yen.

"Once I asked my students to write a composition describing the spring season. Several of them wrote about Master Cheng Yen—they said that the Master is the spring of Hwalien; if the Master had never come here, the people of Hwalien, especially the aborigine girls, would still be suffering in the long winter of their life."

"Our lives are not pre-determined and cannot be foretold.
But our lives can be formed by our own vows."

— *Master Cheng Yen* —

Miss Shin-chow Hwang had graduated with the first class from the Tzu-chi Junior College of Nursing and was now working in the Buddhist Compassion Relief General Hospital as the head clinical administrator of nurses.

She was very young and pretty, with a round face and an impish look in her large, almond eyes. There was a trace of lipstick on her narrow mouth but no other makeup. Her hair was tied back, and perched on the back of her head was a starched nurse's cap with a thin line of blue trim. Wispy dark bangs fell over her forehead, almost reaching her thin, curving eyebrows.

She sat on the edge of an armchair, prim and neat in her white uniform. Attached to the left side of her blouse was a name tag that displayed a picture of her in a red blouse. She appeared very much at ease, ready to answer questions from both of us, in Chinese and also in English.

Our question was simple: since a trained nurse could find a job in almost any hospital, why was a beautiful young girl like her staying in Hwalien instead of a larger city?

With a sweet smile, she began to talk, "In the summer of 1989, I had just graduated from high school and was about to take a test for entrance to college. I was studying in a library in Taipei, and reading a newspaper while taking a break."

She paused, and then her voice became filled with emotion. "Leafing through the paper, I was captured by a picture of Master Cheng Yen. Together with her picture was an article, describing the Buddhist Compassion Relief General Hospital and announcing the opening of the Tzu-chi Junior College of Nursing.

"I stared at the Master's picture and couldn't look away. How frail she looked in the picture, and yet she had done so much for the people who were but strangers to her. Her picture had an effect on me that I could not fathom. A deep emotion whelmed up in me, and when I finally forced myself to glance away from her picture, I began to read and reread the article.

"The article quoted several of the Master's sayings, and one of them shook me: 'Our lives are not predetermined and cannot be foretold. But our lives can be formed by our own vows.'

"I soon began to cry and made a vow: if I should pass the qualifying examination and be accepted by the Tzu-chi Junior College of Nursing, I'll be a good student and then, after graduation, a good nurse in the Buddhist Compassion Relief General Hospital.

"The next day I traveled to Hwalien. A taxi brought me from the train station to the school ground. I stood unmoving in front of the large, white building and the dark mountain ranges behind it, with my mouth open and my heart beating in my throat. When finally able to lift my feet, I walked towards the building and could hear my steps echoing in the open space. Growing up surrounded with the continuous noise of the city and the crowded conditions, I thought that I had found a paradise on earth. Once I entered the school building and talked with the personnel, I decided to study as hard as I could to pass the qualifying examination.

"I passed the examination and was accepted. I enjoyed my years of schooling here. After graduation, I started to work in the Buddhist

The Tzu-chi Nursing College

Compassion Relief General Hospital, and each day has brought me the gift of helping others.

"However, even though I respect and love the Master and have the opportunity to be close to her when she visits the hospital, I never became a Buddhist. I'm not a Christian either. I've been viewing all religions from a distance, but still don't have the intention of moving closer to any of them. You know, religion is like a faraway mountain, and I just don't have any desire of climbing it. Not yet."

Raising a hand to push back her bangs, Miss Hwang smiled peacefully. "I'm not alone in feeling this way. We have many doctors and nurses who are devoted to the Master, living their lives following her teaching, carrying out their duties as instructed by her, and yet are hesitating in becoming Buddhists.

"Neither the Master nor her followers ever told us that we should become committed to Buddhism. And the strange thing is, since there is no one to push us, most of us are studying the books on Buddhism willingly. Perhaps when I'm older and can truly understand Buddhism, I'll become a Buddhist."

The Master and the nursing students

Lifting her head, Miss Hwang said, "I like all the doctors and nurses here, and I enjoy every moment working among them. The most joyful moment of our days here is at sunset. The doctors, nurses, and some patients will gather in the corridors and stairways. Someone will strum a guitar or sing a note, and everyone else will join in. After a while our songs will fly out of the windows and go beyond the hospital ground, as if proving that our love for all beings is traveling to reach the farthest corners of the world."

PART TWO

WISDOM OF THE MASTER

CHAPTER EIGHT

"To see oneself lightly is to have wisdom,
and to regard oneself as all important is otherwise."

— *Master Cheng Yen* —

A TAXI BROUGHT US THROUGH the papaya grove and stopped at the beginning of a tree-lined path to the Abode. After taking a few steps, we saw someone in a gray robe waving at us from the other end of the path.

We rushed forward. Shuen Sheh-fu's smile was as warm as the morning sunlight. She handed me a piece of paper and said, "I typed the questions you gave me in the train. But the Master hasn't had time to look at it. The Master has been extremely busy, and is now talking to someone about the winter relief. But she will be able to see you at nine o'clock as scheduled, in her office."

Master Cheng Yen's office was not at all what I had imagined. It was not a private office but a work-room shared by six other people. It was not a restricted area either; there was a constant flow of her disciples and followers coming and going.

Instead of heavy sofas and teakwood tables, there were only three cushioned rattan chairs plus two low rattan tables, one draped with a white crocheted tablecloth, the other covered with a sheet of glass. There was no artwork on the walls, but two maps—one of China and the other of the world. The only ornament in the room was a small blue-white pot containing a single-stem plant that was blooming with little red flowers.

Three of the workers in this room were young girls wearing white blouses and gray sweaters; the other three were nuns. They were writing, typing, or talking on phones. They didn't stop when Master Cheng Yen appeared at the door of her bed-chamber, holding a sheet of paper.

"I'm sorry that I haven't had time to read your questions," the Master said after we had greeted each other by bowing and bringing our hands forward with palms together. "But please go ahead and ask me whatever you wish."

She sat on a rattan chair. After gathering her gray robe and arranging a knitted gray afghan around her legs, she placed the sheet of questions on her lap. A few of her disciples and followers quickly formed a semicircle to stand behind her, and among them was Shuen Sheh-fu. I sat on the chair next to hers and opened my notebook.

Shuen Sheh-fu stands behind the Master

At that moment a middle-aged man and a young girl walked into the room—he in a blue suit and carrying a black leather bag, she in a nurse's uniform and holding a metal stand with an I.V. bottle hanging from it.

"Here comes my doctor and nurse," Master Cheng Yen said with a helpless sigh. "Please forgive me for the interruption."

From behind the Master, Shuen Sheh-fu said, "Our Master has been sick for several days, suffering from a cold and running a high fever. But she refuses to rest; she insists that she must go on with everything as scheduled."

The doctor checked the Master's pulse, then went on to take her temperature. "Thirty-nine point two (102.5° F)," he said, glancing at me with a frown. "Master, you ought to be in bed instead of sitting here giving someone an interview."

With a frail smile, Master Cheng Yen waved away the doctor's advice. The nurse took her right hand, guided the needle into a vein. A few drops of blood appeared, a stark contrast to the paleness of her very thin hand. I flinched, sharing the pain that had to be felt by the Master. Looking up, I met the Master's eyes, which seemed to be saying, "I've grown used to it, and my pain is unimportant."

At that moment I remembered what the Master had said in one of her books: "To see oneself lightly is to have wisdom, and to regard oneself as all important is otherwise."

My heart was laden with a deep sense of guilt: I should see my interview lightly and stop regarding the book that I want to write as all important!

"Master Cheng Yen, perhaps you should rest . . . ," I mumbled.

"It's all right," the Master uttered gently. "I don't like to rest."

I looked at the Master's face and remembered the words of an art professor who had taught me to paint portraits: "There are beautiful faces, meaningful faces, and faces that are like a lighthouse."

My professor had defined the third kind of face in detail: "It is a quiet face; it never calls attention to itself, but sends out beams to illuminate a dark world."

And then he had said, "Paint a beautiful face and you should receive a few compliments. Capture a meaningful face and you'll make the viewers think. Discover a lighthouse-face and transfer it onto your canvas with success—then you shall become an artist."

Master Cheng Yen's face was beautiful, with striking features, meaningful because of her expressive looks, and at the same time, the face of a lighthouse, glowing with an inner radiance produced by love, kindness, mercy, compassion, and the determination to turn her Buddha-nature into actions for the benefit of this needy world.

Sitting with her arm extended, a needle taped to the back of her hand releasing medication from an intravenous tube, the Master waited for me to start the first question.

I picked up my notebook and pen. The doctor and nurse had left, and around us people were busy working. A soft chanting, accompanied by the sounding of a chime and the sound of a wooden fish being struck, could be heard in the distance. The faint scent of incense lingered in the air but was overpowered by the fragrance of jasmine that bloomed all year round in the surrounding field.

As I prepared to ask the first question, several microphones suddenly appeared at the same time. They were held in the hands of Shuen Sheh-fu and other disciples of the Master and also the Master's followers.

I became very nervous. In the past years, the Master's words had been recorded on tape, transferred into written form, turned into books in Chinese and then translated into different languages. There were people in every corner of the globe waiting for more words of wisdom as their guidelines in life. If I asked foolish questions, it would be a disappointment to all of them.

"Some of us are born with the drive to accomplish.
Such drive is rooted deeply in the soul;
this yearning to accomplish is carried over
from the previous life."

— *Master Cheng Yen* —

"During a lifetime," I asked, "some of us can accomplish much more than others. Are those that accomplish a great deal born with a goal in life, or is such a goal acquired in the later years as a result of searching?"

The Master thought carefully, then began to answer. Her voice was soft but clear and unhurried, resembling the steady ringing of a silver chime. She said, "First, I must talk about Yea, or Karma, which is created by our actions and feelings in a previous life.

"Whatever we did, and however we felt in an earlier lifetime, has not vanished. Our actions are carried to this life as a part of our soul and will dwell permanently in our subconscious.

"For instance, let us suppose that you and I had met in our previous lives. How did I act towards you? Did I do something to make you like me? Or did my behavior give you a reason to resent me? Your emotion at the time, either fondness or resentment, will remain in your soul and travel with you to this life. And in this life, whatever I did previously will continue to stay; it will remain in my subconscious.

"Let us say that in the previous life I acted mean, and you despised me. And let us also suppose that you and I meet again in this life. Although strangers, something in your subconscious will create a feeling in you, telling you that I'm not a likeable person. And at the same time in the depth of my soul I'll find you rather undesirable.

"With such negative feelings hidden in our souls and subconscious, it will be difficult for us to get along. There will be conflicts without an obvious cause, and it will be very trying should we attempt to build a friendship.

"And, of course, the opposite is also true—two strangers can become extremely fond of each other upon the initial meeting for no apparent reason. And also for no apparent reason, they will discover that they can work together in great harmony as a perfect team.

"The above example tells us that whatever is a part of the soul will remain unchanged; therefore some of us are born with the drive to accomplish. Such drive is rooted deeply in the soul; this yearning to accomplish is carried over from the previous life.

"Let us look at this one step further. If a person's uppermost goal in life is to help people and benefit mankind, and if his body should perish before that goal is obtained, then instead of forgetting that goal, his soul will continue to strive. And if his soul should become the soul of another person through reincarnation, it will definitely propel this new body to move unknowingly, naturally, and subconsciously towards a direction coinciding with the direction of the other body in another lifetime.

"And eventually, when the goal of serving people and helping mankind is reached, then although the soul has been striving throughout several lifetimes, only the body which is currently housing this soul will be known as a great accomplisher, born with a mission in life.

"However, the subconscious yearning in a person's soul is not alone responsible for his accomplishment; it also takes constructive modification and positive reinforcement.

"We already know that a person is born with Yea, or Karma, a powerful yearning in his soul that can be neither created nor destroyed. And now we must also realize that a person can always develop Yuan, which is the outcome of a series of actions aiming at the reinforcement and modification of the Yea, or Karma.

"For example, let us suppose that upon our first meeting, you and I instantly feel repulsed towards each other—which will be Yea, the Karma. But then we both decide that we must better our relationship. With such a decision in our hearts, we continue to be nice to each other, and eventually become more or less friends— that will be Yuan.

"And if you and I should start our relationship with instantaneous fondness because of the inborn Yea, and we continue to reinforce it with various actions of trying to please each other, then we can easily become great friends with the created Yuan. Just like the forming of a friendship, an accomplishment of any kind is based on two factors: the inborn Yea, or Karma, and the cultivated Yuan, or positive reinforcement.

"But we must remember that not all Yuan are positive reinforcements. It can be negative just as well. At times, the Karma is good, but we can ruin it with negative actions or negative Yuan. Our Karma is changeable; it can be improved with positive Yuan and worsened with negative Yuan."

The Master had been coughing while talking. When she paused, a young girl brought us hot tea. As the Master sipped at the tea, I looked at my notes and reached a new understanding:

Yea is Karma and Yuan is the modification of Karma. Without such modification, our Karma would become absolute, and all matters would be predetermined. Therefore, we would travel on the same path in the same direction from one life to another.

I shivered, realizing for the first time how important it is for a person to do his best in life for the sake of improving Karma. With negative actions, a person's Karma will become worse with each lifetime, and eventually he will be born into a hell on earth or somewhere worse than earth.

And I also remembered reading about another explanation of Karma, which was called the Law of Cause and Result.

Karma is like a seed, therefore the Cause. Yuan is like the farmer's planting hands and the sunshine and the rainfall, therefore the modifying force. With Karma and Yuan working side-by-side, the outcome is the harvest, which is the Result.

Each of our actions will lead to an after effect, and every harvest is started with a seed. Therefore a Karma, the Cause, will always create a certain Result. At the same time, every Result can be traced back to Karma, the Cause.

However, the Result of a Cause can become the Cause of another Result—a cotton plant is the Result of a cotton seed, but the same cotton plant is also the Cause of fabric that is made of cotton; and then the cotton fabric is also the Cause of a cotton dress . . . and it will go on and on.

The Master put down her teacup and smiled at me to let me know that she was ready for the next question.

"All religions are high above manmade restrictions,
and a good religion knows no boundary—
be it racial, national, or geographical."

— *Master Cheng Yen* —

I asked, "In the past thirty-two years, I've lived in Mississippi, Kentucky, Tennessee, Hawaii, California, and Michigan, in large cities and also very small towns. Why do many people there consider Buddhism a religion of the East and Christianity a religion of the West?"

The Master answered without hesitation, "Those dominated by this kind of thought are influenced by their social environment and family trait—a person's religious view is intermingled with his habits in life.

"Both Christianity and Buddhism are for everyone everywhere. It will be very easy to understand when we think of religion as a way of life: we can be of different races and living in various places, and yet leading the same loving and merciful life.

"Buddhism did not originate in China, but in northern India. Buddha, which means the Enlightened One, appeared at one time as an Indian prince born in the sixth century BC, in Lumbini Park, at Kapilavatthu, on the borders of today's Nepal. As a young man, he witnessed the sufferings in life, spent many years searching for the truth, and eventually reached enlightenment and became Buddha.

"For the next several decades Buddha traveled in India with a few disciples, sharing his wisdom with people, showing them the ways to enlightenment, until his death at age eighty."

The Master was coughing again. Covering her mouth with a hand, she waited for the coughing spell to subside.

She coughed for a long while, then closed her eyes to rest. Waiting, I thought of what I had read that was a glorified version of what she had said:

In the Sakya tribe of India, there was a young prince who was well-educated in fields including logic, literature, religion, medicine, fighting skills, and many more. He was brave and intelligent, fond of dwelling in deep thoughts.

When traveling with his father outside their magnificent palace one day, he saw farmers in a field toiling in the scorching sun. The farmers' old bony oxen were being whipped to drag their feet forward while pulling a heavy weight, their skin bleeding, their flesh raw. And there were worms being dug out of the soil, becoming food to the birds; their bodies were torn, and their lives ended while they were still struggling.

The prince was shocked by what he saw. "Why must all living beings hurt one another?" he asked himself and began to search for an answer.

The prince soon traveled out of the palace again, without his father but with a few followers. He noticed an old man walking with the help of a stick, suffering great pain with each step. He also saw a sick person lying on the street, moaning and struggling in helpless agony. At the end of the journey, he saw a funeral of the poor. The cadaver was swollen and beginning to decompose; the stench was unbearable. The cries of an entire family shattered the air, the torment of being parted forever from their loved ones fueling their grief.

The prince was astounded by a sudden realization: old-age, illness and death will embrace everyone—rich or poor, noblemen or peasants.

Soon after that, the prince left the palace in the middle of the night, followed by only one servant. When beyond the boundary of his father's kingdom, he stopped at the banks of a river, first removing all his jewelry, then his elegant garments. He then drew his sword and used it to cut off his long hair. He put on simple clothes worn by the local monks, then informed his servant to take everything piled on the ground back to the palace. He instructed the servant: "Tell my family that I'll spend the rest of my days searching for a way to free all living beings from endless suffering!"

The prince spent years talking to the wise people of India and also meditated each day for long hours. His mind finally became clear—all beings are born with a Buddha-nature inside. But such nature is hidden behind worldly desires such as greed, hatred, and lust. Once the worldly desires are removed, the Buddha-nature will appear, and a person will reach the state of Nirvana, where all souls are spared from being reborn, where there is only ultimate happiness for all.

Buddhism continued to blossom in India after the death of Buddha. What he had said during his lifetime was written into scriptures by his disciples. In the next centuries, these scriptures were handed down from one generation to another, while monks and nuns used them as a foundation for teaching. And through the years, Buddhism gradually reached other nations that were near the Indian border.

Buddhism traveled along the Silk Road, which passed through the boundless territories in Central Asia to connect the West and the East. The Silk Road was opened during the Han Dynasty, which lasted from 140-87 BC. Buddhism was also introduced to China during the early part of the Han Dynasty through Central Asian countries.

At this time, the people of China were suffering as they had been for thousands of years. Before long, the rich and poor, noblemen and coolies, all embraced Buddhism. Starting with the Han Dynasty and continuing for the next several hundred years, Buddhist scriptures were translated into Chinese.

The Master opened her eyes and began to talk again, picking up where she had left off.

"After the ancient scriptures were translated into Chinese, we came to know Buddhism and were deeply touched by Buddha's supreme wisdom and his selfless love for all beings. Since the Chinese have enough intelligence to adopt a foreign religion and make it our way of life, why can't the Westerners do the same?

"Those who have trouble accepting Buddhism need to know that to become a Buddhist does not mean to adopt superstition. They also need to see some of the things that the Tzu-chi Foundation members are doing. Eventually, the world will realize that being a Buddhist is to live one's life in a way far above the worldly norm.

"Among my friends, there are Catholic priests and nuns, Protestant preachers and ministers. We respect one another, and while together, we enjoy the harmony. Yes, for those who truly understand religion, it is agreed that all religions are high above man-made restrictions, and that a good religion knows no boundary—be it racial, national, or geographical."

The doctor had returned with his nurse. As soon as the Master finished her last sentence, they began to take her temperature and feel her pulse. They then checked the intravenous tube and removed the needle from the back of her hand.

"Please don't talk too long," the doctor said, putting an adhesive tape on the Master's hand. "You still have a fever and really need to lie down and rest."

The doctor and nurse continued to take care of the Master, and I began to drift back into what I had learned.

Buddhism started to travel from the East to the West centuries ago. There are more than a billion Buddhists now, distributed in every region of the globe. People are turning towards Buddhism because it is a religion of peace. Nowhere in history has it been stated that there was a war caused by Buddhist crusaders. Nor has there ever been any man persecuted by a Buddhist organization for his beliefs in other religions or the expression of them.

The doctor and his nurse prepared to leave. "Master, please promise me that you'll rest," the doctor said pleadingly at the door.

The Master nodded her head. But as soon as the doctor and nurse were gone, she smiled at me calmly and asked softly, "What is your next question?"

CHAPTER NINE

*"We take care of the aged, not because they are related to us,
but because we respect old age itself.
And we watch over the youngsters, not because
they are our offsprings, but because they are innocent and helpless and in need of merciful loving care."*

— Master Cheng Yen —

"MASTER CHENG YEN," I said. "Please give me your interpretation of Confucius' saying: We must take care of all the old folks as if they were our own parents and tend to all the youngsters as if they were our own children."

The Master nodded her head, answered unhurriedly, "To take care of all the old folks as if they were our parents and to watch over all the youngsters as if they were our children is not only the traditional thought of China but also the spirit of true Buddhism.

"In the eyes of the Buddhists, all beings are equal. Naturally, we are willing to give our love and merciful care to them regardless of who they are and what they are.

"We respect the aged, not because they are related to us, but because we respect 'old age' itself.

"And so we take care of the elderly as long as they have reached a respectable age, even when they are not our blood relatives.

"In our eyes, what makes children loveable is the fact that they are children. Even when they are not carrying in their veins our blood, they are not less than what they are.

"And so we tend the youngsters of the world, not tracing their origins but looking at the fact that they are innocent and helpless and in need of merciful, loving care.

"The saying of Confucius has become much more than just words to our Tzu-chi Foundation members. The members are constantly acting out these words. In the mind of each of them, there is this golden principle: Under heaven all elderly are my parents and grandparents, all people around my age my brothers and sisters, and all youngsters my children and grandchildren.

"As volunteer workers in the Buddhist Compassion Relief General Hospital, the members address the aged patients not by names, but as Grandpa and Grandma, or Baba and Mama.

"When giving out relief money and goods to the needy in other nations, the Tzu-chi Foundation members also consider the non-Chinese their own parents, siblings, and children.

"A group of the Tzu-chi Foundation members has just returned from South Africa. They described the bloodshed that had taken place, and told me that they were heartbroken at the sight of the suffering of the young and the old. In the hearts of these members, the African old men and women, young boys and girls are but their own fathers and mothers, sons and daughters.

"To be a member of the Tzu-chi Foundation, a person must obey ten rules, and the first rule is to Honor Thy Parents.

"Times are changing. China has become modernized. Taiwan is westernized in almost every way, and the old family ties are weakening. During the time of Confucius, when there were four generations living under the same roof, this family was the envy of its neighborhood. But now many of the old are nothing more than burdens to the young, and are unwelcome in the young couples' homes.

"However, in the homes of the Tzu-chi members, when an old couple have several married children, each with his or her own home, this old couple is in great demand—all the children and their spouses want them instead of pushing them to the homes of others.

"As far as tending to the young is concerned, we are not only taking care of their physical needs, but also their emotional ones.

"We are establishing schools for the young, and in these schools we are giving out scholarships. The recipients can be anyone—they don't have to be either Chinese or Buddhists.

"The Tzu-chi Foundation members have also formed a Mother-and-Sister Association. There are one-hundred-thirty ladies, paying regular visits to the students in various schools. All children need attention and someone to talk to. Such needs of the youngsters in Taiwan are fulfilled not only through their biological mothers and sisters, but also the Tzu-chi Foundation members who have for them a strong sense of motherly and sisterly love.

"Yes, we have followed Confucius' saying in teaching, and also carried out the teaching in action. One of our Tzu-chi Foundation members even composed a song, telling the world that under heaven everyone should be loved, trusted, and forgiven."

The Master paused. I had heard the song in the Tzu-chi Hall of Taipei. With it echoing in my memory, I began to daydream: If all political leaders with the right to declare war would think of other people's sons as their own sons, there would be less war. If all people who are about to commit a crime would think of their potential victims as their own parents or siblings or children, there would be much less crime.

"A person's true nature is like pure water in a peaceful lake,
undisturbed and gentle and serene.
An outside force can create a turbulent wave,
causing the water to become cloudy for a while,
but when the force is gone and the aftereffect ceased,
the water will return to tranquility."

— *Master Cheng Yen* —

"The sun shines upon us, and then its light is hidden behind clouds. When the clouds move away, we can always find the sun unchanged. Master Cheng Yen, is the eternal sun love and mercy, and the passing clouds the negative forces?" I asked.

The Master looked at me deeply, "Why do you ask such a question?"

"Well, my question is based on the assumption that love and mercy exist in the hearts of all men, that even when social environment and political situations change, such love and mercy remain unchangeable."

The Master continued to look at me, and I rephrased my question, "A certain ruler at a certain period of time can force those under his rule to replace love and mercy with prejudice and persecution. When this ruler is no longer in power, can those ruled by him become loving and merciful again?"

The master answered slowly, "Only the unchangeable is called the Truth, and the Truth is: love and mercy are always there, and they can only be concealed by outside forces momentarily."

The Master looked at me questioningly, "Do you know the meaning of 'A person's true nature' and 'the Buddha-nature in a person's heart?'"

"Yes." I began to quote from the Master's book: "A person's true nature is bright and clear like a mirror, and it is the nature of Buddha. The worldly desires and negative forces can soil this mirror with a layer of dust, but the dust cannot destroy the mirror. When the dust is removed, the mirror will once again become clear and bright. . . . And a person's true nature is like pure water in a peaceful lake, undisturbed and gentle and serene. An outside force can create a turbulent wave, causing the water to become cloudy for a while. But when the force is gone and the aftereffect ceased, the water will return to tranquility."

The Master nodded her head, smiled and continued, "Clear and pure, peaceful and bright, a person's true nature is unchangeable. However, the dust on a mirror and wave over a lake can taint a person's true nature and produce much sorrow. Nevertheless, although on the surface a person's daily life can be disturbed and soiled, beneath the thin veneer his true nature remains good and stable. He can remove the disturbance and cleanse the stain with two forces: one is his merciful conscience, the other is his selfless love.

"A person's conscience is as powerful as the rays of summer sun shining through layers of cloud. Once the conscience is awakened, it will start to act, and the impact will drive away all evil influences.

"There are two types of love in a person's heart: one is called 'unconditioned love,' and the other is 'conditioned love.'

"Conditioned love is rather selfish. Its light has only unsubstantial power, and it shines only on confined areas. The light of conditioned love is changeable. It can easily lose its glow, and while creating illumination, it also forms shadow—it leads to competition, yearns for control, demands reward.

"Unconditioned love is selfless. It knows no limit. Its light shines over all beings and reaches all areas. It cannot be changed, dimmed, or destroyed. It is a light that creates no shadow; it is non-competitive, non-domineering, and it does not ask for anything in return.

"Because a person has in him the Buddha-nature, merciful conscience and selfless love always exist in his heart. These two elements have the power to strengthen his morals and guide him back to his principles.

"Once a person's merciful conscience and selfless love start to work, his true nature will soon resume sparkling like an immaculate mirror and a tranquil lake. The clouds will be pushed aside, and his love and mercy will shine like the eternal sun."

"While praying, a person should pray to no one but himself."

— *Master Cheng Yen* —

"How can a person's prayers be heard, by whatever force wherever the force may be?" I asked.

The Master answered slowly and carefully, "In reality, praying is but a person's way of contacting his true self.

"It is only natural to pray when a person is in trouble, or in need of help, or in search of an answer. We Buddhists do pray fervently and often. But a true Buddhist submits himself to only three elements: Buddha, the Ways of Buddha, and the Teachers of the Ways of Buddha.

"Let us suppose that when a Buddhist prays, he prays to one of the three elements:

"Can he pray to the Ways of Buddha? No. Because although the ways of Buddha are useful in life, no 'ways' can hear a prayer.

"Can he pray to the Teachers of the Ways of Buddha who are but monks and nuns? No. The monks and nuns are merely human beings, and it is not sensible for one human being to pray to another.

"So a Buddhist can only pray to Buddha. And it is very easy to pray to Buddha when a person needs help.

"Let us say that a man has sinned and now needs forgiveness. It is useless to ask a prayer book to forgive him. The monks and nuns have vowed to never reveal confessions, but still it will be embarrassing to face this monk or nun in the future. So the easiest is to tell his sin to Buddha and imagine that Buddha has forgiven him.

"But such forgiveness can only exist in his imagination; he cannot be certain what Buddha really has in mind. When supposing that Buddha will punish him someday and somehow, he will dwell in fear and anxiety.

"He will feel much better if he talks to himself and finds a solution. He can be greatly relieved if he does something to right the wrong; only after that can he truly feel forgiven.

"Asking for forgiveness is only one of the numerous pleas in prayers. But just like asking for forgiveness, in all prayers a person should pray to himself instead of to Buddha."

The Master paused to drink tea. I remembered what I had learned from one of her books:

In Buddhism, one does not believe in a creator or a supreme being. All living beings are responsible for their current conditions: the world is the way it is, because all the elements in it have interacted throughout time and caused the world to be as it is today.

And in Buddhism, one does not believe that Buddha is God; instead, it is said that Buddha is a man who has reached enlightenment, and all men will become Buddha once they are also enlightened.

Therefore a Buddhist has to pay for his own sin; sins can be erased or reduced only with good deeds, and there is no easier way. And a Buddhist has to answer for his misfortune, since his present situation is the result of his sins in another lifetime.

A Buddhist will not scream, "Oh, God! Why did you make this happen? What is the purpose of this? Please do something to better my situation!"

Instead, he will ask himself, "What did I do in either this lifetime or a previous lifetime to cause this? What can I do now to keep it from happening again in this lifetime or a future lifetime?"

The Master put down her teacup and went on, "Let me give you more examples of how the true Buddhists do not pray to anyone but themselves:

"In 1991, people in China suffered a flood. Those of us in Taiwan didn't pray to Buddha and ask Buddha to save them. Instead, a group of the Tzu-chi Foundation members went to China, representing all of us, to distribute relief to the needy.

"Our recipients were scattered in three provinces: Anhui, Jionsu, and Honan. We gave them enough rice to live on for the next five months, enabling them to survive until the next harvest. We also gave the farmers seeds and fertilizer so that they could farm. And we issued cotton robes among them to help ward off the cold. We built over 3,000 homes for the homeless, ten schools for the children, and over a dozen nursing homes for the aged. Besides material help, we also gave them emotional support—we talked to them, listened to them, sang to them, and comforted them.

"When the autumn of 1993 began, the people in Hunan Province suffered another serious flood, the worst in the past hundred years. Once again we did not pray to Buddha but discussed among ourselves and decided what actions to take.

"A group of the Tzu-chi Foundation members hurried over before winter arrived and immediately visited two towns in the most deprived areas of the province. We had brought money and now tried to buy cotton robes, blankets, and rice. With the help of many of the local officials, the food was purchased, and the robes and blankets were being made in factories in four different towns.

"The factories were not responsible for shipping. As soon as the robes were made, it would be our duty to pick them up. Each thick robe was a bulky package, and there were over 200,000 robes. It would require more than fifty trucks to ship the robes to the homes of the needy. One of the mayors, who was especially helpful, promised to take care of the shipping.

"He asked for help from the Liberation Army. The high officials agreed to loan us fifty trucks. Because the trucks had to be engaged for ten days, a lot of paper work was needed to transfer the higher officials' consent to the commanders in the headquarters who had direct control of the trucks. Winter was approaching, followed by the biting cold; the needy were waiting. We had urged the factories to hurry with the making of the robes, but never imagined the mountainous amount of paper work it would take to move the trucks; it took longer than the making of the robes.

"The factory told us that all robes would be made by December 3, and we must pick them up no later than December 5. When it was the afternoon of December 3 and we still didn't know where the trucks were, the mayor became sick with worry.

"He decided to go to the army headquarters and talk to the officer in charge. He couldn't start the journey until mid-afternoon. It was many miles away and would take over two hours by car to get there even on a normal day, and he must cross the Bridge over Yangtze River which was usually time-consuming.

"In the beginning of his trip the traffic was terrible. His heart sank as he looked at his wrist watch. The officer in charge would not hesitate to leave at five o'clock sharp, although he had called to say that he was on his way.

"The mayor began to pray fervently in the car. He prayed ardently, calling the name of Master Cheng Yen: 'Please help me arrive in the headquarters before the officer is gone! Please make my dealing with this man a success!'

"Like a miracle, the driver was not slowed down by any of the traffic for the remainder of their journey, nor did they have to stop at any of the traffic lights that stood between them and the army headquarters.

"They reached the headquarters a few minutes before five. The Mayor stated his purpose to the officer in charge, saying that he was pleading for the Tzu-chi Foundation. The answer he received was that even for the Tzu-chi Foundation, no trucks could be sent out without either a written or verbal order from at least one of the higher officials. And then at one minute before five the officer stood up to leave.

"At that very moment the telephone rang. The departing officer stopped at the door, turned and walked back to his desk, answered the phone, and his expression changed. He said to the mayor that one of the higher officials had given the order and the trucks would be ready on the following day.

"The mayor could not explain the miracle. He is now firmly convinced that his prayers to Master Cheng Yen were answered.

"I keep telling him and everyone else that the miracle has nothing to do with his praying to me, that this unlikely occurrence was caused by his sincerity, and that when someone is truly sincere, it will create a force.

"In reality I had nothing to do with either hearing his prayer or performing a miracle. I was in Taiwan during the time, and the mayor was in the outskirts of Nanjing City, and between us there was not only the Pacific Ocean but also a vast stretch of land. I didn't hear a single word, although I shared his determination in having the winter robes shipped to the people who were shivering in the cold.

"The mayor's determination was so strong, and his selfless love was so powerful that they created an invisible force. That force could have reached the higher official in charge, and caused the man to pick up the phone.

"And so when people ask me about praying, I always tell them to pray to their own hearts where their true self stays. Because in a person's heart, his true nature is the nature of Buddha.

"A person can find not only Buddha in his own heart, but also the Ways of Buddha, and the Teachers of the Ways of Buddha—all of these three precious elements in Buddhism.

"The word 'Buddha' means 'The Enlightened One' or 'The One Who Is Awakened.' Once a person is wakened by his sincerity and selfless love, he becomes a Buddha. And at that moment he will be able to hear his own prayer, receive his own plea, and then grant his own wish."

The Master stopped. I stared at her. I could see in my mind's eye a worried mayor in China, praying urgently in a car. His earnest voice could be heard by his driver, and his anxiety cast a strong influence on the man. The driver drove in concentration, avoiding the traffic, making it through before each traffic light changed to red. But how did the phone happen to ring a few seconds before five? Could the mayor's sincerity and selfless love really create a force strong enough to reach the mind of this high ranking official and give him the incentive to pick up the phone?

My eyes met the eyes of the Master. Once again, I was positive that she had read my mind.

With a smile, the Master added, "A true prayer is not said in a voice which is meant to be heard by anyone outside of oneself. It is said in a voice which is meant for one's own heart. Once a person's heart hears his prayer, so will the rest of the world."

"While dying from a natural cause, at the end it appears
that all living beings have a look of peace.
Perhaps at the door to the other world the dying get a glimpse
of a place that is magnificent in its beauty."

— *Master Cheng Yen* —

"Master Cheng Yen, why are we afraid to die?" I asked.

"Among the things feared the most by living beings, death ranks the highest. Why? Because most of us neither understand death nor have enough knowledge about life.

"Most of us see death as the death of the physical form, a form of flesh and blood. But within each physical form there is a great amount of energy, which is nourished by wisdom—we call such energy the Life of Wisdom.

"Each of us has two types of life. The Life of Physical Form is momentary, but the Life of Wisdom is everlasting. It will not perish, but becomes stronger with each lifetime. It cannot be weakened by illness, nor will it cease to be alive simply because the physical form is no longer breathing."

The Master paused, coughing softly.

I thought, How comforting it is to know that the things learned in this lifetime will not be wasted! And a child prodigy is a living proof for the Life of Wisdom.

The Master continued, "We should not be afraid of death. While dying from a natural cause, at the end it appears that all living beings have a look of peace. Perhaps at the door to the other world the dying get a glimpse of a place that is magnificent in its beauty. But of course at the time of death, the dying do not know that they might be reborn and start to suffer all over again. . . ."

I thought, When a baby is born, he cries and screams even before the doctor gives him a whack. Perhaps at the door to this world all babies are peeking at a long hard road.

The Master went on, "A person with any kind of religion is searching for the source of life and the whereabouts of life after the death of a physical form. As a result of such searching, all religions point towards the same direction—life itself does not die with the death of the physical form.

"When living beings are afraid to die, it is because they do not know what death is. A religious person has no such fear, because he knows that he will live on through his Life of Wisdom."

"Human beings have endless desires.
We should develop a noble desire such as the ambition
to benefit mankind.
A desire that will soil our heart and soul must be abandoned,
and if a person should have trouble abandoning it,
all he needs to do is work in a hospital and
absorb what is taking place around him."

— *Master Cheng Yen* —

"We human beings," I asked, "are always desiring material things and emotional fulfillment, such as money and fame. Master Cheng Yen, how can we ignore such desires?"

"Every human being has to have his share of desires, and it goes beyond material things and emotional fulfillment. Incorrect desires are the root of misery, but at the same time there are desires that should not be abandoned.

"A desire can be an ambition and a yearning, or an obsession and a lust.

"Ambition and yearning can become a positive driving force. With ambition a person can reach a worthy goal, and with yearning a person can accomplish a noble mission.

"Obsession is the dust that gathers on a clear mirror, and lust is the wave that takes away the tranquility of a lake. An obsessed person will descend from his moral standard, and, when possessed by lust, a person will detour from his principle of honor.

"A person's heart is pulled towards the direction determined by his desires, and a person's true nature is often soiled by the wrong kind of desires such as lust and obsession.

"If a person can change the negative type of desires into positive ones, then his heart can be released from the pulling pressure and his true nature can become once more pure and free.

"When a person already has a positive desire in his heart, he should nourish it, work hard for it, and march in full force towards its fulfillment.

"Thousands of years ago, Buddha gave up his position as a prince, left his magnificent palace, and parted from his family including his loving parents, beautiful wife, and newborn son. His heart was guided by a noble desire—to find a path that will lead all living beings from endless sorrow and pain.

"And the Tzu-chi Foundation members also have the desire to serve people—to grant happiness to those who are sad and to lend a merciful hand to whoever is in pain. Such desires have fulfilled the lives of many members who used to feel their existence void of meaning, and such desires have also provided many men and women with a reason to face each day.

"Desires for worldly possessions are not easy to relinquish; the want for money and fame is difficult to curb. But it is not impossible—all a person needs to do is become a volunteer worker in a hospital and absorb what is taking place around him.

"The Tzu-chi members have trained their minds to observe all that is happening. When working in the Emergency Room of the Buddhist Compassion Relief General Hospital, they came in contact with the critically ill and the seriously wounded and often witnessed the death of a physical form.

"'When life on earth is but temporary, why should we desire earthly possessions?' They began to think this way and soon forgot their desire for things that cannot be taken to another life.

"And then they were transferred to the Rehabilitation Center. While helping those either mentally or physically handicapped, what they saw reminded them of what I have been teaching:

"'In this world, no one has permanent ownership over what he has, not even his mind and body. In this world, everyone is only leasing things for the time being, including his mind and body.'

"Watching the physically handicapped struggling to gain the full use of their arms and legs, they realized how fortunate they were to have the full use of their bodies. Observing the mentally handicapped battling to utter a few words or gather some thoughts, they began to see that the right to use their minds to the fullest potential was a privilege. It dawned on them that for the physically and mentally handicapped all the precious gems in the world are useless, nor is there any use for fame or wealth.

"A desire for emotional fulfillment can be very difficult to abandon when the desire has become either a lust or an obsession. But once again, when a person has trouble abandoning such desire, all he needs to do is work in a hospital and keep an absorbing mind.

"The Tzu-chi members worked in the Maternity Ward. There they saw the mothers suffer the pain of giving birth . . . even a normal birth. When it was a difficult birth and the mother suffered more, she always insisted that if only one life could be saved, it had to be the life of her baby.

"In the waiting room there were anxious fathers. They might be poor and uneducated, but they always had dreams for their children—the children will have the life that they themselves do not know, and they will do all they can to provide such life for their children.

"Seeing the selfless love of a mother and a father, the Tzu-chi members began to regret that they had not been treating their parents well enough. They had all argued with their parents and at times had been rude enough to break their parents' hearts.

"And then they went to the Geriatrics Ward, where they were shocked by the difference between the Geriatrics Ward and Pediatrics Ward. In the Pediatrics Ward, each child was surrounded by worried adults—there was seldom an orphan. In the Geriatrics Ward, there were so many lonely, old people—most of them looked like aged orphans.

"When a child was sick, his parents could always take a leave of absence from work. But when an old woman or old man was sick, most of the children would have to work or do more important things—so they claimed.

"The sad sight of the sick and lonely old people saddened the Tzu-chi members. They became aware of the fact that when the parents are giving an unlimited amount of selfless love to the children, the children are giving back very little love in return. Their true nature is awakened by their conscience. Those with living parents couldn't wait to rush back home and throw themselves into their parents' arms. Those whose parents were dead regretted that the love which they always had in their hearts did not awake soon enough.

"At this moment, they could also see clearly that there is no love as noble and selfless as the love of parents—when compared to such love, the love based on passion and lust is unworthy of pursuit."

CHAPTER TEN

"Wisdom is an inner force that is kind and virtuous.
It shows in a person's proficiency to differentiate good from evil.
And it can be seen in his aptitude to separate right from wrong."

— *Master Cheng Yen* —

A YOUNG GIRL APPEARED, carrying a tray. She placed two bowls of soup on the rattan table for the Master and me, then continued to serve us snacks in small separate dishes.

"This is called Tse-ba," Master Cheng Yen said, pointing at a plate which contained tiny rice-balls that seemed to have been made in a mold. "The aborigines taught us this dish. We take a section of bamboo about two inches in diameter and one foot long, wash it, then fill the center with seasoned raw rice. The bamboo containers are steamed until the rice is done, then are split open with care and the long tubes of rice are cut into sections."

We began to eat. The rice-balls were delicious with a faint fragrance of bamboo. I ate heartily while the Master nibbled the food with little appetite.

"I can live on food like this for the rest of my life," I said, picking up my soup bowl. "If I could learn to cook like this, it would be easy to become a Buddhist."

"But Buddhists do not have to be vegetarians," the Master said. "A Buddhist must not kill or give orders to kill. But when non-vegetarian food is already prepared, it is not a sin to eat it. However, all the Sheh-fus and I are vegetarians for life, of course."

Continuing to eat, I glanced up at the wall-clock. It was 10:15. We had been talking for over an hour. The Master had used her will power to conquer the coughing spells but still coughed now and then. I remembered what the doctor had said—she still had a fever and needed to rest.

"Master Cheng Yen," I said, putting down my soup bowl. "If you don't mind, I'll proceed with my questions while finishing my food."

She looked at me reassuringly, "You really don't have to rush."

Soon the food was taken away and the interview resumed.

"Master Cheng Yen, we are granted the privilege of using our bodies and minds, and the difference between the clever and the not-so-clever is the result of an uneven distribution of these gifts.

"Since the clever are blessed with better gifts, do they also have a greater obligation in using their minds? And since the not-so-clever are not gifted with much, can they just sit back and relax instead of striving to conquer their handicap?" I asked.

A frown wrinkled the Master's smooth brow. When she spoke, there was a touch of disappointment in her voice, "It is wrong to say that the rights we have are 'granted,' 'distributed,' 'blessed,' or 'gifted.'

"We have to earn our rights; they are not gifts. If a person does not work diligently to improve his mind during this life, then in his next life he will not be born with a greater intelligence—we can predict our future by looking at our current behavior.

"But when a person is born with great intelligence in this life, then in his previous life he must have worked hard to develop his mind—we can trace our past by examining our present status.

"Besides what we are born with, we must also continue to absorb and digest—to learn. A child can be born as a fast learner, but even a genius has to be educated. We have heard that a child at age seven can go to college, but we have never heard that a child is born with the knowledge of a college graduate.

"Karma is the result of all moral and immoral volition. Karma creates either good or evil transmigration, based on our actions. And Karma is the moral kernel in each being which survives death for further rebirth or metamorphoses.

"When we are born with an unlimited right to use our mind as the result of a good Karma, we need to strive for wisdom instead of cleverness; the two are totally different.

"Cleverness is but a function. Wisdom is the true nature in us—the nature of Buddha.

"When a person is clever, he is not necessarily wise. But when a person is wise, he is always clever.

"Cleverness is not always good. It can be used by anyone towards a wrong goal. At times it can become the means of acquiring personal gain at the cost of others. Even cunning is a sign of cleverness.

"A clever person can create problems at home and be a nuisance to society—while at the same time developing a bad Karma for himself in his next life.

"Wisdom is an inner force that is kind and virtuous. It shows in a person's proficiency to differentiate good from evil. And it can be seen in his aptitude to separate right from wrong.

"A wise person strives to serve others, to benefit society, and to contribute to mankind—throughout his current life, he develops a good Karma for himself in the life to come.

"You asked about the obligation of those born with a right to use their mind to its greatest capacity.

"The clever should cultivate his cleverness and turn it into wisdom. He should use his mind for the goodness of mankind instead of himself. He must try his best to uproot his greed, malice and lust, and carry out deeds of kindness, compassion, mercy and selfless love. By doing so, in his next life he may become wise instead of merely clever.

"Once wise, a person usually knows that he should cherish his hard-earned wisdom. He is capable of safeguarding the result of his effort in a previous life, and making certain that his wisdom does not deteriorate. He will continue to learn and improve himself, so that after the death of his physical form, and if not reaching the state of Nirvana, he will be born again with a good Karma.

"And you asked if the not-so-clever can sit back and relax instead of striving to conquer his handicap.

"When a Karma is already bad, we cannot afford to make it worse.

"When a farmer is given the seed of a poor crop, he has to work extraordinarily hard.

"He must fertilize, water, weed, and toil to protect the sprout from bad weather and expose it to a proper amount of sunlight. It is only then that a farmer can gather a harvest better than the seed's original potential.

"And when carrying the seed of his current harvest to the next planting, he will begin with a healthy and vigorous seed—a good Karma. Similarly, a considerable amount of effort must be used to insure a highly developed mind."

Master Cheng Yen and the author

"When a person's hands are filled with the packages of today,
he will not have a spare hand to pick up a package of yesterday."

— *Master Cheng Yen* —

Looking at the next question that I had written, I remembered writing it at home right after reading a book on the thoughts of Master Cheng Yen. She was quoted to say that in order to move forward, a person must not look back.

"Master," I asked, "how can we not look back? Sometimes the call of the past is so strong that we cannot avoid hearing its voice . . . even when the voice is filled with anger and regret and grief."

The master's voice was firm and strong, "In order to forget the past, a person has to look at the present.

"When a person concentrates on living the present moment, he will not be able to spare his attention for the past.

"For example: when a person's hands are filled with the packages of today, he will not have a spare hand to pick up a package of yesterday.

"In order to advance, a person must take steps. When his right foot moves forward, his left foot has to let go of the old ground and follow the right foot's path.

"A person will not get anywhere if his right foot steps forward but his left foot is glued to the same spot.

"Nor can a person progress into the future if only half of him starts a new life while the other half lingers in a life that is long gone.

"A person should not live in yesterday, nor should he live in tomorrow. The only reality is today and this current moment. Give it your full attention, and the past will disappear, and the future will arrive in due time to become the present."

"Knowing is easier than doing."

— *Master Cheng Yen* —

"Master Cheng Yen," I said, "My next question was motivated by the Four Classics of China, in which the ancient scholars debated the question, Which is easier—To Know or To Do?

"As of this day, this argument is still being carried on; some think it is difficult to know what we want to do, but rather easy to do it once our mind is made up; the others think it is always difficult to do things, although we can easily know what we want done.

"Master Cheng Yen, which do you think is easier—Knowing or Doing?"

Master Cheng Yen says, "Both Knowng and Doing can be easy,
provided that the pursuer longs for knowledge,
and the doer yearns for accomplishment!"

The Master thought carefully. Time ticked on. And then she answered with a sigh, "If I must choose one over the other, then I will have to say that in my opinion Knowing is easier than Doing.

"To know something can be a private matter. When reading, researching, collecting information, or thinking, trying to reach a conclusion . . . the chances of encountering opposing forces is minimum.

"We acquire knowledge, and then we know what we want to do. But once we start working towards the goal, we are no longer on our own. There are very few things that we do, which do not involve other people. . . ."

The Master paused. A dark shadow moved across her face, disappearing the next instant without a trace.

I remembered what Dr. Tseng had told me about the building of the Buddhist Compassion Relief General Hospital. For Master Cheng Yen, Knowing what she wanted to do had been easy; there had been no struggle or debate; the knowledge of wanting to build a special hospital had come to her effortlessly. But the Doing had taken seven long years, during which she had encountered opposition and difficulties beyond imagination; tears had been shed, sleepless nights endured, and she had even suffered a minor heart attack.

I looked up from my notebook. Studying the Master's face, I could find only love, mercy, wisdom, forgiveness and peace. Shaking my head in disbelief, I envied her mastery in turning a deaf ear to the calls of a formidable yesteryear.

With another sigh that was barely audible, the Master added in a whisper, "Knowing can be difficult too, if the person is not sincere in acquiring wisdom. Doing can become even more strenuous, if the person is not enthusiastic in seeing things done."

The next moment the Master squared her shoulders, lifted her chin, and at the same time clenched her left hand into a fist. Giving a wave of the fist, she raised her voice, "On the contrary, both Knowing and Doing can be easy, provided that the pursuer longs for knowledge, and the doer yearns for accomplishment!"

*"To turn compassion into action is a road,
and we Buddhists are fellow travelers.
The road is long and wearisome, but we can keep going
as long as we have courage in our hearts."*

— *Master Cheng Yen* —

"Master Cheng Yen, my next question is how to turn compassion into action . . . but please first allow me to explain.

"It happened on a day soon after Shang and I arrived in Hwalien. We were at the seashore, and we saw a pushcart, selling sausages that were being cooked on a rotisserie. Other than the peddler, there were several men, eating and talking while walking around the stand. There was also a dog. It was almost bald from mange. Its ribs were sticking out from underneath its furless skin. Its eyes were large and watering, staring at the sausages that hung from the rotisserie. It was taking in the aroma with its mouth open, revealing a pink tongue that was wet with salivation.

"When the dog neared the men, none of them hesitated to give it a kick. It seemed such a natural thing for them to do. They simply raised their booted feet and brought the weight down on the dog, all the while laughing and enjoying their food.

"It must hurt a lot, because the dog moaned deeply—a sound that escaped through his throat from deep inside his body.

"Master, I shared the dog's misery. I could feel his hunger, and knew his pain and agony. I could almost hear him asking: 'I'm not a bad dog. Why do all of you dislike me so much? Why won't any of you give me just a small bite of something?'

"Master, I wanted to buy some sausages for the dog, but was hit with many questions: What will the people think of me? Will they laugh at me? Or will they think that I am crazy since there are only very few people on this island who feed stray dogs?

"Master Cheng Yen, I didn't do anything to help the poor dog. I can still see him in my mind. And the image of him will not fade. I will always wonder what happened to him in the end, and when will his suffering end. And I will continue to hate myself for not giving him at least one good meal as a temporary relief.

"Master, how can a person immediately turn his compassion into action without thinking about so many other things?"

The Master looked away from my tearful eyes and answered softly, "To turn compassion into action is not the problem of one person, but the problem of the entire human race.

"When a person wants to do something, even when he wants it badly, there is always other people's opinions to consider.

"And people do like to criticize, and they like to point fingers too—these actions are but habits of the human species.

"In order to turn compassion into action, a person has to be brave . . . he has to be *very* brave.

"With courage, he can proceed to conquer the psychological barrier that stands between compassion and action, and disregard other people's viewpoints and criticisms, then do what he thinks is good and right.

"After taking the first step, he must hold on to his courage. He cannot afford to lose it; he has to reinforce it, because he will need plenty of it in order to continue with his conquest.

"In this world, suffering is found everywhere. Actually, all living beings are suffering . . . in various locations, in different ways.

"The pain and agony you saw in that dog can easily be found in other beings. The ill treatment received by that dog is the treatment which is received by many of those living throughout every region of the globe.

"A Buddhist respects life itself, regardless of its physical form. We wish that, someday, somehow, every human being will be willing to respect every other living creature.

"'To turn compassion into action' can be viewed as a road, and 'All living beings becoming free from misery' is the destination. We Buddhists are but fellow travelers. The road is long and wearisome, but we can keep going as long as we have courage in our hearts.

"Marching forward, we can use endurance and patience as our traveling companions. We will parade through all difficulties and eventually reach our goal."

"When the Inferior Self is forgotten
and the Superior Self takes over, then a person can
gain super energy and force himself to go on."

— Master Cheng Yen —

"Master Cheng Yen, you never sleep more than four hours a night, and you do not waste any of your waking moments. I heard that resting is considered wasting time as far as you are concerned. You make daily visits to the patients in the hospital, and you do a million other things . . . including taking time to talk to me. How can you force yourself to go on when your body is exhausted?"

The Master answered with a smile, "Forcing oneself to go on can become a habit, like any other habit that we form. It can, however, be reinforced by environment.

"I've been working like this for over thirty years now. Throughout the years, I've taken on numerous tasks, and I consider each task a reinforcement of my habit.

"A person's environment is the training ground for his body and mind. When environment demands, a person's body can produce more strength, and the ability to tolerate can gradually sprout in his mind.

"Of course, at times the body will feel the burdens of life, and the mind will have the tendency to weaken.

"For example: there are times when I am already exhausted and someone comes to tell me that I must talk to so-and-so. The first thought that crosses my mind is, "Why must I do this when there is no strength left in me?"

"But then after I have forced myself to face the individual and start talking to him, I will find myself enjoying the conversation. There will be a newly gained strength in my body, and I will forget that I ever hesitated to talk to this person.

"The feeble body and the impotent mind belong to a person's Inferior Self. A body that knows no exhaustion, and a mind that knows only determination, belong to a person's Superior Self. When the Inferior Self is forgotten and the Superior Self takes over, then a person can gain super energy and force himself to go on."

"A giver must be grateful to the receiver.
When your gratefulness is sincere, the receiver will know
that you are not only giving him a gift, but also your respect."

— *Master Cheng Yen* —

"Giving is viewed as a good deed,
and a giver is always considered a good person.
But beneath the wings of such goodness
is the indispensable supporting wind—the receiver.

— *Master Cheng Yen* —

"Master Cheng Yen, before my next question, I must tell you something."

The Master nodded her permission. I looked down at the dark blue coat that I had on and said, "Not knowing a cold wave was blanketing Taiwan, my husband and I had not brought any heavy clothing, and had shivered in the wind and rain. Observing this, the Tzu-chi members offered us sweaters and coats. We accepted some, but felt rather uncomfortable. We decided that this coat and the sweater I am wearing, plus the sweater Shang has on, must be returned to their owners as soon as possible, although they have insisted that we are welcome to take the clothing home.

"Master Cheng Yen, one has to learn to become generous in order to enjoy the act of giving. But it is not easy to be a receiver either. How can a proud person learn to accept without feeling that his pride is being wounded?"

The Master laughed softly. "In order to accomplish this, our ways of thinking must be changed—on the part of the giver as well as the receiver.

"If a person thinks of himself as a giver, only a giver, and nothing less than a giver, then his arrogance will be sensed by all others, including those to whom he intends to give things.

"With self-respect, most of us would rather be without things than receive from an arrogant giver.

"I often tell the members of the Tzu-chi Foundation that when giving, you must be grateful to the receivers. When your gratefulness is sincere, the receiver will know that you are not only giving him a gift, but also your respect.

"If a giver does not feel such respect towards the receivers, then it is his duty to develop such feeling.

"A true giver is offering two things at the same time—the present and his highest respect.

"And when a true giver sees that his gift has been accepted, he will immediately give the receiver another gift—his hearty thanks.

"Two years ago, the Tzu-chi members went to China to help the flood victims. The members and I were criticized severely by some of the people in Taiwan: the people in China are our enemies! Why help the enemies when there are plenty of needy on our own island?

"Troubled by such criticism, some of the Tzu-chi members were frustrated. I told them that the situation only proves that to give is a rare privilege which has to be earned by conquering all obstacles.

"I also told them: such privilege can never be yours without the help of the receivers—they are paying a high price to make it possible; without their suffering, how can you have a chance to help remove their pain?

"Giving is viewed as a good deed, and a giver is always considered a good person. But beneath the wings of such goodness is the indispensable supporting wind—the receiver.

"The concept that 'a receiver is in debt to the giver' has to be changed. Such change may take a little time. But once it takes place, we can all agree that 'a giver is in debt to the receiver.'"

Master Cheng Yen smiled at me meaningfully, "And then, why should any receiver feel too proud to receive?"

CHAPTER ELEVEN

"If a person doesn't know how to use money,
his money will use him."

— *Master Cheng Yen* —

THE LONG-HAIRED CAT was pure white and quite large, wearing a red collar with tiny bells hanging from below its chin. In long, slow strides, it moved towards the rattan chair next to mine, leapt up and curled itself into a ball. Its topaz eyes were half-closed, its tail moving back and forth.

"It was given to me about ten years ago. It's name is Shan Lai, which means 'Goodness Arrives,'" the Master said.

Shan Lai, Goodness Arrives, reminded me of two stories:

The first was about Buddha as a young prince leaving his palace around 500 BC riding a white horse. The second was about the Guardian of Earth as a Korean monk sailing to China during the 8th century AD in a boat while accompanied by a white dog. It is believed that both Buddha and the Guardian of Earth are still among us, taking various physical forms to show us the way to enlightenment, and wherever they go, each of them is accompanied by a pet that is pure white.

"And here comes Show Show," the Master said, pointing at another cat who had just entered the room.

It was a Siamese, also wearing a red collar with bells. It moved lightly and fast, headed directly towards the Master, then jumped

The author with the Master's white cat—
Buddha had a white horse, and the Guardian of Earth
was a Korean monk who traveled to China
accompanied by a white dog.

up to land on her lap. It did push-pulls before lying down and closing its blue eyes.

"Show Show, Charm Charm, is also a gift from someone about a decade ago," the Master said, her hands gently stroking the Siamese. "My cats are vegetarians. They don't even kill mice. Show Show and Shan Lai like to walk behind any mice, following them step-by-step but never get too close. And the mice never try to run from either of them."

Looking at Show Show, I thought of a documentary film about cats. The cameraman had gone to Thailand and filmed the temples and monasteries. Siamese cats were seen everywhere with the monks. According to the legend of Thailand, when a cat purrs, it is actually chanting out a Buddhist prayer. We continued with our interview in the presence of Shan Lai and Show Show, who continued to purr.

* * *

"Master Cheng Yen, what is your definition of 'money?'" I asked.

The Master answered briefly, "Money is a tool. With it, we can do many things. Other than being a tool, money is nothing."

In one of her books the Master had written: "A person has to know how to use the money earned by him. If he doesn't know how to use money, his money will use him."

And in the same book she had also reminded people that according to the teachings of Buddha, a person's money eventually comes into the possession of five other parties: government, natural disaster, thieves and robbers, war, and children.

She had explained that no matter where a person lives or what period of time he lives in, his money will eventually fall into the hands of either one of these five parties or be divided among all of them.

She had explained further: When living under the rule of any government, we always have to pay a tax. Many of us have lost our homes because of natural disasters. Thieves and robbers can appear in various forms and rob us in different ways. We are paying for the war of the world directly or indirectly. Our children share our money either before or after the death of our physical forms.

"Our physical forms can last only a lifetime, and that is the only time we can hold on to our share of the money," she had said. "But if we can use our money to benefit mankind, the good Karma created with money will stay with us forever . . . and it cannot be taken from us by any of the other parties."

"It will take the actions and thoughts of many lifetimes
for a person to improve his soiled soul,
and his soul has to be completely purified
before he can escape the Wheel and the Round."

— Master Cheng Yen —

"Master Cheng Yen, my next question is about the Wheel of Transmigration, also known as the Round of Existence. But first, please allow me to refresh my limited knowledge, so you can correct my mistakes."

The Master nodded and I went on. "According to the teachings of Buddha, a living being's soul was pure in the very beginning when the world was young. But then he began to act and think, and his harmful actions and wicked thoughts soiled his soul.

"In each life, a being is born with a soul that has traveled through other lifetimes. During this lifetime his mind and body will once again react to environment and all the accessory conditions and add a new dimension to his soul. Upon the death of his physical form, his soul will not die, and upon rebirth the soul will enter another physical form which is not necessarily human. Once more, his physical form will act and think and change his soul in either positive or negative ways while suffering the unavoidable agonies of a mortal being.

"This constant revolution is the Wheel of Transmigration and the Round of Existence, commonly called the Wheel and the Round. It is said that a soul can escape such revolution only when it becomes pure again. Once escaped from the Wheel and the Round, a soul will go to the state of Nirvana, where eternal bliss and absolute happiness can be found."

I looked at the Master. When she did not correct me, I asked, "Master Cheng Yen, how can a physical form help purify his soul and escape the Wheel and the Round?"

The Master said, "Our world is old. Therefore, there is an old soul in every being, even a very young being. Within each of us there is a soul that has traveled many lifetimes on a road paved by behaviors and thoughts carried out through various physical forms.

"When all the previous thoughts and behaviors were merciful and kind, the road already leads towards the state of Nirvana. When a person has such a soul, in his current life all he needs to do is to carefully complete the last section of the road.

"But if all the past behaviors and thoughts were merciless and selfish and damaging to mankind, then the road leads towards endless suffering. When a person has such a soul, in his current life and also the many lives to come, he will have to work hard in order to change the direction of this road.

"A person should always do good deeds and think good thoughts to help purify his soul, although it will not make an immediate difference. A person cannot help his soul to escape the Wheel and the Round with one action or one thought, and perhaps not even with the actions and thoughts of an entire lifetime. Usually, it will take the actions and thoughts of many lifetimes for a person to improve his soiled soul, and his soul has to be completely purified before he can escape the Wheel and the Round."

Dharma Master Cheng Yen

"All fears can be removed
by revealing the Buddha-nature in our hearts."

— *Master Cheng Yen* —

"Master Cheng Yen," I showed her a pamphlet containing information on bone marrow donation in Taiwan, "according to this pamphlet, in Taiwan and during different times, various organizations have tried to convince people that donating bone marrow will not endanger a person's health. But the fear is universal, and the majority continued to refuse such donation.

"And then you, Master Cheng Yen, asked people to donate their bone marrow, and the members of the Tzu-chi Foundation started a bone marrow donation movement. It is said that immediately the bone marrow donation became a great success, and no one can figure out how the success was achieved.

"Master Cheng Yen, since fear is a strong barrier between compassion and action, and there is a deep-rooted fear for donating bone marrow, how did you succeed in removing such fear?"

The Master answered calmly, "I removed such fear by revealing the Buddha-nature in everyone's heart.

"In everyone's heart, there is this selfless love—the love of Buddha. Once such love is revealed, the person will be able to do what Buddha would have done if placed in the same situation.

"When a soul descends from the state of Nirvana by choice, it is called either a Buddha or a Bodhisattva. In the bygone days a Buddha appeared as an Indian prince, and a Bodhisattva emerged as a Korean monk. As of this day, Buddhas and Bodhisattvas continue to appear in different physical forms, and most of the time we won't even know we are facing them.

"The Buddhas and Bodhisattvas are on earth not only to enlighten us but also to save us from suffering. Our sufferings can be divided into many categories, such as the lack of material substances, spiritual fulfillment and sound health.

"When saving people from the lack of material substances, a Buddha or a Bodhisattva will give them an opportunity to earn money, food, clothing and houses. When saving people from the lack of spiritual fulfillment, a Buddha or a Bodhisattva will apply various methods. For example, when a person is caught in a net of confusion, he will be shown a light of wisdom. But the achievement of a Buddha or a Bodhisattva depends on whether the person being helped is willing to accept such wisdom—there are plenty of us deaf to golden words.

"When saving us from the lack of sound health, a Buddha or a Bodhisattva will do all he can to remove the illness. Some of the illnesses can be cured by medicine, some cannot. As of this day, there is still no medicine to take the place of bone marrow.

"The Tzu-chi Foundation members and I explained to the people that by giving only a part of the healthy bone marrow in our body, we can save another person's life. And we advised everyone to put away their fear.

"A person's willingness to accept advice is decided by his Karma, whether the adviser and the listener were compatible in their previous lives. When the same advice is given to the same person by two different advisers, at times one advice will be accepted, the other rejected.

"It just happened that, when the others advised people, no one was willing to listen, but when I and the Tzu-chi Foundation members counseled people to do so, the advice was willingly accepted.

"In only two months, our call for bone marrow was answered by almost ten thousand donors. We will soon have an auction, selling jewelry and other items collected from compassionate people, and the money will go to the Bone Marrow Center.

"On the week of the donation, there were long lines waiting to donate their bone marrow. When asked why they are no longer afraid, their answers were the same: Master Cheng Yen said it will not hurt us, and the Master will not want to see us hurt.

The Master smiled broadly, "People's eagerness in donating bone marrow is also based on the wisdom that they have collected throughout the years: it is a person's privilege to give; when giving, a person has to be totally selfless. Yes, there is this Buddha-nature in everyone's heart. Once revealed, there will be no fear in serving mankind . . . it may be saving them from poverty, sorrow, or an illness through the giving of bone marrow."

"We are all fish in a tank with holes;
time is the water that keeps seeping out,
and once it is gone all our physical forms must die.

— *Master Cheng Yen* —

"Master Cheng Yen, the Tzu-chi Foundation members meet once a month. When you spoke during each meeting, your words were recorded and gathered into books. At the beginning of one year you wished to develop greater courage, wisdom, and strength. In another year you wished to set proper goals and acquire knowledge to obtain them. Another year is almost over. Master Cheng Yen, what are some of your plans and wishes for the coming new year?"

The Master let out a long sigh, revealing the accumulated exhaustion of more than three decades. "At this very moment, except for looking forward to the opening of the medical college, I do not have any special plan or wish. I'm only doing the best I can for today and this very moment."

After a brief pause, she added, "However, I do have some plans and wishes that will never change; among them, I would like to see all living beings saved from suffering.

"I would also like to see all living beings learn to treasure their living moments . . . life is so short and fleeting!"

The Master paused. I recalled in one of the books she was quoted to say that we are all fish in a tank with holes; time is the water that keeps seeping out, and once it is gone all our physical forms must die.

The Master continued softly, "I would like to see Buddha's words accepted by all living beings, and every living being carrying out Buddha's teaching. Then hatred will be replaced by love, and cruelty replaced by mercy, selfishness will turn into selflessness, and violence become peace. By that time the purity and goodness within each living being will be revealed, all lives will be treated with respect, and every ordinary earthly creature will become a saint."

A saintly glow brightened the Master's face. Nodding and smiling, she said firmly, "Yes, that is what I wish and plan for the future."

"A writer's writing has to be proven to the readers
through speaking and behaving;
the three cannot contradict one another."

— *Master Cheng Yen* —

"Master Cheng Yen, what can a writer do for the Tzu-chi Foundation?" I asked.

The Master answered after thinking the question over with care. "When a writer has a sincere and impartial heart and can use her pen to describe life objectively and truthfully, and when the readers are willing to accept her writings as the words of someone who has absorbed life, then this writer has carried out a good deed for the Tzu-chi Foundation.

"The Tzu-chi Foundation needs writers . . . not for advertising, but for sending out messages and enabling people to understand the Foundation—its true spirit, its history, and its current function and future goal.

"And a writer has to do more than just writing. Whatever she or he has written has to be proven to the readers through speaking and behaving; the three cannot contradict one another."

I met the Master's penetrating eyes. The next moment I realized what she was telling me: As a writer, a person has certain responsibilities to society. If she expects her book to have a moral value, such a moral standard must also appear in her spoken words and physical conduct.

I glanced at the wall clock. It was almost 11:30. The Master, who seldom gave interviews, had allowed me to interview her for two and a half hours.

She had been extremely patient all this time. After answering each question, she had asked if the answer was clear enough. She had encouraged me to keep asking, saying that if the answer had created more questions in my heart, she wouldn't mind answering more questions.

As I closed my notebook, she said slowly, "Buddhism is not the easiest to understand, and it ought to be made simple and down-to-earth. If it could be applied to daily life, it would be practiced by more people . . . especially the younger generation.

"Twenty-five hundred years ago and in northern India, Buddhism was a simple religion dealing with a manner of living and a down-to-earth way of life. But when the scriptures were brought to China and translated into Chinese, some became complicated and confusing. And then the scriptures became worse when fantasies and mythological fabrications were added to frighten or impress people.

"Well, my disciples and I have been trying our best to bring Buddhism to its simple original way, and I hope you've understood everything we have discussed."

The Master began to cough again. Show Show, the Siamese cat, peeked at me through half-open eyes. Shan Lai, the white Angora, stretched and yawned.

"Thank you, Master Cheng Yen," I said, putting away my pen. "I truly appreciate this interview. . . ."

The Master interrupted me, "You don't have to go. I feel very strong right now, and we can talk for a while longer."

And then she leaned forward and asked with obvious interest, "Tell me about your life in Michigan."

I described Bark River: the glistening winter, the delightful spring and summer, the colorful autumn, the absence of neon lights, the low rate of crime, our few but true and sincere friends, the beautiful deer, the wild rabbits and other wild animals that roamed outside our humble home, the hermit-like lifestyle that Shang and I have treasured in the past decade. . . .

The Master listened with full attention. When I stopped, she said, "I didn't know anything about you and your wish in writing this book until two days before you arrived. Actually, I don't think I am worthy of this writing. I didn't create the Tzu-chi Foundation without the help of many people. All that has been achieved is the accomplishment of a society, a nation, and a race."

The Master glanced at my notebook. "Will you let the readers know that the credit of spreading Buddha's teaching belongs to the Tzu-chi Foundation members and not an insignificant person named Cheng Yen?"

I smiled. "Master Cheng Yen, I will let the readers know that you are a thread that is woven with love and mercy, and that each of the Tzu-chi members is a pearl. They are strung together with you in their hearts, and then the Tzu-chi Foundation is formed and functioning as an unit."

She tilted her head to one side, "But the value of a string of pearls rests in the pearls themselves. A thread is but a thread, not really worth much mentioning."

"The thread does not wish to be noticed, I know. She only wants the world to see the pearls," I said. "But before accepting Buddhism, the pearls were merely worthless pebbles. They were nurtured by the mother of pearl and then turned into gems. And as gems they were once scattered in different places. Without the thread, each of them would have had only a minimum value. Master Cheng Yen, the thread is *very* important."

I noticed a look of worry in her eyes, and I added, "When the thread is not made of cotton or silk but love and mercy, it will never break. It will connect the pearls forever. Once connected by your teaching, the Tzu-chi Foundation members will never become scattered again."

Nodding her head, Master Cheng Yen leaned back. She looked very tired, and I hesitated before asking the last question that had just come to my mind.

"Master Cheng Yen, in what form would you like me to write this book about you and the Tzu-chi Foundation?" I asked.

The Master answered without hesitation, "You should write it in a non-fictional form, reporting truthfully and sincerely on people and events."

"People and events?" Repeating after her, I tried to capture the full meaning of the two simple words.

"That's right," the Master's voice was definite and precise. "You should write about the Tzu-chi members whom you happen to meet, and describe their accomplishment. You don't have to use big words or fancy sentences. Some people say that I have created a new sect of Buddhism. That is not true. I am bringing Buddhism back to its original form, which is simple and down-to-earth."

The Master smiled at me one more time, "A simple and down-to-earth book, that is all you need to write."

"People meet and part because of Karma."

— *Master Cheng Yen* —

Shang and I left the Pure Abode of Still Thoughts holding a stack of books that were gifts from the Master. We walked on the tree-lined path accompanied by Ming Sheh-fu. I kept turning and looking over my shoulder, casting farewell glances at the white temple which was being left farther behind with each step.

"Why do I feel a part of me is being left behind?" I asked. "Does the temple really have magic power? My heart is captured by it and reluctant to leave. I would like to become either Show Show or Shan Lai, the two lucky cats who can stay beside the Master."

"I have the same feeling," Shang added. "The magic power does not rest in the temple, but the Master herself. And I keep hearing her farewell words as translated to me by Shuen Sheh-fu: 'People meet and part because of Karma, and we'll see if it is our Karma to be under the same roof again soon.'" Shang was interrupted by the sound of footsteps.

"Wait!" Shuen Sheh-fu called, running after us.

We waited. Shuen Sheh-fu caught up with us, panting and giving me a small red-and-white box. "Another gift from the Master."

I opened the box. It was a small statue of Buddha. The white rock had been chipped out of the mountains that surrounded Hwalien. Buddha sat with his legs crossed, hands in front of his chest, palms down as if giving out love and mercy.

Staring at Buddha's tranquil face, I saw the face of Master Cheng Yen. Shang must have shared my discovery, because he mumbled, "There is no resemblance in the features of the two. Physically, Buddha is three times the size of the Master, but it's the expression . . . peaceful and selfless, forgiving and compassionate. And the two also share the same calm strength . . . like the strength of moonlight that can brighten the world in its own quiet way."

"Please thank the Master for me," I said to Shuen Sheh-fu. "I would like to go back and thank her, but am afraid to do so. . . ." Swallowing the sudden lump in my throat, I continued, "Once going back, I might never want to leave again."

Unable to move my feet, my whole body began to shake. There was such a strong urge in my heart: I want to leave something behind, something valued by me and a part of me, something to take my place and stay in the temple with the Master, so that through it I could also stay with her.

My tear-blurred vision fell on my left hand. A narrow gold band glistened in the sunlight. It was the wedding ring given to me by Shang; he never bought me a diamond because I never wanted one. The band was of solid gold, soft and bendable.

"Its shape can be changed to suit your finger, and I can be changed to suit you," Shang had told me twenty years previously on our wedding day.

Throughout the years, we had both changed ourselves to suit each other, and the ring had never left my finger.

I removed the ring, handed it to Shuen Sheh-fu. "It's for the coming auction," I said. "The auction will take place in Taiwan, and whoever buys this ring will be able to stay much closer to the Master than I. I've been receiving so much from all of you since arriving in Hwalien, and this is all that I can give right now."

I walked away quickly, without giving Shuen Sheh-fu a chance to speak. I only turned one more time to see that both Shuen Sheh-fu and Ming Sheh-fu were waving. I waved back at them, then forced myself to walk faster.

PART THREE
MEMORY OF A MOTHER

CHAPTER TWELVE

"A person's wisdom does not die.
It travels from one lifetime to another,
and becomes stronger with each life."

— *Master Cheng Yen* —

TAICHUNG WAS IN THE HEART of Taiwan, and Ching-shuei, Clear Water, was a small town in its outskirts. As our car descended a high mountain that stood to the west of this town, we saw at the foot of the steep hills rivers running through the valley and rippling in the sun.

"This is Mount Ox-Horse," said Alex Chow, who had accompanied Shang and me to Taichung. "From a distance, it resembles the heads of an ox and a horse. Legend goes that it has absorbed the best of heaven and earth and become a mountain with soul, therefore through the years in the nearby area many great people have been born."

He pointed down towards the valley at a building that was red and gold and glistening. "It's also said that the temple down there is equally responsible for the town's good fortune."

We reached the Purple Cloud Temple and saw raised white letters on two red posts:

The Temple of Purple Clouds in Master Cheng Yen's hometown

Purple sky extends toward the east
when heavenly music is coming near.

Clouds of magnificent hue arrive from the west
as a new wisdom is shared by mankind.

I told Shang what they meant, "Buddhism traveled from the western lands towards China, then enlightened the suffering Chinese like purple clouds brightening a dreary sky."

The temple was an overwhelming edifice with its brightly colored carvings at the tip of five curled roofs. Two of the roofs were covered with carved figures. There were a pair of triple-layered pagodas on either side of the massive entrance, each with eight-sided tops curving upward.

An ornate building stood behind the temple, its thick pillars carved with flying dragons and its horizontal beams hung with red lanterns. The roof was crowded with carvings of phoenix, tigers and other figures, both human and animal, all painted in bright colors.

Alex went on, "The Purple Cloud Temple was built by the Japanese who occupied the island from 1885 to 1945. During those fifty years the Taiwanese were not allowed to become politically active. Because of that, they turned towards Buddhism for comfort. Having always been Buddhists, the Japanese encouraged the Taiwanese to do so. Master Cheng Yen was born during the Japanese rule, and her first glance of a Buddhist temple was this one."

We left the temple and drove around Clear Water, through narrow alleys and curving lanes. "Although now a tourist attraction the town has not changed much in the past decades," Alex said, "except that the rice fields have reduced in size and a few of the old houses have tumbled down. But only people who are much older than I can tell you what Clear Water was like in the years when the Master was a child—people like the Master's mother."

✳ ✳ ✳

The Master's mother, Mrs. Wong, met us in the Tzu-chi Hall of Taichung.

Shang left us to take pictures in the other parts of the Hall, and she and I were left alone.

Soft music could be heard coming from unseen speakers, surrounding us with the songs that told of love and kindness, mercy and compassion. Softer than the music was the sound of chanting coming from somewhere at the end of a long hall outside the office. There was no incense or candle. The air was faintly scented with fresh flowers blooming in pots. The sun shone through the many windows that were tall and wide, casting warm light upon us and reflecting upon the polished wooden floor.

Mrs. Wong said, "I'm almost eighty . . . actually, seventy-nine. I worked the entire day yesterday, at the Foundation's auction in Taichung. I fainted from exhaustion and people became worried; they took me to the hospital. This morning, the doctors wouldn't let me leave until I received vitamin B12 intravenously."

She had on the dark blue uniform of Tzu-chi Foundation members, wore steel-rimmed glasses, and the eyes behind them were bright. Her hair was combed straight back and tied into a bun.

Mrs. Wong, Master Cheng Yen's mother, being interviewed

Her only jewelry, other than a pair of pearl earrings, was a boat-shaped pin symbolizing the Tzu-chi members' mission: to transport all earthly creatures from life's bitter sea. Her skin was smooth with only a few wrinkles. She was so thin that her face had a gaunt look. She had a high forehead and prominent cheekbones; her lips were thin and mouth narrow. When she smiled, neat tiny teeth were revealed.

"Mrs. Wong, you know Master Cheng Yen better than anyone else. Please tell me about her without exhausting yourself." I suggested, "Would you like to start from her birth?"

Without hesitation, Mrs. Wong started to speak. Her voice was so strong that it was difficult to believe it belonged to an aged, fragile lady.

"She was born on May 14, 1937, to a couple in Clear Water. Her mother was a kind woman, her father a tailor . . . not a tailor of clothes, but a tailor of buttons. During those days, all buttons were handmade and a form of art. . . ." Mrs. Wong went on to describe the buttons that were made of silk or cotton and shaped like butterflies.

Mrs. Wong also described a period of time when Taiwan was Japan's first colony. The Japanese were proud of the colonization, and made the island a model of economic growth.

"At the time, her parents already had two daughters, the first named Chin-yua, Magnificent Moon, and the second Chin Yu, Magnificent Jade. They named her Chin-yun, Magnificent Cloud," Mrs. Wong continued with a proud smile, "I know, because I was her aunt . . . married to her father's younger brother, who was in the business of running a small theater that featured Taiwanese opera."

Mrs. Wong narrowed her eyes, looked through her glasses at a faraway wall, and seemed to be looking at the bygone years. "Chin-yun was born a beautiful baby, neither wrinkled nor red. Her eyes were dark and bright, like two pools of water containing wisdom carried over from a previous life.

"Yes, I believe in previous life. I was already a Buddhist at that time, just like most of the people in Taiwan."

Mrs. Wong talked of the island's being shrouded in Buddhism under Japanese rule, that the Japanese and Taiwanese shared a similar writing system as well as the teachings of Buddhism and way of life.

". . . I fell in love with Chin-yun, my newborn niece, at first sight. I was childless at the time, although my husband and I had already been married for quite a few years.

"I went to the Purple Cloud Temple to pray to the Goddess of Mercy, asking for a child just like Chin-yun. In those days everyone asked for things from Buddha or the Goddess of Mercy, and no one had yet thought of searching for Buddha or the Goddess within oneself.

"I kept praying, and soon my brother-in-law and sister-in-law learned what I was praying for. When Chin-yun was eleven months old and I was still childless, they told me that I could adopt her."

Mrs. Wang looked at me, her thin face brightened by a proud smile. "Chin-yun was already walking on the day we adopted her. My husband and I loved her dearly. It was unusual for a man to treasure a daughter the way my husband treasured her. It has to be Karma—we must have known and loved her in previous lifetimes.

"As a toddler, Chin-yun already knew how to return our love. She laughed a lot and soon began to talk. Her joyful laughter and innocent words brought endless happiness to us and enriched our lives.

"Soon after adopting Chin-yun, I became pregnant and then gave birth to my first child. A total of three more followed. But even after my husband and I had these children, we continued to think of Chin-yun as the most precious child among all . . . we had completely forgotten that she was adopted.

"She was a perfect child who never needed scolding, but constantly observed and read the minds of the grownups. Oh, yes, I do recall one occasion when I had to reprimand her.

"When Chin-yun was four or five, she fought with a neighbor's child. I told her that no matter what happened she must control her temper, that to fight with anyone was absolutely wrong.

"Chin-yun looked at me sadly without arguing, then gave me her hand with palm up and waited for me to administer the thrashing. I picked up a ruler but didn't have the heart to hurt her. I barely touched her palm, then let her go.

"Chin-yun loved not only us, but also her brothers and sisters. Merely a child herself, she was helping me to take care of the babies.

At age five she was walking around with a baby strapped to her back. And it was also during this time that Taiwan was being bombed."

Mrs. Wong described the bombing. It was disastrous. Each family had a bomb shelter, usually dug in the shadow of grapevines or under the branches of a large tree. Upon the sound of an air-raid, the family would drop whatever they were doing and run for the shelter. They would hide in the dark hole and listen to the bombs fall, while the ground shook and the roof of the shelter trembled, threatening to collapse at any moment.

Mrs. Wong said, "When the all-clear sounded and we came out of the shelter, we could always see the horrible effect of war—the ground was covered with the dead and the dying, and they were not only human beings but also dogs and cows and other living things. Clear Water was a much smaller town than it is today. Everyone knew everyone else then. We would try to save the wounded, and their cries of agony would tear at our hearts and linger in our ears for the rest of our days.

"And we would also attempt to comfort those who had lost their family members. But no comforting words could heal the hearts that were broken by the loss of their loved ones.

"Besides the loss of lives, there was also the loss of worldly possessions. We would see houses demolished into piles of rubbish and remember how proud their owners had been only a short while before the air raid.

"We would catch glimpses of bicycles and rickshaws melted by the heat of the bombs, also furniture and clothing turned into ashes by flame. Beside these useless things people stood crying, murmuring that they had toiled and saved for years to buy them.

"I didn't think much about it at the time and only realized years later that Chin-yun was an observing child with wisdom carried over from previous lifetimes, and that the war affected her to a great extent. Walking among the dead and the wounded must have caused her to see the impermanence of life. Witnessing the easy destruction of material things, she must have acquired an understanding that no one could hold on to his worldly belongings.

"And when she was six years old, life became even more difficult. Taiwan had become a major navy base for Japan. Now Japan was losing the war and was no longer able to see to Taiwan's economic growth. Her father's theater was not doing well; very few people had money for entertainment. I worked hard from morning to night. Chin-yun was helping me with all the household chores, including gathering firewood while carrying a younger child on her back.

"When she was six and a half, we decided that she had to go to school. I was not in good health. Without her help, I would have to work much harder. But her education was important to us."

With a deep sigh, Mrs. Wong talked briefly about the schools in Taiwan during the Japanese rule:

Ever since taking over the island in 1885 AD, Japan had promoted elementary education with studies in Confucianism, science, and the Japanese language. They had also created a farmer's association as a means of improving agronomic technology. But they had avoided creating an intellectual climate. Middle schools had not been started until 1915, and a university had finally been established in 1928.

Mrs. Wong said, "Chin-yun was a good student. Her teachers liked her a great deal. They called her an Oh-she, in Japanese it means a Delight. She was up at dawn every morning to study, then went to the nearby foothills to gather firewood. She had four younger siblings, and she always studied and worked with one of them strapped to her back. Before going to school, she would have gathered enough wood for me to burn in the stove for the rest of the day.

"In 1945, when Chin-yun was eight years old, the war was reaching its end. The bombing became worse. There were usually several air raids a day. During one of them she and I were separated. We had run into different shelters. When the raid was over and we found each other, she held me tightly and cried hard, 'Mama! I thought I would never see you again!'

"I can't describe the expression of hers at that very moment. It was not the expression of a child, but that of an adult with superb wisdom—the wisdom to know that life is fragile, that loved ones can easily be separated forever by the hands of Karma.

"And then in the eighth month of 1945, the war was over. The Japanese left Taiwan. We were ruled by the Chinese for the first time in fifty years. Chin-yun started the third grade. Now the schools in Taiwan no longer taught in the Japanese language. She studied diligently and continued to work hard at home. I was in very poor health, and she took care of the four youngsters as if she were their little mother.

"Chin-yun was a good cook. After school she cooked supper, washed clothes, ironed, and cleaned house. No matter what she did, she did it thoroughly, making sure that she had done the best she could. And she took care of me. Whenever I needed the care of a doctor, she would run a long way to fetch him. She did everything with no one to help her except her maternal grand-mother—my mother—who lived with us.

"Between 1945 and 1947 things changed for the better. Taiwan's economy began to flourish. As a result, my husband's business branched out. Within a short time he opened six more theaters scattered in various cities and towns such as Fon-yuen, Taichung, Clear Water, and Tan-tze.

"While under the Japanese rule, only Taiwanese opera was performed in the theater that we owned. But now we showed movies as well as Taiwanese operas, and the movies brought in much more money. We soon moved to Fon-yuen and prospered as the trade expanded.

"In 1949 when Chin-yun was twelve, the Nationalist Party moved its government to Taiwan, the population increased, and the theaters became more crowded. My husband became very busy with our seven theaters.

"By this time, we were finally able to hire maids, and Chin-yun no longer needed to do the household chores. After school, instead of playing with the other girls, she would go to her father to help in one of the theaters. In the beginning she only worked in the concession stands, making and selling snacks to the customers. But before long she was able to do everything—from collecting tickets to balancing books. And she stayed in the theaters a great deal, sometimes studying in her father's office, most of the time keeping her father company.

"When Chin-yun became a teenager, her beauty blossomed. She had a lovely face with faultless features. She was slender, and she moved gracefully. When she looked at people, her eyes were captivating without her trying to do so . . . in the depth of her large eyes there was something special, as if she could look into the souls of everyone.

"Chin-yun never used any makeup. She wore her hair long and straight. She wasn't trying to attract any attention, but when she walked by, men and women, old and young, all turned their heads.

"There were many eligible young men in the social circle of which we had become a part. While helping her father take care of the seven theaters, Chin-yun had plenty of chances to come in contact with boys her age and even older men. However, she never showed any interest in them and never had a boyfriend. She was cold to them, her attitude a protective wall keeping her admirers at bay. Everyone in Fon-yuen knew her as the Shaw-nue, the Girl Devoted to her Parents.

"I cannot explain her attitude towards men. Perhaps it was the days during the bombing that affected her way of thinking, or perhaps it was the wisdom she had carried over from a previous lifetime: she seemed to realize that with all the love she carried in her heart she should not limit or restrain it by the demands of a marriage. Her dreams for the future were different from those of any other girls her age—instead of a husband and children she was waiting for a chance to love in a much grander and holier manner.

"But, being ordinary parents, her father and I had only ordinary dreams for her and were certain that someday she would marry. We gave her ordinary gifts too, such as fine jewelry. On one occasion we gave her a gold chain with a small diamond hung from it . . . in those days, diamonds were rare and costly. We considered the diamond a good-luck charm and asked her to wear it around her neck and never take it off.

"We loved our Chin-yun deeply and couldn't forget that as a child she had lived a hard life. Therefore we wanted to give her as much as we could to make up for those days. Her clothes were of the best material and all of them custom-made—her father and I insisted upon it."

Mrs. Wong tilted her head to one side, thought, then continued with a smile, "I cannot recall the exact year . . . maybe it happened when Chin-yun was seventeen, or maybe she was even younger. Anyway, regardless of her chilly attitude towards all men, a handsome young man of Japanese ancestry sent over a matchmaker to ask her father for permission to marry her.

"Loving Chin-yun more than the average father would a daughter, her father acted against tradition and left the matter to Chin-yun's decision. Chin-yun turned down the marriage proposal and said firmly that she never wanted to listen to another matchmaker's words in the future."

Mrs. Wong sighed. Her thin face seemed even thinner now, and her eyes were darkened by a sad memory. "But I do remember the exact year when I was seriously ill. It was 1952, and Chin-yun was fifteen years old. I had an ulcer. It was so critical that everyone thought I was going to die very soon. The doctor suggested an operation, but in 1952 patients rarely survived stomach operations.

"I struggled between life and death. Staying beside my sickbed, our Chin-yun did something incredible. It changed her life, and years later it also affected the lives of millions of people. . . ."

Mrs. Wong paused, closed her eyes and leaned back to rest. Someone approached from down the hall carrying a tray on which sat two small cups and a pot of hot tea. For the next few minutes we sipped tea without exchanging words, listening to a new song coming from the hidden speakers and breathing in the fragrance of flowers.

CHAPTER THIRTEEN

"When a promise is made to your heart,
sooner or later your heart will remind you
to carry out that promise."

— *Master Cheng Yen* —

MRS. WONG seemed to have regained her strength. She opened her eyes, leaned forward to rest her elbows on the table, and smiled at me apologetically. "Old age is such a nuisance. I try to block it out by not thinking about it, but still it haunts me mercilessly."

She took a sip of the now lukewarm tea and continued with a sigh, "In one of her books, my Chin-yun talked about the length of life. She said that the more a person does, the longer he lives. . . ." Mrs. Wong went on to quote her daughter's words: "One third of a person's life is wasted in sleeping. If a person sleeps four hours less every night, he can gain sixty extra days in a year. In thirty years, he will acquire five additional years of life."

Mrs. Wong smiled, "A dying person will be willing to pay a doctor a fortune for five additional years of life. But by sleeping less, a person can prolong life at no cost at all. Chin-yun sleeps only four, never more than five, hours per night, and all her disciples are doing the same."

I stared at her, "Are you telling me that you sleep only four or five hours per night?"

Mrs. Wong shook her head, "No, I would like to, but can't. I'll doze off during the day if I don't sleep much during the night. But I try to do as much as I can during my waking moments. I'm a commissioner of the Tzu-chi Foundation, which means I must visit people and collect donations from families at whatever amount they are willing and able to offer."

She pointed at the gold pin on her lapel and said proudly, "I earned my right to wear this pin. It has nothing to do with the fact that Master Cheng Yen is my daughter. Well, she doesn't believe in special privileges. She still works to earn her daily keep, and her old mother has to work hard in order to be a Tzu-chi commissioner. . . ." Pausing in mid sentence, Mrs. Wong suddenly remembered what we were talking about before the tea. "Ah, I was going to tell you what happened in 1952!"

She put a hand over her stomach and frowned deeply. "Stomach ulcer can be so painful! It was like having a fire burning inside me! In 1952, my ulcer was getting worse. I ate very carefully, but it didn't help. When I began to spit blood, the doctor said that the ulcer had perforated the stomach lining; therefore I must have an operation. But he couldn't guarantee anything. At that time, most of the people we knew who had stomach operations died.

"My Chin-yun began to pray. Having spent her childhood years in Clear Water, she remembered watching people pray in the Purple Cloud Temple and believed that when a person's prayer is sincere and selfless it would be answered.

"She prayed for my recovery and also made some serious promises to her heart:

"'I'll trade twelve years of my life for Mama's health. And if Mama gets well, I'll be a vegetarian for the rest of my life!'

"She prayed fervently day and night, and one night she had a dream.

"She saw a small temple with a door in the center and two doors on either side. She watched herself entering the temple. There was a large statue of Buddha in the middle of the room. She glanced toward one side of the statue and saw a bamboo bed. She looked closer and found me lying there. The next moment she saw herself squatting beside me, facing a small earth stove and holding a fan, fanning the flame. She recognized the contents in the pot placed over the fire; it was herb medicine.

"As her dream continued, she heard the wind blowing softly outside the open door. She turned and saw white clouds flying low, like a flower descending from heaven.

"Staring at the white flowering clouds, she saw in their heart the most beautiful lady she had ever seen. The lady produced a glowing bottle and poured out a small packet. Silently, Chin-yun knelt and reached for it. Wordlessly, the lady waited for her to take hold of it, then gradually vanished like a shadow upon the fading of light.

"Still in her dream, Chin-yun unwrapped the packet and found a small dosage of powdered medicine. She mixed the powder with some liquid and fed it to me.

"Chin-yun continued to pray the following day. The same dream recurred the next night. Once again the low-flying clouds descended from heaven and entered the triple-door temple, and then in the heart of the clouds appeared the beautiful lady with the glowing bottle. For the second time in her dream, Chin-yun fed me the medicine.

"On the following night, Chin-yun dreamed the same dream for the third and last time. She told me it was like watching the same movie over and over again, and it always ended with her feeding me the medicine."

Mrs. Wong paused, lifted her head, and looked out the upper part of the high window at the clear blue sky. There was not a cloud. The sky seemed mysteriously high and faraway.

"There are so many things that are beyond reasoning; my recovery from the ulcer was one of them. I never had an operation, but in the past four decades I've been living with a healthy stomach. My doctor could not explain it then, and still there is no doctor able to give me an explanation."

Mrs. Wong withdrew her gaze from the sky, met my eyes, and answered my silent question, "Yes, Chin-yun carried out her promise and became a vegetarian at age fifteen. She has never taken one bite of meat, fish, chicken, or any kind of eggs since then."

I asked, "Was it then that she decided to become a Buddhist nun?"

Mrs. Wong thought for a while, then shook her head. "No, she didn't know much about Buddhism at the time. Her becoming a vegetarian was the result of listening to her own heart—she had promised her heart that she would become a vegetarian if I became well, and her heart reminded her to carry out that promise."

Mrs. Wong leaned back from her chair and closed her eyes once more to rest.

Soft music continued to pour out of the hidden speakers, but the chanting had stopped. Two pots of gardenias were placed next to the window, and the sun intensified their fragrance. A lone bee, who had entered the room but now couldn't find its way out, buzzed from one white flower to another, like a lost child searching for its home.

Mrs. Wong opened her eyes and resumed talking. "For the next three years, life went on smoothly. We still had seven theaters. The economy was booming. People crowded in every day for movies and Taiwanese operas, especially on weekends. My husband was extremely busy. Since I had recovered from illness, Chin-yun had been spending more time with her father, helping him run the business.

"While working, she always dressed well. Her clothes were specially designed. Her shoes always matched her purse. Her face was clean from makeup. Her hair had grown to be very long. Although it was fashionable to have a permanent, she still wore it straight and most of the time loose. Her only jewelry was the gold chain around her neck with the diamond hanging from it.

"At age eighteen, she had become even more beautiful, far more striking than when she was a little younger. But still she had no boyfriend. Men admired her, but her remoteness forced them to admire her only from a distance. Her reputation as the Girl Devoted to Her Parents reached near and far."

Mrs. Wong stopped. All of a sudden her eyes became tearful and her lips tightened into a straight line. Silently, she turned her head towards the window where the gardenias stood.

The searching bee had settled in the heart of a flower and become content. It was still in the warm sunlight; its brown body contrasted to the white flower but matched a petal that had yellowed. Staring at the withering flower, Mrs. Wong sighed deeply, then started talking again. "A flower loses its petals one by one. A man's health also declines step by step. Always healthy, my husband suddenly suffered a minor heart attack when Chin-yun was almost nineteen.

"It didn't seem that serious. He had pain in his chest and a shortness of breath, and then it was over and he felt fine. The doctor didn't warn us, and we didn't pay much attention to it." Gesturing towards the gardenias, Mrs. Wong said, "We were looking at the whole flower in bloom and ignoring one yellowing petal."

The sorrow in her aged eyes deepened as she continued. "And then another petal turned yellow; my husband had the second heart attack about a year later, and it was much worse than the first one. His health declined rapidly after that; the flower was wilting but we didn't know. Now the doctor said that he had high blood pressure and there was nothing that we could do.

"Every day, he still went to the theater in Fon-yuen, and Chin-yun usually went with him. She was now the main force behind our booming business and the supervisor of all seven theaters; she often traveled to other cities and towns for her father."

Mrs. Wong swallowed, her voice turning hoarse with emotion. "One day in June of 1960, my husband woke up with a bad headache. He went on with his daily chores, then after sharing a vegetable meal with Chin-yun, he left home for one of our theaters named Kwong Hwa, the Glory of China.

"Chin-yun left a while later. Arriving at the theater, she saw her father in the office, lying on the sofa. She sat beside him, and he told her that his head was hurting terribly.

"Immediately, Chin-yun sent someone to fetch our family doctor. The doctor measured my husband's blood pressure and said it was extremely high, and he also gave my husband a shot. Then he left without saying what Chin-yun must or must not do.

"Chin-yun had learned to measure blood pressure and had the equipment. She waited for a while, measured her father's blood pressure and found it somewhat lower than before. The office was a noisy place. She could hear people laughing and talking in the theater. She also noticed her father twisting uncomfortably on the sofa. So she told our pedicab driver to get the pedicab ready.

"In those days, automobiles were rare in Taiwan and taxis were unheard of. There were only about two gas stations in the entire island, and even if we owned a car, it wouldn't be of much use. Pedicab stations were everywhere, just like today's taxi stations and bus stops. Owning a pedicab was the symbol of prosperity, and we were fortunate to have one.

"The pedicab driver and a few other men in the theater helped Chin-yun move her father onto the pedicab. Chin-yun sat beside him. It was not a long journey, but his condition deteriorated with every passing moment. When they reached home, she helped him to get off the pedicab, only to discover that he was no longer able to climb the steps. She supported him, and they struggled to enter the front door. Once inside, he collapsed.

"At this time, the entire family had gathered around him. We carried him to bed. As he stared at us with his mouth open, we realized that he had lost his ability to speak.

"We sent for the same doctor again. The man came, examined my husband, then turned towards Chin-yun, 'If only you had not moved him!'

"The doctor went on to tell us that it was the moving that worsened my husband's condition—something about all the blood being rushed into his brains.

"My husband remained unconscious for the rest of the day, and the next day he died."

Tears fell from Mrs. Wong's eyes, rolled down her thin cheeks, were caught in the lines above her mouth. She removed her glasses, opened her purse and took out a white handkerchief, slowly drying her face.

Afraid to embarrass her, I looked away. She sniffed softly, and the air in the room was thick with sorrow. The music seemed to have turned into a mourning song. The chanting had resumed, but it, too, sounded like the chant of death.

*"All living beings, rich or poor, powerful or powerless,
beautiful or plain, handsome or otherwise,
are destined to die, and the dying process
starts at the moment of birth."*

— Master Cheng Yen —

*"Nothing lasts forever except Karma,
which determines the whereabouts of our souls."*

– Master Cheng Yen —

Mrs. Wong recaptured her composure and continued softly. "Watching my husband die, I fainted. When I regained consciousness, I saw all the family members crying except Chin-yun. Her eyes were wide-open but dry, her face white like wax, and her lips bloodless. And I heard her mumbling, 'It's all my fault. If I hadn't moved Baba, he would still be alive. I should have never fetched the pedicab. It was such a silly thing to do. It was my decision that caused blood to rush into his brains and led him away from life. . . .'

"Chin-yun stopped murmuring when she noticed how weak I had become. She also looked at my aged mother who had also become ill at the sight of my husband's death.

"Throughout the funeral and the burial, Chin-yun remained dry-eyed and white-faced. She did all that was needed, taking care of all the arrangements—however, she moved like an efficient zombie. It seemed like a part of her was no longer with us. I looked on helplessly, not knowing how to make her whole again.

"Long after her father's burial, Chin-yun still wasn't eating, nor was she sleeping. She was so thin that her face looked almost transparent. I was terribly worried. I went to my mother, who was ancient and wise, and asked for advice.

"My mother said that aged monks and nuns are usually clever and willing to help, so we brought Chin-yun to see a monk in one of the many local temples. When the monk asked Chin-yun how he could help her, she said, 'Please tell me where the soul of my father is!'

"The monk asked for her father's name and a detailed report on his death. She told him everything, including what she had done and the guilt she still felt.

"The monk started a ritual. He burned incense, lit candles, and also meditated for a long while. When he finally opened his eyes, he said to Chin-yun, 'I've found the soul of your poor father. He is a prisoner in Won Ze Chen—the land of the dead who didn't deserve to die.'

"Chin-yun was greatly shocked. It increased her sense of guilt ten-fold, and it took her a long time to gather enough wisdom to disregard the monk's words.

"Some time later an old monk named Mew-Kwan Sheh-fu arrived at Fon-yuen Temple and started a series of sessions teaching the scriptures regarding the Guardian of Earth. A friend came to us and told Chin-yun that she ought to attend some of the sessions. One day, riding her bike, Chin-yun stopped at the Fon-yuen Temple and paid Mew-kwan Sheh-fu a visit.

"She asked Mew-kwan Sheh-fu the same question: 'Where is my father's soul?'

"The monk looked at her kindly, told her not to think troublesome thoughts, then handed her a book: 'Read it, and you'll know where your father's soul is!'

"Chin-yun hurried home and started to read. When she finished, she was able to face a truth: all living beings, rich or poor, powerful or powerless, beautiful or plain, handsome or otherwise, are destined to die, and the dying process starts at the moment of birth.

"However, still wishing to know the whereabouts of her father's soul, she returned to the Fon-yuen Temple and ran into a girlfriend who was shocked by her bony body and bloodless face and sad expression. 'Chin-yun, I know a way to free you from pain,' her girlfriend said. 'Come with me to another temple named the Temple of Kind Clouds, where a wise middle-aged nun is teaching the scriptures regarding the Emperor Liang Wu. Once you have captured the meaning of the scriptures, you'll know where your father's soul is.'"

Mrs. Wong paused, hesitated, then said apologetically with her head cocked to one side, "This middle-aged nun of the Temple of

Kind Clouds played an important part in Chin-yun's life. It's better not to mention her real name. Can we just call her Kind Clouds Sheh-fu, the same as the name of her temple?"

I nodded and Mrs. Wong went on. "Chin-yun developed an instant liking to Kind Clouds Sheh-fu. She listened carefully to the scriptures that centered on the story of an ancient Emperor:

"The Emperor was tormented by the death of his beloved wife and kept dreaming of her. In his dreams she appeared either as a snake or a dragon, always suffering great agony because of her impaired Karma. The Emperor began to pray for her soul and gather monks and nuns to perform litanies in her name until she appeared in his dream again, no longer as a snake or a dragon, but as a beautiful woman. She thanked him for what he had done, told him that she must purify her Karma with her own doing, then departed forever. When he awoke, the Emperor became an enlightened man.

"Chin-yun absorbed the wisdom contained in the story, combined it with the truth acquired from the other book and obtained an enlightenment: nothing lasts forever except Karma, which determines the whereabouts of our souls.

"With such enlightenment, Chin-yun embraced Buddhism but was still troubled by a question: why does Buddhism appear always in words but seldom in action?

"Trying to find the answer, she went to the Temple of Kind Clouds every day and had long talks with Kind Clouds Sheh-fu. The two studied Buddhism together, and the idea of becoming a nun gradually took shape in Chin-yun's heart."

Mrs. Wong shifted her position in the chair and drank more of the newly refilled hot tea. When she resumed talking, her voice was once again strong like the voice that she had when we first started the interview.

"Chin-yun was no longer lost. She became very busy. Rising early, she took care of the household chores, making certain that I, her grandmother, and her siblings, were fine. She then started to read books on Buddhism. She also meditated and prayed. She calmed her mind and collected her thoughts by chanting Na Mo Ah Mee Tol Fo, reminding herself to behave like the Enlightened Ones.

"She read and prayed until it was time to take care of our seven theaters. None of the other children was trained to run the business, therefore the burden of our livelihood was entirely on Chin-yun's delicate shoulders. She finally came to me and asked if I was willing to sell some of the theaters. I told her that I'd rely on her decision. She soon sold two of our theaters, deposited some of the money and used the rest to buy gold bars, which she kept in our home in a safe place. I never even checked with the bank to see the total amount of money or looked into the hiding place to see the gold. I no longer had a stomach ulcer, but I didn't do much except wake in the morning, eat three meals, then wait for the day to end. I didn't know until many years later just how hard my poor Chin-yun had struggled.

"During this time, my Chin-yun was caught between the calling of two forces: her wish to become a nun and her obligation to her family."

Mrs. Wong continued to talk. No longer narrating in the first-person, she had stepped out of herself and looked at the whole occurrence objectively. Her words had become the words of a story-teller, and I continued to take my notes accordingly.

CHAPTER FOURTEEN

*"A woman's world is not within the boundary of her home.
Equal to men, women are also entitled to serve society,
the nation, and all mankind."*

— Master Cheng Yen —

*"A person, man or woman, should love all living beings,
instead of just one individual or a handful of them.
And a person, man or woman, should love
without expectation, instead of expecting
the love to be rewarded or returned."*

— Master Cheng Yen —

A S MRS. WONG'S VOICE filled the room, the music faded, the chanting no longer existed, and the walls disappeared. Looking up now and then from my notebook, I found the image of her turning into a blur and the city outside the window diminishing. I was transferred to the summer of 1960, to a small town called Fon-yuen, and a position where I could remain unseen while keeping a watchful eye on Chin-yun Wong, a beautiful, long-haired girl who was only twenty-three.

172

*　*　*

"I love my family!" Chin-yun Wong said to herself on that summer morning. Her family was still sleeping soundly. As usual, she was up earlier than the servants.

Looking out the window at the summer sky that was pink with the first rays of sun, she proceeded to dress and continued to murmur, "Poor Mama is not in good health. My brothers and sisters have not yet learned to be on their own. My grandmother is old and weak. After Baba's death, I've been taking care of all of them . . . not only because I love them but also because it's the obligation of the eldest child. No! I can't follow my heart's liking!"

Shaking her head, Chin-yun went on to begin another day of serving her family, starting with grocery shopping—refrigerators were uncommon and the woman of the house had to buy food every morning.

Chin-yun walked through the town of Fon-yuen and soon reached the open market. Peddlers gathered alongside a narrow street, crowding the next few blocks. Each shopper carried a basket made of bamboo or rattan; Chin-yun's was a large rattan one. When she finished with the shopping, and wishing to be freed from the heavy load, a shopper could always find, among the children of the peddlers, some errand-boy to deliver the basket.

Chin-yun shopped in the rising sun that had quickly heated up the tropical island, dwelling in deep thoughts as she did the selecting, bargaining and buying. When finished, it was still early. She paid a boy a few coins and gave him her home address. As he walked in one direction carrying her basket, she headed in another.

She arrived at the Temple of Kind Clouds, went to Kind Clouds Sheh-fu, her friend and the master in charge, who was wearing a kind smile and a flowing gray robe.

After exchanging greetings, Chin-yun asked, "Kind Clouds Sheh-fu, please tell me what kind of women are the most fortunate under heaven?"

Kind Clouds Sheh-fu answered without hesitation, "The most fortunate women are those carrying grocery baskets."

Chin-yun was puzzled. Tilting her head to one side, she asked, "That's strange. I carry a grocery basket every day. Why don't I feel fortunate? As a matter of fact, I feel miserable!"

"You should go home and figure it out. When you understand what I mean, then come to me again," Kind Clouds Sheh-fu said and walked away.

With her mouth open and eyes wide, Chin-yun glared at the master's back. When the master was out of sight, she turned and went home reluctantly.

Kind Clouds Sheh-fu's puzzling words lingered in Chin-yun's mind for the rest of the day and remained a riddle for days to come. She tried her very best to solve the mystery, but the answer stayed beyond her grasp.

Life went on. Chin-yun rose at dawn, carried her rattan basket to the open market, shopped, then went home to oversee the servants preparing breakfast. After breakfast she read, meditated, and prayed until it was time to go to one of the family-owned theaters.

However, whatever Chin-yun was doing, she was also thinking: Why is a woman carrying a grocery basket the fortunate one?

Summer ended and autumn began. Early one morning Chin-yun was once again walking with a basket in her hand, heading for the open market. Her thoughts followed the same route:

Can a woman be fortunate because she has the grocery money to buy whatever she likes? If that is what the master means, then I doubt she is right. I strongly disagree that a woman's right is limited to spending grocery money! I definitely object that a woman's world is within the boundary of her home! In my opinion, women are equal to men and are also entitled to serve society, the nation, and all mankind!

When nearing the market, Chin-yun let out a deep sigh:

If only I could step out of the four walls of my home and begin to serve first my society and my country and then all of mankind!

Chin-yun glanced at the basket she was holding, and the next moment she was astounded by a sudden enlightenment:

A woman is fortunate when she carries a grocery basket for not only her immediate family but also for all living beings!

Motionless and almost breathless, she stopped in the middle of the busy street. Unaware of the passing pedicabs and bicycles and people, she went into a deep contemplation:

Yes! I should broaden my field of loving. It is not enough to love my family that consists of only a few individuals. I must love my society and my country where there are many men and women, old and young, rich and poor, healthy and ill. But that is not enough either. I must love all living beings, because all lives are equal, and all beings are worthy of being respected and loved!

Thinking how wise Kind Clouds Sheh-fu was, Chin-yun smiled. She hastened towards the market on weightless feet, her mind filled with delightful thoughts:

I'll go to Kind Clouds Sheh-fu as soon as the shopping is done. She will be pleased to know that I've finally figured out why a woman carrying a grocery basket is the fortunate one!

She stopped in the middle of the street and vocalized her determination:

"I'll tell her that I've decided to take upon myself the largest grocery basket under heaven! In my basket there will be food to feed the bodies of all living beings, wisdom to nourish their minds, and love and mercy to heal their wounded hearts!"

Chin-yun frowned when she realized that at this moment she had only paper currency for meat and vegetables, but not even one ounce of spiritual wealth for the mighty items on the shopping list in her heart.

She thought, then lifted her chin and clenched her hands into fists.

"I am not worried, nor am I afraid," she said as she looked up at the clear sky. "I have much to learn about Buddhism and a long way to travel before picking up that invisible basket. When the time comes, I'll know exactly what to do!"

"While loving, a person should be selfless instead of self-centered;
more than satisfying himself, his love should bring
happiness to the loved ones."

— *Master Cheng Yen* —

Chin-yun Wong made up her mind to become a Buddhist nun and function through Buddhism to accomplish what had been accomplished in China throughout the centuries only by men.

Living within the four walls of her home, it was impossible to become more than an obedient daughter and a loving sister. She saw the necessity of leaving home, but also knew that she would not be allowed to go if she should share her decision with her mother.

"Please help me," she went to Kind Clouds Sheh-fu and pleaded. "I want to find a new home, a true home, and an eternal home . . . a home for my temporary physical form, and a home for my everlasting soul. My family can survive without me. They will not be short of any monetary thing because they have plenty of money. Besides, I'm sure that once I am gone, my brothers and sisters will learn to take care of everything. Please find me a temple that is far from Fon-yuen—the farther the better; the best would be a temple located at the opposite end of the sky and the other side of the sea."

She kept visiting Kind Clouds Sheh-fu and pleading. When the autumn of 1960 neared its end, Kind Clouds Sheh-fu was touched by her persistence and promised to find her a temple where the master in charge would take in a novice nun.

An ideal temple was found in Si-tze, a small town in the outskirts of Taipei. It was called Jin-shew, the Temple of Still Meditation.

Chin-yun did not want to leave without saying goodbye to her family, but she knew that if any of them should find out that she was going away to become a nun, it would be impossible for her to walk out of the door. She decided to run away. However, young and trusting, she told a few of her close friends where she was going, assuming that they would never betray her.

She packed only a few pieces of clothing and left for the train station in Fon-yuen. She boarded the waiting train and looked nervously out the window for fear that any of her family members would be there by chance. She breathed with relief when the train pulled away from the station, her heart filled with wishful thinking: perhaps they will not come after me, because I know they truly love me. And they ought to know that while loving someone, it is more important to see the loved one happy than keeping her home to satisfy themselves.

She arrived in Taipei, took a bus to Si-tze, and found the Temple of Still Meditation. The master in charge was an old nun who had been notified of Chin-yun's coming by Kind Clouds Sheh-fu. Chin-yun settled in the temple and believed that she had parted forever from the days when she carried a grocery basket large enough only for one family.

* * *

In Fon-yuen and in the house of the Wongs, things were in a turmoil.

"My precious! My Chin-yun! Where are you? Are you all right?" Mrs. Wong walked from room to room, screaming and crying.

Missing their beloved elder sister, the four younger children were also sad and worried. They helped their mother search the town, but they couldn't find Chin-yun anywhere.

Unlike the family members, a few acquaintances and friends thought differently of Chin-yun's disappearance.

Several of them were looking for someone to blame. "It was your deceased husband's fault! He spoiled Chin-yun too much! Who has ever heard of letting a girl decide that she didn't want to marry anyone? When the first matchmaker came to your house, your husband should have accepted the proposal. Chin-yun would have become someone's wife when she was still a teenager instead of a problem today!"

And a few of them were worried about other things. "Mrs. Wong, you trusted Chin-yun too much! You should have never allowed a daughter to take care of the family's business and fortune! Did she run away with all the money that you had?"

Mrs. Wong cried louder. "What does it matter whose fault it is? And who cares about money? I only want my Chin-yun back!"

But the distrusting friends insisted that Mrs. Wong should know what Chin-yun had taken. In order to silence them, Mrs. Wong searched Chin-yun's room. After opening one of the desk drawers, Mrs. Wong found cash money stacked in piles. Opening another drawer, she saw deposit slips, receipts, canceled checks, envelopes, stamps, and change money all arranged neatly. It didn't take her long to find a heavy box containing bars of gold.

At the sight of all the monetary things, Mrs. Wong felt a stabbing pain in her heart. "My poor child! I would feel much better if you had taken everything! Without taking anything, how can you live?"

Mrs. Wong fainted. Panicking, the children sent for the family doctor, who arrived and gave Mrs. Wong a shot. When she returned to consciousness, Mrs. Wong continued to cry.

"Also while loving, a person should cultivate pure thoughts instead of thoughts contaminated with lust, infatuation, jealousy or domination."

— Master Cheng Yen —

"Under heaven, the worst a person can do is to dislike his lot and give less than the very best to his responsibility."

— Master Cheng Yen —

Chin-yun was content in the Temple of Still Meditation.

She spent the first two days adjusting to the environment. On the third day she already felt a part of the temple. With eagerness, she carried out the chores assigned to novice nuns, knowing that it was the first step towards serving mankind.

Before the third day was over, she looked up from the chore she was doing and saw her mother entering the arched doorway. She couldn't believe her eyes. Blinking, she watched her mother running across the temple grounds followed by the nun in charge.

"Chin-yun! My precious girl! Have you any idea what you put me through?" Mrs. Wong cried as she ran.

"Mama!" Chin-yun gasped, dropping what she was doing. "How did you know where I was?"

"Silly child! You shared your secret with some friends. Your secret was but a conversation piece for them. One of your friends talked. And I only wish that she had talked three days earlier!"

The next moment Mrs. Wong took Chin-yun in her arms, held her tightly and cried harder. Chin-yun had no regret for what she had done but felt terribly guilty for the distress that she had brought upon her mother and the rest of her family. Burying her face against her mother's shoulder, she could not hold back her tears.

Looking up, Chin-yun saw, through her blurred vision and over her mother's trembling shoulder, the expression of the nun in charge of the Temple of Still Meditation. Her heart sank, knowing that she had no choice but to go home with her mother.

Traveling silently beside her mother, Chin-yun asked in her thoughts: does Mama know that, while loving someone, a person should not dominate the loved one's life, because domination is as wrong as lust, jealousy, and infatuation?

* * *

On the morning after returning home, Chin-yun picked up the old rattan basket and resumed her familiar chores.

She shopped for food in the open market, tossing into her basket the things needed by her family. The basket was soon filled, but Chin-yun's heart remained empty.

Besides food items, there were also other things in the market. Clothes, shoes, teacups and dishes . . . and mirrors. Chin-yun looked into one of the mirrors on a stand and caught a glimpse of her face: an unpleasant face with the eyebrows gathered into a frown and the corners of the mouth curving down.

She looked away from the mirror and glanced around the market to study the faces of other shoppers. She found some faces brightened with satisfaction while others were darkened by discontent. The former belonged to those taking pride in serving their families, and the latter were the faces of those detesting what they were doing.

The comparison was like lightning cutting across a murky sky. Chin-yun raised a hand to smooth her eyebrows and looked into the mirror once more. She was pleased to see herself smiling. Shaking her head, she whispered to her reflection, "Under heaven, the worst a person can do is to dislike his lot and give less than the very best to his responsibility!"

She continued with a sigh, "Someday and somehow, I'll be free to carry out the mission that's rooted in my Karma. I'll be in charge of a basket so large that its contents can fulfill the hunger and curb the thirst of all living beings. But as of this moment, I will do what I can, and do it with love and contentment!"

CHAPTER FIFTEEN

"When you are determined to do something,
now is as good a time as any!"

— *Master Cheng Yen* —

"The river has nothing to say about its destination;
Karma decides the direction of its flowing.
Living beings are like the water;
Karma determines the course of their traveling."

— *Master Cheng Yen* —

MRS. WONG reminded me to keep in mind that Kind Clouds is not the real name of Chin-yun's friend. "According to the Buddhist teaching, once becoming a monk or a nun, a person must give up his original name and receive a new name from his master—a name followed by the title Sheh-fu which means 'teacher.' I would like to name this nun after the temple where she was a master."

She continued with her narration, and we became lost in Chin-yun Wong's early life. Someone refilled our teapot, but we did not pause to drink. The tea soon turned cold as the faraway chanting remained unheard and the soft music ignored.

* * *

Chin-yun Wong stayed home for the next year, serving her family without mentioning any future plans.

In the beginning, worried that Chin-yun might run away again, Mrs. Wong kept a watchful eye on her. But time gradually lessened her concern, and she finally relaxed, believing that Chin-yun had given up the idea of becoming a nun and that she visited Kind Clouds Sheh-fu merely as a friendly gesture.

The friendship between the two had intensified. Kind Clouds Sheh-fu told Chin-yun that in the earlier years she had stayed in Japan, and the lifestyle of the Japanese monks and nuns was different from that of the monks and nuns in Taiwan. Other than praying and teaching, the Japanese religious men and women also did many things to benefit their society. "After returning to Taiwan, I found it difficult to get used to the lifestyle here. I would like to see the nuns in my temple doing the things that are being done by the Japanese monks and nuns, but it is hard to change things in a town where tradition must be obeyed."

Kind Clouds Sheh-fu's words had a deep impact on Chin-yun. On the next visit Chin-yun told her friend, "When I become a nun, I will change tradition, and my followers will be not only respectable but also useful!" With the enthusiasm of a twenty-four-year-old, Chin-yun went on, "As a nun I will strive towards two goals. The first is to work for every morsel—my followers and I will not live on anyone's donation, and we will not eat on the days we haven't worked. The second goal is to serve all living beings under heaven and teach Buddhism to all, regardless of their age, gender, wealth, education and profession."

The older nun did not say anything but nodded her approval.

Another summer turned into autumn, and it was time to harvest rice. Early one morning, Chin-yun, as usual, went to the open market. Her rattan basket was soon filled with meat and vegetables, and she hired an errand boy to deliver the basket to the Wong house. Empty-handed, she walked towards the outskirts of Fon-yuen and reached the Temple of Kind Clouds. The Temple was surrounded by a rice field. Ordered by their master, the nuns were busy harvesting. They looked up from under their coolie hats and, recognizing Chin-yun, waved.

Working among the nuns was Kind Clouds Sheh-fu. She saw Chin-yun and called with a smile, "Would you like to help?"

Without hesitating, Chin-yun borrowed a hat and joined them. The autumn sunlight was warm, the breeze soft. The sky was clear and cloudless. Birds, flying to this tropical island from colder lands, created a variety of formations overhead. Chin-yun looked up occasionally, enjoying the tranquility and beauty as she worked beside Kind Clouds Sheh-fu, moving across the rice field.

Stopping to stretch her aching back, Kind Clouds Sheh-fu looked at Chin-yun. "Do you still want to become a nun? And if you do, would you like to run away with me?"

Chin-yun, stunned by the sudden question, did not reply. Of course she still wanted to become a nun. But remembering how she had been caught in the Temple of Still Meditation, she shivered.

Kind Clouds Sheh-fu continued, "I've been thinking about finding a temple far from here to start things anew. If you want, we can leave together, right now!"

"Right now?" Chin-yun asked. It would be much less frightening to run away with someone who was already an experienced nun, but she was totally unprepared. "I have nothing in my pocket except the autumn wind!"

"Then you simply must travel with just a pocketful of autumn wind," Kind Clouds Sheh-fu said. "Should you go home to pack, you'll never be able to leave."

Chin-yun looked into the eyes of her friend, and the next moment found a sudden courage. "You're right! When you are determined to do something, now is as good a time as any!"

After a brief discussion, they decided that since Chin-yun had nothing, Kind Clouds Sheh-fu must pack something for the two of them and take the small amount of money she had saved. They left their coolie hats beside a pile of harvested rice and walked out of the field; Kind Clouds Sheh-fu returned to the temple and Chin-yun headed for the highway that stretched between Fon-yuen and Taichung.

Ching-yun stood waiting on the highway in the bright sunlight, her long hair flying in the wind, her heart beating in her throat. Every time a pedicab or a bicycle approached she was afraid that it carried someone she knew. It did not take Kind Clouds Sheh-fu long to pack, but to Chin-yun it was ages before her friend appeared with a small bundle. "Let's go to a train station," Kind Clouds Sheh-fu said, pointing first at one end of the highway and then the other. "We have to choose between the Fon-yuen Station and the station in Taichung."

"I imagine the station in Taichung will be safer for us," Chin-yun said.

"We'll go to Taichung then," Kind Clouds Sheh-fu agreed.

They waited for the next pedicab to appear, stopped the driver, jumped onto it and ordered in unison, "Take us to Taichung Train Station and hurry!"

Taichung, located in the central part of the island, was a much larger city than Fon-yuen. The station was crowded. There were long lines in front of the two ticket counters, one for the passengers going south, the other for those going north.

"Are we going south or north?" Kind Clouds Sheh-fu asked.

"I don't know," Chin-yun said, then added, "Why don't we let our Karma decide for us? If the southbound train comes first we'll go south, otherwise we'll go north."

Kind Clouds Sheh-fu had no objection. They checked the schedule and found out that the next train passing Taichung was coming from the north and going to the south. They joined the southbound passengers standing in line and purchased two tickets to Kao-shung, a city on the south end of the island.

The train passed many rivers. Looking out the window and down the bridge, Chin-yun said, "The river has nothing to say about its destination . . . its Karma decides the direction of its flowing. Let you and I be like the water, and let our Karma determine the course of our traveling."

They arrived in Kao-shung. Following their instincts, they did not stay but went to the bus stop. Divided by the Central Mountain Ranges, the east of the Taiwan island was known as the back of the mountain, the west the front.

"Shall we head for the east or the west?" Kind Clouds Sheh-fu asked. "Do you prefer the front of the mountain or the back of it?"

"Last time I headed for the front of the mountain. I stayed in the Temple of Still Meditation for only three days before Mama found me," Chin-yun said. "Maybe this time we should try the back of the mountain."

They bought two tickets to Tai-tung, a city on the east coast of Taiwan, and had no money left after buying food during the journey. Kind Clouds Sheh-fu said, "My second elder brother is a dentist in Tai-tung. I didn't mention him earlier because he and I are not very close. But it seems necessary now that we stay with him for a while."

They spent the night with Kind Clouds Sheh-fu's brother but became restless the next morning. When he gave them money, they insisted that they would pay back the loan, then went to the train station again. "Where shall we go?" Chin-yun asked, standing facing the ticket counters and looking up at the names of various cities and towns. "We must decide . . ."

She stopped in mid-sentence upon hearing a male voice calling, "Shaw-nui," the Girl Devoted to Her Parents.

"Shaw-nui!" the same voice called again from the other side of the station.

Chin-yun saw a man running towards her from across the crowded station, yelling, "I saw your long straight hair from a mile away and thought it was you!"

Chin-yun recognized the old man as one of the friends of her deceased father. Knowing that there was no way to escape, she waited for him to come nearer.

"Shaw-nui!" the man looked from Chin-yun to Kind Clouds Sheh-fu and could not hide his suspicion. "Does your mother know where you are?"

Chin-yun read the man's mind—he had guessed that she had run away from home again to try once more to become a nun. Thinking quickly, she decided to bend the truth. "Yes, Mama knows where I am," she said, trying her best to convince the man. "I'm on vacation from all the household chores."

The old man studied her a while longer, blinked his eyes in disbelief, and finally said goodbye. He went to a parked motorcycle and hesitantly rode away. But just when Chin-yun breathed with relief, he zigzagged through the crowd and stopped at her side.

"Shaw-nui, you are not lying to me, are you? Does your mother really know where you are? You better not be running away from home like you did last year!"

Chin-yun's heart sank. So she had not fooled the wise old man after all. For the next minutes she tried her best to convince him, and when he left reluctantly, she realized that, although she had saved herself from being escorted back home right then and there, as long as he knew she was in Tai-tung, she was no longer safe from the reach of her mother. "Kind Clouds Sheh-fu," she said, "We must leave Tai-tung this very moment!"

Kind Clouds Sheh-fu nodded. "We have more than enough money for two tickets on the train. Where shall we go?"

Chin-yun did not know. They talked until deciding that they must go towards the direction decided by their Karma. Kind Clouds Sheh-fu looked up at the places listed above the ticket counters and her eyes suddenly widened. "The next train goes to Deer Field, a village near the city of Hwalien . . . why does the name make me shiver?"

Staring at the name, Chin-yun's face was brightened by a broad smile. "Deer Field is a village that existed over two thousand years ago in northern India! After walking away from his palace and becoming a monk, meditating for many years and becoming enlightened, Buddha gave his first sermon in Deer Field!"

"Deer Field it is then!" Kind Clouds Sheh-fu said, sharing Chin-yun's excitement.

"Two tickets to Deer Field!" they said at the same time to the man behind the counter.

"Nothing will be done if we just stand and wait
for a helping hand to reach down from among the clouds."

— *Master Cheng Yen* —

"What kind of place is Deer Field?" Chin-yun asked the porter when the train came to a stop.

The man shrugged, "A barely inhabited village with two or three small stores." He waited for Chin-yun and Kind Clouds Sheh-fu to get off the train, then shouted after them, "And you can find all of them right on the same block as the train station!"

Ching-yun and Kind Clouds Sheh-fu looked around. A train station was usually the most crowded place in town, but the Deer Field station was abandoned. In front of one of the three stores, they saw a group of villagers in tattered clothes, obviously local residents.

"Do you have a temple anywhere?" Chin-yun asked one of them.

The villagers did not answer but stared at the newcomers. Outsiders seldom entered the village, and it was unusual to see a beautiful young girl in the company of a nun. "Yes," one of the women said when she recovered from surprise, pointing towards a high mountain. "We have only one temple, and you can find it near the mountaintop."

Chin-yun thanked the woman and turned to Kind Clouds Sheh-fu, "Are you ready for mountain climbing?"

"Do I have a choice?" Kind Clouds sighed.

It was mid-morning when they reached the foothills. The narrow path was overgrown with weeds that scratched their legs. Sunlight sifted through trees growing wild on both sides, the low branches cutting their arms and faces. They climbed until noon, and their clothes were soaked with sweat, their bodies covered with bruises.

"This has to be it!" Chin-yun pointed at a small dwelling.

"But it is not a temple!" Kind Clouds Sheh-fu uttered in disappointment. "It is only one of the Divinity Houses built by the Japanese!"

Chin-yun nodded. The Japanese had, during the fifty years when they ruled Taiwan, built many Divinity Houses alongside country roads for travelers to stop and rest, take shelter from bad weather, and pray. "Let us take a closer look," she said. "There ought to be someone inside."

Moving closer, they saw words written on the battered door saying that the building had been a Divinity House during the Japanese rule but was now one of the many branches of the Temple of Kindness and Mercy, a famous temple in the city of Hwalien.

"May I help you?" a male voice asked.

Astounded by anyone being there, they looked up at a monk approaching from inside the temple, his hands together with palms touching.

Chin-yun and Kind Clouds Sheh-fu exchanged glances. They were tired and hungry, and they had nowhere else to go. "Will you let us stay?" Chin-yun asked. "We won't be a burden to you."

"Where are you from?" the monk asked.

"We are from . . . ," Chin-yun paused, then continued vaguely, ". . . from where we are from."

The monk looked at them with piercing eyes, trying to decide whether they were trustworthy. He finally nodded his head. "All right, you may stay. But I must warn you: I don't have much to offer."

Chin-yun and Kind Clouds Sheh-fu were led through the small temple and shown the inner rooms. They quickly discovered that the monk was right about his having very little to offer. Although there were separate sleeping quarters for men and women, neither of the two rooms was bigger than a broom closet. The ceiling was so low that they could barely stand up straight. The room for women was filthy and needed a good cleaning.

"We'll need some water," Chin-yun said, looking for broom and mop.

"You'll have to go to the other side of the hill, where there is a waterfall," the monk answered. "We have no running water."

"And I guess there is no bathroom either?" Kind Clouds Sheh-fu asked.

"You are right," the monk said. "The bathroom, too, is at the other side of the hill . . . anywhere you like."

"Well," Chin-yun began to roll up her sleeves. "We better get started if we want to get our room cleaned—nothing will be done if we just stand and wait for a helping hand to reach down from among the clouds."

They traveled many times between the two sides of the hill, carrying buckets of water. When they were about to collapse, the monk reappeared, looked at the spotless room in surprise, then nodded his approval. "Can the two of you sing?" he asked.

Chin-yun and Kind Clouds Sheh-fu looked at each other in disbelief. The monk had to be joking if he expected them to sing a song right now!

The monk explained, "The villagers like to pray . . . not simply pray, but sing out their prayers. Well, can the two of you sing?"

"Yes," Chin-yun answered. "We used to sing out our prayers in the Temple of Kind Clouds. And we often sang while working in the rice field."

Relieved, the monk continued, "That's great! With my sandpaper voice, it's impossible to lead the prayers. With the two of you singing the lead, our prayer meetings will be more interesting, and the villagers will come to this temple more often."

The sun was setting, and it was getting dark quickly. "Where is the light switch?" Chin-yun asked.

"There is no electricity," the monk answered as he walked away. "I can give you an oil lamp and some candles. But oil is rather costly and so are the candles. I suggest that the two of you go to sleep early and rise after daylight comes."

Chin-yun and Kind Clouds Sheh-fu stared after the monk, then faced each other and began to laugh.

※　※　※

In Fon-yuen, Mrs. Wong was talking to her deceased husband's brother who was Chin-yun's father by birth.

"How am I to live without my Chin-yun?" Mrs. Wong asked her brother-in-law. "Since you let me adopt her when she was eleven months old, she has been my most treasured child!"

"You have four other children," Mr. Wong said. "You have to learn to live without Chin-yun . . ." He stopped at the sound of someone knocking on the door.

An old man entered, walked directly toward Mrs. Wong. "A few days ago I was passing the train station in Tai-tung. . . ." He described his conversation with Chin-yun. "Has she returned from vacation?"

"What vacation? She ran away again!" Mrs. Wong said; her barely dried tears resumed falling. "But what is she doing in Tai-tung, and who is this nun?"

Mr. Wong said thoughtfully, "I heard that the master of the Temple of Kind Clouds also disappeared—I won't be surprised if she is this nun. We should pay a visit to the nuns in that temple and see if their master has some relatives or friends in Tai-tung."

"After taking the first step, a person must hold on to his courage.
He cannot afford to lose it; he has to reinforce it,
because he will need plenty of it to continue his quest."

— *Master Cheng Yen* —

"We are living an easy life when compared to the life led by Buddha when he first left his palace," Chin-yun said, washing her face with the ice-cold spring water. She was wearing a gray robe, one of the three robes packed by Kind Clouds Sheh-fu. But her hair was still uncut, reaching her thighs.

"Yes. . . ! We are having an easy life . . . with so much fun!" Kind Clouds Sheh-fu said, her teeth clattering. "And this is only . . . the end of autumn. Wait until winter comes, and our fun will . . . double!"

They tried to joke away their difficulties in getting adjusted to the new life. They continued washing, reminding each other that one day Buddha was a prince living in the most fabulous palace in India, and the next day he was sitting underneath a palm tree in coarse clothes.

"And Buddha ate only sparingly, taking in no more food than it was necessary to keep himself alive," Kind Clouds Sheh-fu said, drying her face with a ragged towel.

"Unlike Buddha, we've been eating well," Chin-yun said, pointing at the two empty baskets placed beside the spring water. "I'm sure both baskets will be filled before the day is over."

They left the spring water, brought their toilet things back to the temple, and started down the mountain on the narrow path carrying the baskets woven with young bamboo that grew around the temple. The sun was peering down from the mountaintop, the forest wakening in front of their eyes. The birds were singing, small animals running and stopping to peek from behind trees. The air was fresh and fragrant with wild flowers. A faint scent of food entered their nostrils as threads of smoke rose from the village and reached the pathway.

"The villagers are cooking breakfast," Kind Clouds Sheh-fu said, inhaling deeply. "They would be honored if you and I were willing to join them."

"But we will *not* join them!" Chin-yun said with a firm shake of her head. "My first goal after becoming a nun is to earn my daily food—I will not eat on the days I have not worked!"

"In that case, I will not eat without working either," Kind Clouds Sheh-fu sighed. Although she was older and an experienced nun while Chin-yun was younger and a lay person, soon after their journey had started she had begun to follow Chin-yun's instruction as if it were the other way around. Sighing once more, Kind Clouds Sheh-fu added, "But if we should eat with the villagers, it wouldn't be imposing on them. We taught them singing and praying, and they owe us at least a few meals."

Chin-yun pretended that she had not heard Kind Clouds Sheh-fu's comment. They reached the foothills where rice fields spread like a patched quilt. The harvest was over and the planting season had not yet begun. In the deserted fields, plants and vines had grown wild; some were edible. They had asked the villagers and received permission to pick whatever was left on the ground.

"I found a sweet potato!" Kind Clouds Sheh-fu shouted in delight when she spotted something half-buried in the ground. She squatted quickly and began to dig with her fingers.

"Where there is one sweet potato, there are usually several more!" Chin-yun said, squatting beside her friend.

Glancing down, Chin-yun noticed her fingers. They were no longer the fingers of a young lady with an easy life. The nails were broken, the fingers calloused. There was a large blister on the back of her right hand, a result of cooking. The past flashed across her mind. Was it yesterday or a lifetime ago that she carried a rattan basket to shop for her family? All she had to do was point at the things she wanted and the peddlers would put them in her basket. When the basket was filled, an errand boy would deliver it to her home, and the raw meat and vegetables would be cooked by a maid.

"But I've traded the small basket for a much bigger one—instead of providing for one family, I'm on my way to providing for the world! I've taken my first step, and I must hold on to my courage. I cannot afford to lose it; I have to reinforce it because I will need plenty of it to continue my quest," Chin-yun said as she continued to dig.

Few people in China liked sweet potatoes; they were planted by the villagers for their pigs. But for Chin-yun and Kind Clouds Sheh-fu the sweet potatoes were a treat. When there were no more sweet potatoes to be found, they moved on to another field. Luck was with them on this day. They soon found some peanuts on the vines, unnoticed by the owner. After that, they selected carefully among the wild plants, picking only those that they knew were not poisonous. By the time the autumn sun reached mid-sky, their baskets were filled.

"We can go back to the temple now," Chin-yun said, leading the way towards the steep path. "After eating the first meal, we'll pray and read the scriptures. We'll eat our second meal before sunset, then wait for the villagers to arrive with their candles and oil lamps. We'll teach them songs and prayers, and interpret for them the scriptures that are hard for them to understand. Then we will rise at another dawn, to meet the beginning of another day."

Struggling behind her, Kind Clouds Sheh-fu coughed weakly. "Another day and another night . . . and soon it will be winter. It is only the end of autumn, but it is already very cold on this high mountain. We have only three thin robes between us. How can we survive the cold weather?"

"Don't worry. When winter comes, we will know what to do," Chin-yun said, frowning. She was glad that Kind Clouds Sheh-fu was behind her and could not see her face. Stopping for a moment to straighten her sore back, she looked up towards heaven.

She did not ask heaven what she should do, for she knew that the answer had to come from within her own heart.

CHAPTER SIXTEEN

"I must forget the past! I must look at only the present!"

— Master Cheng Yen —

SORROW FILLED MRS. WONG'S EYES, deepening the lines between her brows, adding a seasoned look to her otherwise ageless appearance. Waiting for her to resume talking, I glanced at the table and saw a large plate filled with sliced fresh fruit; someone had brought it in without my noticing it. The air was sweetened by the scent of peaches, apples, bananas, and guavas, plus the fragrance of gardenias. The bee had left the flowers and was now circling above the plate, buzzing restlessly. The ever-present music sounded like a lullaby, and the chanting had a hypnotic effect. The bee landed on a wedge of ripe peach, stilling his wings into silence.

Mrs. Wong continued, "My brother-in-law and my husband's friend and I rushed to the Temple of Kind Clouds, telling the nuns that Chin-yun seemed to have left with their master and we needed their help. One of the nuns recalled the day of the harvest when she looked out the window and saw Chin-yun working beside their master. Another nun said that she had seen their master returning to the temple to pack all her belongings. We begged them to check into Kind Cloud Sheh-fu's background and learned that she had an elder brother practicing dentistry in Tai-tung.

"We found the dentist's address, and the following day my brother-in-law and I were packing for the trip. We had to bring enough warm clothes, because autumn had already turned into winter."

* * *

The winter of that year was colder than usual. The temperature in Deer Field had dropped to the fifties, with a chilling wind blowing down from the high mountains. Leaves on the tropical trees clung to the branches, creating a canopy that kept the winter sunlight from shining through.

The walls of the tiny temple were thin, allowing the force of the chilling wind to fill the rooms. And then, in the middle of December, the rainy season began. The roof leaked, creating puddles and turning the dirt floor to mud. Everything was damp; fungus began growing in the dark corners.

"I wonder if they are poisonous?" Kneeling on the ground, Chin-yun pointed at a bunch of white mushroom among the fungus that had grown next to where Kind Clouds Sheh-fu was lying. "If not, I can make a pot of mushroom soup. . . . In this weather, it is almost impossible to find peanuts, sweet potatoes, or any edible vegetables."

Kind Clouds Sheh-fu did not answer, but gathered her limited strength to turn her head towards the white mushrooms. Her movement caused the straw underneath her to rustle. The rustling continued as her lean frame shivered beneath two thin quilts given to her and Chin-yun by the monk next door.

Chin-yun moved closer to her friend, leaned forward, and placed a gentle hand over the sick nun's forehead. "Your fever is gone. You'll be well soon," she said, forcing cheerfulness into her voice and trying to hide her worry.

Kind Clouds Sheh-fu turned her head from the dark and damp corner, met Chin-yun's eyes and caught the anxiety. "I don't . . . think so. I'm afraid you'll be alone in this place . . . soon. And I'm sorry, for leaving you. . . ." Her frail voice turned into a low moan, followed by a painful expression that suddenly appeared on her thin face.

"Is your stomach hurting again?" Chin-yun bent lower and placed both hands on her friend's midriff.

Kind Clouds Sheh-fu was too weak to nod. She blinked once, meaning yes.

Watching her friend suffer, Chin-yun's heart ached. Kind Clouds Sheh-fu had been sick for quite some time. The cold weather was only part of the reason; the major cause was hunger.

The monk next door had offered to share his food with Chin-yun and Kind Clouds Sheh-fu. Chin-yun had refused to accept because the food was purchased with money donated by the villagers before the rainy season began. Ever since the slippery path became impossible to travel, the villagers had stopped coming to the temple, and none of them knew that Chin-yun and Kind Clouds Sheh-fu were on the verge of starvation.

"It's my fault that you are sick!" Chin-yun mumbled with guilt. "My stubbornness!"

Struggling hard, Kind Clouds Sheh-fu managed to utter, "I respect your stubbornness, my friend."

Kind Clouds Sheh-fu's forgiving words intensified Chin-yun's guilt. She continued to massage her friend's stomach, wishing that her love could be carried in her touch and create the impact of medicine and food—both equally needed in easing her friend's pain.

"I wish I could find some medicine for stomach-ache, and food such as rice . . . a large bowl of soft steaming rice! Perhaps when the monk next door comes to offer us his food again, I'll accept. And if only I had something to sell . . . ," Chin-yun murmured, until she too began to shiver.

Another gust of wind had penetrated the thin walls through unseen cracks, scattering the rain from the leaking roof in all directions and spreading a few cold drops onto Chin-yun's bare neck.

Chin-yun had on only a thin cotton robe. It had been a new gray robe when Kind Clouds Sheh-fu packed it in Fon-yuen, but it was now tattered and faded. She withdrew a hand from her friend's stomach to pull the lapels of her own robe tighter. Her fingers touched something cold and hard, and she lowered her eyes to examine.

"Ah!" she gasped.

A diamond hung from a gold chain, sparkling against her skin tanned by the sun while laboring throughout the warmer months.

She stared at the glittering stone, and her thoughts flew back to the past.

She was only a teenager when her parents gave the necklace to her. Some of her girlfriends owned jewels of jade, amber, coral, and pearls, but she was the only girl in Fon-yuen wearing a diamond. She had never taken the necklace off, and it had become so much a part of her that she had not noticed its existence until this moment.

"It represents the love of my Baba and Mama. . . ." Whispering, she took the diamond in her hand.

Tears burned her eyes. She blinked quickly. Sinking her teeth into her lip, she thought: No! I must forget the past! I must look at only the present!

"Baba and Mama . . . ," her voice became hoarse when she continued, ". . . will you forgive me for parting from your gift of love?"

The wind continued to howl; the rain splashed against the walls. Listening, she tried to capture the voice of her father. But her father did not speak in the wind. The answer she searched for came from within her own heart: Chin-yun, go ahead and do what you must!

"My friend," she said to Kind Clouds Sheh-fu, "I must leave you for a while. It is early morning now, and I may not come back until night. But I will be back."

"According to the teachings of Buddha,
the sun represents courage, the moon wisdom.
My dear ancient moon, please give me the wisdom
to go forward instead of backward!"

— *Master Cheng Yen* —

The rain soaked through Chin-yun's robe. For a while, the wind sent her long hair flying, but then her hair became wet and heavy and glued to her forehead, face, and neck.

She struggled down the narrow path, holding on to the trees to keep herself from slipping down the muddy slope. By mistake, she grabbed a thorn. The sharp needles pierced into her fingers and palm. She let out a low wail, but labored on while sucking on the torn flesh.

The journey became easier once she reached the foothills. She continued towards town and was soon nearing the train station in Deer Field. She stopped at a distance from the first store, combed her tangled hair with her fingers, and used the back of her hand to wipe the dirt off her face. She noticed that the lower part of her wet robe was covered with mud, but there was nothing that she could do. Lifting her head and squaring her shoulders, she wished that people would see her pride and not her appearance.

The owner of the store, a middle-aged man, was surprised to see her. "What brought you down from the high mountain in this weather, long-haired girl? Have you suddenly decided to buy food instead of looking for it in the field?"

"No," she said, slowly shaking her head. "I didn't come to buy. I have something to sell."

Reaching back with both hands, she tried to unfasten the necklace. Her cold fingers touched her warm neck. She quivered. It was not caused by the icy touch, but the memory: more than a decade ago, her father had fastened the necklace around her neck as her mother watched with a smile.

Tears burned her eyes when she realized that her mother was far away and her father's fingers would never touch her neck again, and she would soon be parted forever from their gift of love.

Blinking, she forced back the tears. Swallowing the lump in her throat, she was determined to ignore the memory.

"How much would you give me for this?" she asked, reaching across the counter with the necklace held in her trembling hand.

The man took the necklace. He had never seen a diamond before, nor could he tell gold from brass. Glancing up, he saw the urgent need in Chin-yun's eyes and decided to do her a favor. "My little girl might like to wear this glass thing or put it on her doll. I'll give you three hundred dollars."

Chin-yun opened her mouth. "It's not glass. . . ." She stopped.

It would be useless to explain. This man could not afford the price of diamond and gold. She calculated quickly in her mind. This kind man was offering what was equivalent to almost seven U.S. dollars! It had to be much more than he had ever paid for any of his daughter's toys.

Smiling at the man, she said, "All right. I'll take the three hundred dollars."

The man tossed the necklace into the nearest drawer and closed it with a bang. That sound brought new tears into Chin-yun's eyes. "Goodbye, my gift of love. Farewell, my sweet bygone days!" Mumbling, she dashed away from the counter to look for the things that she needed.

There was not much to buy, definitely no medicine for stomach-ache. Fumbling with the money in her robe pocket, Chin-yun tried to decide what to do. She heard a train coming, and the next moment the store was vibrating as if in an earthquake. An idea came to Chin-yun. She thanked the store owner with a deep bow, and walked out into the pouring rain once more.

The train station was only a few steps away. She looked at the listed prices for a ticket to Tai-tung. The First Class and Second Class tickets were far too expensive for her. She purchased one for the Third Class, where the passengers were not guaranteed to have seats. Holding the ticket, she went to the end of a long line. Those ahead of her were peasants carrying farm products or caged chickens or ducks or piglets, each person dripping wet like she and in a bad mood. The train came and the line broke. She was pushed away from the door. Her feet and her long robe were stepped on. She quickly realized that in order to survive, all humbleness must be cast aside. She elbowed her way into the train.

Standing between a case of dried turnips and a cage of noisy geese, she breathed in the unpleasant odor—a combination of wet hair, muddy shoes, animal wastes, sweaty bodies, tobacco, and foul breath. People around her were shouting over the sound of the train. Her ears were ringing and her head pounding. She closed her eyes and saw once again the past flashing across her mind:

She was dressed in silk, sitting in the First Class section where the seats were cushioned and protected with starched white slipcovers. A porter came with a kettle of boiling water, aiming perfectly from a distance at the teacups secured onto the arms of each seat and containing fragrant tea leaves.

"Miss Wong, traveling again on your father's behalf?" in her memory she heard someone asking politely.

"Young woman, will you get out of my way?" the voice of a man barked impatiently as he tried to get through, snapping her back from the past.

Stepping out of the way, Chin-yun opened her eyes and sighed: the past is gone forever. She was no longer a rich girl traveling for the booming business of her father's theaters.

"Go away, you silly memories, and stop haunting me!" she said without knowing that she had raised her voice.

The people nearby looked at her strangely. She smiled at them to cover her embarrassment.

The train reached Tai-tung. Chin-yun got off and was grateful that the rain had stopped. She walked to the market district, bought medicine, then headed for the grocery store.

"Chin-yun Wong!"

Jumping at the voice, she turned and saw two young nuns from the Temple of Kind Clouds. Her first impulse was to run. But the street was crowded, and the nuns were only a few steps away.

"Chin-yun Wong," one of them grabbed her arm. "We know that our master, Kind Clouds Sheh-fu, went away with you. Where is she? We've been looking for her and we want her back!"

"She is . . . ," Chin-yun searched but could not find a way to avoid telling the truth. "She is in a temple not far from here."

"How is she?" the other nun asked demandingly. "We have not heard from her, and we are worried! She was never too healthy, and we don't think she ought to be away from her temple for such a long time!"

"She is sick," Chin-yun answered truthfully, showing them the medicine in her hand. "But I've been taking good care of her."

"We want to go to her," the first nuns said.

"Will you take us to her?" the second added.

"I've not finished shopping," Chin-yun said, wishing that they were in a hurry. "It may take quite a while."

"We have plenty of time," the first nun said.

"We'll shop with you," the second nodded.

Chin-yun entered a grocery store with one nun on each side. With a sigh, she began to shop. She and Kind Clouds Sheh-fu had not tasted rice for more than a season. Nor had they any oil to cook whatever edibles that they could find. She bought a bottle of peanut oil and spent the rest of the money on coarse rice.

The nuns followed her closely. She had no choice but to take them to the station, then on to Deer Field. They were astounded by the remote and underdeveloped small village. They climbed the mountain, falling several times on the steep path.

Kind Clouds Sheh-fu was asleep when they arrived. The visiting nuns called her name; she opened her eyes and, seeing them, smiled. Chin-yun watched Kind Clouds Sheh-fu take the medicine. After that, as the three enjoyed their reunion, Chin-yun went out to fetch water, then started cooking supper. "White rice! Each grain soft and chewy! How delicious!" Kind Clouds Sheh-fu said, enjoying each bite wholeheartedly. "I feel much better already!"

"This is like a party and a festival feast," Chin-yun said, delighted by her friend's speedy recovery and proud of the fine meal she had to offer.

The nuns from Fon-yuen were unimpressed by the simple meal. There was no table, and they were squatting above the mud ground. They looked around and frowned at what they hadn't noticed before: the beds were no more than a bunch of straw gathered in one corner of the room, and it was getting dark, but there was no light.

"Kind Clouds Sheh-fu," one of them asked, "will you come back to Fon-yuen? We still don't have a master and we need you."

"Yes, Kind Clouds Sheh-fu," the other joined in, "We all miss you. Have you forgotten how comfortable it is in our temple?"

Kind Clouds Sheh-fu looked at Chin-yun, remembering the easy life she had had as the master of a good-sized temple and the devotion she had received from many disciples. "Chin-yun, shall we go home? Maybe once in Fon-yuen you can convince your mother that you want to live in the temple with us."

Chin-yun put down her rice bowl and shook her head, "No. I can't go back. Mama will never allow me to stay in the temple. Besides, I haven't accomplished a thing since leaving home."

After hesitating briefly, she decided to share her secret with her friend. "I promised myself that I'll never go back to Fon-yuen unless I have accomplished something meaningful!"

Looking up, she looked at Kind Clouds Sheh-fu's gaunt face and added, "But *you* can go back. You need to go back for your health."

"No way!" Kind Clouds Sheh-fu said. "As long as you are not going back to Fon-yuen, I won't either! Actually, I've left Fon-yuen in search of a new temple, and if I should go back without finding it, it would be a defeat!"

The wintry night had deepened during their discussion. The rain had long ceased. The clouds had been swept away, revealing a bright moon. Chin-yun brought the rice bowls out of the temple, and, walking in the moonlight, she cut across the hill and reached the spring water. She washed the bowls slowly, looking up, taking in the moon's beauty and also giving the two nuns another chance to persuade Kind Clouds Sheh-fu. She couldn't help thinking that eventually Kind Clouds Sheh-fu would be persuaded. And she began to consider the possibility of going back to Fon-yuen with her friend. Life would be so much easier. There would be no more struggling. Her mother and siblings would be happy to see her. . . .

With a firm shake of her head, she freed herself from the net of tempting thoughts.

Staring at the moon, she whispered, "According to the teachings of Buddha, the sun represents courage, the moon wisdom. My dear ancient moon, please give me the wisdom to go forward instead of backward!"

When she returned to the temple, Kind Clouds Sheh-fu greeted her with a cheerful smile. "Since I won't go back with them, they will stay with us for a day or two."

"And in a day or two Kind Clouds Sheh-fu just may come to her senses!" one of the visiting nuns added.

Chin-yun had to spread the limited straws into a thinner layer to cover enough ground for four people to sleep on. They shared the two cotton quilts, which were thin and threadbare and had been in the temple longer than she and Kind Clouds Sheh-fu. During the night, she was awakened several times by the turning and twisting and moaning of the two visitors. Knowing that they could not sleep, she remembered that she and Kind Clouds Sheh-fu had been the same way when they had first arrived. The next moment she blocked out the memory together with the sound coming from the visitors and fell soundly asleep. Morning came. Breakfast was a meager meal. Swallowing the thin rice gruel mixed with a few pieces of wilted vegetables and half-rotted sweet potatoes, the visiting nuns exchanged glances.

"Kind Clouds Sheh-fu, are you strong enough for a short train ride? Let us go to Tai-tung to buy a few necessities such as food. Don't worry about money; I'll pay for everything," one of the visitors said.

"Why, yes, I think I am more than strong enough," Kind Clouds Sheh-fu answered, sounding stronger with food in her stomach and exhilaration in her heart.

"And I'll stay here with you, to keep you company," the other nun said to Chin-yun.

Chin-yun looked at the visitors and read their minds. They and Kind Clouds Sheh-fu had obviously discussed this among themselves and reached the conclusion that, if left alone, Chin-yun just might disappear. "I don't need anyone's company. I'll be perfectly all right by myself!" Chin-yun said.

They ignored her. She gave Kind Clouds Sheh-fu another dose of medicine, helped her dress, watched the two descend the mountain, then kept herself busy in the company of the remaining nun.

The shopping trip took Kind Clouds Sheh-fu and her disciple almost a whole day. They returned at nightfall, their arms loaded with food and their faces glowing with excitement.

"Coming back to Deer Field from Tai-tung, we had a fascinating train ride!" Kind Clouds Sheh-fu said. "We met the most interesting man!"

The visiting nun took over where Kind Clouds Sheh-fu had left off, "The man was dressed somewhat like a monk. He was rugged-looking but very nice. We didn't want to talk to him at first, but then he started to tell us a story, and it intrigued us. He told us that he lives in Fragrant Rice, a small town close to Tai-tung. He said that there is a high mountain called Mount Orchid, its peak hiding in the clouds. He also said that in the mountain there are gigantic snakes, but they don't harm people because they are tamed by a nameless deity who is wise and kind and rules the entire rocky mountain with an iron fist. . . ." The young nun paused to drink some spring water.

Kind Clouds Sheh-fu continued for her friend, "The man said that the deity's home can be found at the edge of a cliff on the east side of the mountaintop. Without sincerity in his heart, a person can see only a crack on the protruding rock barely large enough to insert a hand. But after praying to the deity sincerely, the crack will become an opening wide enough for a person to enter. . . ."

She went on to describe the things that this deity had done for the people in Fragrant Rice. When she ran out of words, the visiting nun who had accompanied her on the trip continued to tell more.

While listening, Chin-yun realized that the stories of deities had been rooted in the hearts of her people throughout the centuries. When unable to prove otherwise, everyone believed that the deities existed. And by believing in them, people had found comfort—they were the only hope for those who were desperate.

Chin-yun's young and innocent heart decided to believe what she had heard but with reservation—she would rather think that this deity was like Buddha, a wise man who had reached enlightenment and achieved sainthood.

After the other nun, who had stayed with Chin-yun, had expressed her regrets in having missed the opportunity of meeting this interesting man who knew the whereabouts of the deity, Chin-yun said, "I sure would like to find this man and ask him to take us to the deity. Perhaps the deity can show me a way towards serving mankind and helping all living beings."

"Let us go find him!" both of the visiting nuns shouted.

"Yes! Let us!" Kind Clouds Sheh-fu agreed.

Staring at them, Chin-yun could not find a reason to say no.

The four of them started to pack. According to legend, upon finding a deity, a person would be able to live on dewdrops and would no longer be in need of rice. Counting on that, Chin-yun took all the newly purchased groceries to the monk next door as a farewell gift.

* * *

In Fon-yuen, Mrs. Wong, and her brother-in-law were on their way to the train station.

It didn't take them long to reach Tai-tung. They soon found the dentist. "We've come from Fon-yuen to see you," Mr. Wong said.

"All the way from Fon-yuen? Has my reputation spread that far? Or is your toothache so bad that your local dentists cannot cure it? Please take a seat and open your mouth wide. . . ." The dentist never had a chance to finish.

"I'm here to find my daughter! Did your younger sister, Kind Clouds Sheh-fu, come to you during the harvest season?" Mrs. Wong asked breathlessly, then went on in a hurry, "And did she come with a young girl with long straight hair? Are they still here? If they are, please tell the long-haired girl to come out!"

"Why, yes, they were here in the autumn," the surprised and disappointed dentist answered. "But they only spent a night here. The next morning they left after breakfast. They never said where they were going. I waited for them to come back, but they never did. As a matter of fact, I, too, would like to know where they are. After all, one of them is my sister, and I am concerned about her."

Anxious to see her daughter in Tai-tung, Mrs. Wong had not slept the night before. During the time in the train she had fantasized taking Chin-yun in her arms. Riding on a pedicab she had been certain that as soon as she talked to the dentist, Chin-yun would be called out from an inner room. The dentist's words disillusioned her. All her strength was gone. She collapsed on the dentist's chair, crying and calling her daughter's name.

CHAPTER SEVENTEEN

"I'll grasp your courage, my fearless Buddha!
And I'll imitate your endurance, my Goddess of Mercy!
I'll also assimilate your bravery, my Guardian of Earth,
who is always unafraid!"

— Master Cheng Yen —

"I sobbed in the pedicab all the way to the train station of Tai-tung, then tried to get a hold of myself as we traveled to Fon-yuen, but my tears wouldn't stop falling . . . how can a mother help crying when she thinks that she will never see her precious daughter again?" Mrs. Wong said, sighing and shaking her head.

The sun had moved to the other side of the sky. The high window, bright with golden light when we started the interview, was now in the shade. The dark glass reflected the two of us in this room—Mrs. Wong dabbing her eyes with a white handkerchief and myself holding a pen. Waving the handkerchief, Mrs. Wong disturbed the slumbering bee. It rose from a wedge of peach, circled the room, decided to go out but kept bumping against the glass. The tapping caused Mrs. Wong to turn her head in that direction. Observing the bee, a melancholy smile appeared on her face.

"Aren't we all just like that bee, trying to free ourselves from sorrow but unable to find the right way out? The only difference between us and the bee is that the bee is not responsible for the existence of the glass, while we use our own hands to place a barrier before happiness!"

I leaned closer to Mrs. Wong and found in her aged eyes a deep wisdom. When she resumed talking, I wrote as fast as I could, trying to capture her every word.

She said, "For some people, the barriers are constructed with worldly desires—the endless wanting of fame, wealth, lust, power, and so on. For me, it was the wish to bring my Chin-yun back. I couldn't accept the fact that she is her own person instead of my child, nor could I face the truth that she has chosen a life in the temple instead of home. Throughout the winter I lived in misery because I couldn't let go of the past. I was determined to make it reappear—I believed that once it reappeared, so would my Chin-yun.

"I spent much of the time lying in bed, grieving for my lost happiness, wishing for it to return. Some of my tears were shed for my deceased husband, the rest for my missing daughter. While mourning, I completely overlooked my blessings.

"My four remaining children took turns coming to my bed, calling me, comforting me, and serving me food and tea. They were grateful when I chanced to be in the mood to utter a few words. They became ecstatic if I felt generous enough to show them a smile. But both my words and my smiles were rare, because I was a foolish bee, blinded by an illusion, bumping my head against a solid glass and crying: Let me out of my grief! Bring me back the past! Give me back my Chin-yun!"

❋ ❋ ❋

"Chin-yun! Chin-yun!" Kind Clouds Sheh-fu called, patting Chin-yun on the shoulder. "It's time to get up!"

Chin-yun opened her eyes. The room was still dark. It was seldom that Kind Clouds Sheh-fu, always tired from work and hunger, couldn't wait to rise. Sitting up from a bed of straw, Chin-yun was surprised by what she saw: both Kind Clouds Sheh-fu and the two visiting nuns were neatly dressed and ready to go.

Chin-yun dressed quickly and hurried out of the temple. The path leading to the other side of the hill was brightened by a brilliant moon. She rushed to the spring water, washed her face and brushed her teeth. The icy water caused her to shiver. Through chattering teeth, she mumbled, while looking up, "My wise, ancient moon, please fill my heart with good sense, so I won't do anything foolish!"

When she returned to the temple, Kind Clouds Sheh-fu and the visiting nuns were already waiting at the beginning of the pathway. The monk next door was still asleep. Chin-yun, having said good-bye on the previous night, did not disturb him. Casting a last glance at the tiny temple, she followed the three nuns to leave the crumbling building that had sheltered her for over a season.

They reached Deer Field at dawn and caught the first train to Fragrant Rice, a town at the outskirts of Tai-tung and half the size of Deer Field. The train station was on the main road, which was also the only road, where the lone store stood with half of the town's population gathered on its porch.

"I see him!" Kind Clouds Sheh-fu shouted, pointing at a man sitting on the front steps of the store.

Chin-yun's eyes widened as the man stood up and walked towards them. He was very tall and massive in size. His monk-like attire was filthy and torn. He needed a shave and his hair was much too long for a respectable citizen. He had bare feet. A giant knife in the shape of a crescent moon hung by its handle from his waist. He was accompanied by a neatly dressed, frail old man who looked kind and wise.

Staring at the knife, Chin-yun was ready to back away. Glancing at the old man, she changed her mind.

"I thought you might come!" the man with the knife said to Kind Clouds Sheh-fu, smiling broadly, revealing his cracked, yellow teeth. "I see that you've brought more friends!"

"We've come to search for the deity, and we'll be grateful if you would lead us to the cliff where the magic gate is," Kind Clouds Sheh-fu went on.

Chin-yun kept a watchful eye on the man with the knife and found him listening with full attention and nodding with enthusiasm to help. She began to relax upon discovering that he never once looked her way, nor did he seem to notice that she and the two visiting nuns were young and not unattractive.

When Kind Clouds Sheh-fu had finished, this giant of a man pointed towards the old man, "My friend goes everywhere with me. He, too, knows the whereabouts of the deity's home."

There were six of them—Chin-yun, Kind Clouds Sheh-fu, the two nuns from Fon-yuen, the old man, and the man with the knife. They walked away from the store. The villagers stared after them, silent and expressionless.

They headed west towards the Central Mountain Ranges and had only gone a short way when they heard the sound of rippling water.

"What is that?" Chin-yun asked, frowning and tilting her head to one side.

"The Wu-lue River," the giant answered casually. "It stands between our village and the mountain. It is about two miles wide. There is no bridge, but the water is not very deep."

As they walked closer to the river, the cascading water became louder. It sounded like a waterfall hitting against solid rocks. Listening carefully, Chin-yun couldn't imagine the water being shallow. They entered a bamboo grove. When they emerged from the green forest, the girls gasped.

The Wu-lue River was the widest and most turbulent river that Chin-yun had ever seen. Large brown rocks were piled alongside the river bank and also protruded from the central part of the river; they looked like water buffaloes captured in the arms of an angry water god, crying for help while getting drowned.

"Can we circle around the river to reach the mountain?" Chin-yun asked.

The giant shook his head.

"You expect us to wade across this horrible river?" Chin-yun asked again.

The man nodded this time.

One of the nuns from Fon-yuen stepped back towards the bamboo grove and said, "I changed my mind about finding the deity."

The other nun also began to back away, "I would rather stay alive than search for the deity."

Chin-yun was ready to join them when Kind Clouds Sheh-fu grabbed her right arm.

"Don't anybody leave!" Kind Clouds Sheh-fu said, her voice unusually strong and confident. "Let us join hands!"

"Don't be afraid," the old man said as he stepped into the water. "I've walked across this river hundreds of times and I'm still alive."

Looking at Kind Clouds Sheh-fu and the old man, Chin-yun mumbled, "Well, I suppose we can give it a try." She reached out with her left hand and took the old man's right hand.

The giant grabbed the old man's left hand. Kind Clouds Sheh-fu took Chin-yun's right hand. The nuns from Fon-yuen exchanged helpless looks and joined the procession reluctantly, holding hands with Kind Clouds Sheh-fu and each other.

"The water is cold like ice!" Chin-yun let out a scream. "And it's reaching my knees! No . . . my thighs . . . my waist . . . my chest!"

"We're getting drowned!" one of the Fon-yuen nuns wailed.

"Something is pulling at my feet from underneath the current! It must be the ghost of a drowned man!" the other nun shrieked.

"Let . . . us . . . pray!" Kind Clouds Sheh-fu pretended to be calm, but her quivering voice betrayed her.

The giant and the frail old man ignored the girls and kept walking. Pulled by them, the girls had no choice but to follow Kind Clouds Sheh-fu's example as they murmured all the prayers they knew while struggling towards the opposite shore.

Chin-yun raised her voice and prayed from the bottom of her heart, "I'll grasp your courage, my fearless Buddha! And I'll imitate your endurance, my Goddess of Mercy! And I'll also assimilate your bravery, my Guardian of Earth, who is always unafraid!"

The old man squeezed her hand. She looked at him and saw him smiling.

"My dear child, you may look funny with your long hair and dressed in a nun's robe, but you certainly know how to pray," he said as they continued to tread through the water. "That's it! A true Buddhist never says, 'Grant me this!' or 'Give me that!' There is no god. Buddha started as a man and ended as a saint. Neither he, nor any other deity, can help a person cross a river or do anything else!"

"In that case," Chin-yun said, staring at the old man, "why are we risking our lives to search for the deity?"

The old man did not answer.

They were now in the center of the river where the water was the deepest. Weeds tangled around their legs, pulling them. The rough current swept them against rocks, bruising them. The water was not all that clean. Cadavers of small animals floated by, and the stench was unbearable. Chin-yun held her breath and looked away from the bloated corpses. Just when she thought that she could not take it any more, the bed of the river began to lift. The water receded—from her chest and finally to her knees.

"We made it!" she shouted with delight when she stood on the bank looking back across the turbulent waters.

The girls glanced at one another and knew that they all looked like drowned rats, with their robes wet up to their shoulders. They took the lower part of their robes and wrung out some of the water, then picked off dead leaves and weeds and anything still clinging to the cloth of one another's clothes. "No time to groom yourselves! We must begin to climb the mountain!" the giant ordered before they had a chance to sit and rest.

"How long will it take to reach the cliff?" Chin-yun asked, tilting back her head. "I can't even see it! Is it hiding behind those clouds?"

"Yes. It's behind the clouds. But it won't take us very long to get there . . . not long at all!" the giant answered vaguely.

"You can't see the mountain peak because you are at the beginning of the journey," the old man added slowly. "Just like a child who, at the beginning of life's journey, cannot visualize old age."

There was no path. The giant led the way, climbing from slope to slope, at times jumping from rock to rock. The old man moved with the agility of a mountain goat, as if weightless. The girls tried their best to keep up but were constantly left far behind.

"Wait for us!" they had to plea again and again.

But the girls soon became quiet. Moving sideways with their backs brushing against the mountain, they were afraid to speak or look down. Only a few inches in front of their toes was a straight drop leading to the river, which now looked like a curling ribbon.

When the old man gave Chin-yun a helping hand, she noticed a tarnished watch on his wrist.

"What time is it?" she asked.

"Almost nine o'clock," he answered.

They inched forward, progressing slowly as they went higher. The girls, who had been shaking when first out of the water, were now perspiring. They tried to rest, regardless of the giant's objection, but quickly discovered that they had to keep moving—while resting, the wind would take away their breath and body heat, and they would feel chilled to the bone.

"A person should treat the current day
as a mountain-climber would the ground under his feet.
There is no time for the step he already took or
the step that is still far ahead.
The only real thing is the present moment.
No past and no future, because the past already had its chance
and the future will soon have its turn."

— *Master Cheng Yen* —

"Each living being has a mountain to climb,
and the climbing is never easy.
After the peak we can only climb up into the clouds of death,
and to be reborn is to be placed at the foot of another mountain.
All the tears and laughter will start over again,
and we will climb on and on and on. . . ."

— *Master Cheng Yen* —

"What time is it now?' Chin-yun asked again.

"Almost eleven," the old man answered calmly.

"Time passes fast when I give all my attention to my feet," Kind Clouds Sheh-fu said. "And all this while, my stomach never ached. Actually, all my troubles have left me. Although my body is tired, my mind is clearer than it has ever been!"

One of the Fon-yuen nuns said, "I used to think that mountain-climbers were fools, but now I have changed my mind. When thinking of the step I am taking at this moment, nothing else bothers me anymore."

Chin-yun didn't speak. Her mind was filled with a new realization: a person should treat the current day as a mountain-climber would the ground under his feet. There is no time for the step he already took or the step that is still far ahead. The only real thing is the present moment. No past and no future, because the past already had its chance and the future will soon have its turn.

"What time is it?" she asked again.

"Five o'clock in the afternoon," the old man glanced at his wrist.

"Is your watch accurate?" Chin-yun asked in disbelief. "We couldn't have been climbing for eight hours!"

"Take a look at the sun, and you'll know that my watch has told the truth," the old man said, pointing at the western sky.

A magnificent view met Chin-yun's eyes. The sky was glowing in gold, red, purple, and orange. Flocks of birds, with their feathers painted by the sunlight into glorious hues, were on home-bound flights. Some of them had already reached their nests among the ancient trees nearby; their chirping filled the air as they began to settle for the night. She looked down and saw that the once ribbon-like river was now a thin thread. Glancing up, she found the cliff hanging right above her head.

She shouted in excitement, "There are no more clouds! I can see the cliff clearly!"

"You are wrong," the old man shook his head. "The clouds are still there, but now you are in them."

"But I don't see the clouds!" Chin-yun said.

"Close your eyes and you'll see much more," the old man smiled.

Chin-yun closed her eyes. The next moment she sensed, on her face and hands, something soft and wet, more tangible than wind but less real than rain. She whispered, "This is wonderful! As if I'll soon be able to fly."

A strange feeling overpowered her, and she asked, with her eyes closed, "Can this be the feeling of a dying man?"

"I imagine so, although I've never died . . . not in this life," the old man's voice seemed to be coming from faraway. "My child, life is like a mountain. Climbing starts at birth and, unless you fall off the mountain before your time, old age is unavoidable, like the mountain top. Look down, and you shall see what you've accomplished with each step."

Chin-yun opened her eyes. Beneath her feet, the village of Fragrant Rice lay peacefully. Was it only a minute ago that she and the other girls arrived at the quiet town? How could it be so far away from them now?

And then she saw the turbulent river. Crossing it had been strenuous but also fun. How she wished that she had not complained! But that moment was gone forever, and she could never recapture it to change it into a different way.

She stared down at the winding path that they had traveled on. She and her friends had talked, sighed, laughed, and cried, and their voices were still echoing in her mind. If only they had known that, once passing it, they would never go that way again, they would have laughed more and wept less!

Chin-yun looked up and met the old man's eyes. They smiled at each other and, for the first time since meeting him, Chin-yun felt able to share his wisdom.

"I think I've realized something: each living being has a mountain to climb, and the climbing is never easy," Chin-yun said. "After the peak we can only climb up into the clouds of death, and to be reborn is to be placed at the foot of another mountain. All the tears and laughter will start over again, and we will climb on and on and on. . . ."

She looked at the old man pleadingly, "How can we be spared from further climbing?"

Sighing, the old man shook his head. "I wish I knew. I imagine it would help if we had climbed our current mountain with love and mercy, so as to avoid stepping on other living beings and to give our fellow climbers a helping hand . . . and so on."

Nodding, Chin-yun began to dwell in deep thoughts.

"The Guardian of Earth constantly travels to hell.
Since he is unafraid, why should we?"

— *Master Cheng Yen* —

The magnificent clouds of the sky faded into pale gray. As the gray deepened into darkness, a tiny star appeared modestly from the east. It was followed by many more humble stars, like a group of novice nuns waiting for their master—the moon. Master Moon softly emerged and stood robed in shimmering white, then stepped up onto a platform and began to govern the heavens with her dazzling glow.

Bathed in the moonlight, the procession of two men and four girls reached the mountain top. Aching all over, panting and ready to collapse, the girls stared at their reward for a formidable climb that had lasted more than ten hours.

The entire mountain top was a wooded plateau. It took them several minutes to realize that this area contained, not several trees, but one giant banyan.

Kind Clouds Sheh-fu and the Fon-yuen nuns had lost their voices. Chin-yun said, with her eyes opened wide, "This tree has to be as ancient as the moon! It has thousands of air-roots; each has rooted and turned into another banyan with hundreds of air-roots! The finest air-root from the youngest tree is thicker than the diameter of a rice-bowl!" Looking around, she asked, "Where is the cliff with the magic gate leading to the deity's home?"

"It's on the other side of the tree," the giant answered, pointing towards the thicket.

"How can we go to the other side?" Chin-yun asked again.

"Like this!" The man removed the long, broad knife from his waist, held it in his enormous hands, and raised it high. Swinging the knife, his massive arms moved with the speed of lightning, and his upper body turned swiftly.

The nearest air-root was cut in two. The man kept swinging his knife, and a path began to appear. Bending low, the others followed him, going deeper into the banyan forest.

Branches and leaves sealed them in and kept moonlight out. They became prisoners in a cage that was pitch black, musty, and wet. The wind continued to scream, sounding like a person laughing sarcastically. Other than their footsteps, there were also the footsteps of other living beings, running away from them in all directions.

"Spider web!" one of the Fon-yuen nuns screamed, waving her arms frantically. "It's all over my face!"

"Bugs!" the other nun yelled, stamping her foot. "They fell on my neck and are crawling down!"

"I see several pairs of eyes staring at me from the darkest corner!" Kind Clouds Sheh-fu almost toppled over. "Can they be the eyes of wild hogs?"

"Let us pretend to be the Guardian of Earth, who constantly travels to hell," Chin-yun said in a trembling voice, trying to be brave. "Since he is unafraid, why should we?"

Suddenly, the darkness ran from the rays of the moonlight, and they were out of the banyan forest. Breathlessly, the girls tried to forget their frightening experience by speaking their hopeful thoughts:

"The cliff has to be only a few feet away!"

"Once there, we'll find the magic gate!"

"The deity will be touched by our persistence!"

"He'll teach us what we've come to learn!"

Following the men, the girls moved forward. The plateau narrowed into a strip, curving like a hairpin, leading to the cliff.

The old man stopped. Pointing at the cliff, he said to the girls, "My children, do you see that white rock protruding from the cliff?"

The girls nodded. The old man continued, "That is the highest point of this mountain, also the journey's end for all mountain-climbers. The rock seems to be closer to heaven than earth. Because of that, all sorts of stories have been invented. . . ." He stopped when the girls screamed at the sight of a moving shadow.

"It's coming toward us!"

"It's shaped like a man . . . a tall man!"

"It is a man! And he is not alone!"

"Two men! Or, two . . . deities?"

Huddling, trembling, gasping, the girls watched the two human forms moving closer. The moon was behind the two forms. Their faces were in the shadow. They had on baggy pants and wide-sleeved shirts. As their pants legs and shirt sleeves flapped in the wind, they appeared to be flying.

"Who are you?" one of them asked. His voice was quite human, with the accent of someone from central Taiwan.

"And what are you doing at this place at this hour?" the second one asked, his accent similar to that of the first one.

The giant explained why they had come, then asked, "Who are you?"

Without answering, both of the human forms burst into laughter. The roaring echoed throughout the plateau, caused the creatures in the banyan forest to stir once more. When they stopped laughing, one of them said, "Looking for deity! So the world is filled with fools!"

"Well, I'm sorry to disappoint you, but my buddy and I are no deities!" the other, who was greatly amused, said. "We are herb dealers. We also sell rattan baskets. Various herbs grow around here. The stems of those climbing palms are ideal for wickerwork and so are the young roots of the banyans. We camp here quite often. You are welcome to rest in our tent."

The herb and rattan dealers led the newcomers to the other side of a large rock. The tent was constructed by interweaving banyan roots with stems of climbing palms. The hosts offered their guests wheat buns, which were dry and hard, and also cold water in a tin jar. The girls were given two quilts for the night, and the four men slept outside the tent.

They were awakened by the sound of birds flying out of the banyan forest. In the dawn's pearly light, they walked to the cliff and searched every inch of the protruding rock.

There was no magic gate. The only cracks that they could see were only wide enough for ants.

The girls began to pray—to themselves and to any force willing to help. But the cracks never widened.

Their hearts were heavy with disappointment. Dragging their aching bodies towards the banyan forest, they were ready to descend the mountain.

"Why go that way?" one of the dealers asked, pointing towards the other side of the plateau. "There is a much easier way, wide and flat and with a rope bridge across the river. In less than three hours you'll reach a seaside town called Scented Harbor, where there are buses to take you wherever you want to go."

The girls looked at one another, then glared accusingly at the men from Fragrant Rice.

The giant shrugged. "How could I know that there is another way? I've lived in Fragrant Rice all my life and have never heard of the Scented Harbor!"

The old man answered with a peaceful smile, "Yes, I know Scented Harbor, which is only a short distance from Fragrant Rice. And I also know the easier way . . . but your trip has not been wasted."

He looked from one girl to another, his aged eyes gleaming meaningfully, "The harder a lesson is learned, the longer it will be remembered. I'm sure none of you will ever search for deities again."

His eyes stopped on Chin-yun, and he continued slowly and clearly, "Perhaps some of you have already realized that all deities are just like Buddha, who lives not in high mountains but in your own hearts!"

CHAPTER EIGHTEEN

"When you want to do something but run into opposing forces,
the strongest force usually comes from your loved ones,
and you cannot fight them."

— *Master Cheng Yen* —

M RS. WONG GLANCED TOWARDS THE WINDOW. The sun had moved to the western horizon, and the city of Taichung had become busy with people going home from work. She narrowed her eyes as if searching for something. "Where is the bee that was looking for a way out but kept bumping into the glass?"

I pointed to an open window at the other end of the room, "It went over there and flew out a while ago."

With a sigh of relief, Mrs. Wong said, "I'm glad. I felt for that poor bee because it reminded me of myself at one time."

✳   ✳   ✳

At one time Mrs. Wong was bumping her head against obstacles and going in circles looking for her daughter. She went to the Temple of Kind Clouds at least once a day, asking the nuns if they had heard from their master. She had no idea that, at this time, her daughter was on the mountain top and about to part from her companions.

The giant and the old man preferred to go home their way—down the steep slope and across the turbulent river. The girls took a well-traveled road, crossed a rope bridge, and arrived in Scented Harbor.

When they walked into the bus station, people stared. Their robes were filthy, their faces and arms and hands scratched and bruised. Everyone frowned at the long broad knife in Chin-yun's hands. Before parting, the giant had insisted that the girls take his knife: they might need it for cutting weeds or fending off any evil force. They had taken turns carrying it but had never had the chance to use it, and now they didn't have the heart to throw it away.

Seeing people's expressions, the girls knew that they must find a place to wash and change. The nearest place was the home of Kind Clouds Sheh-fu's brother, so they purchased four tickets to Tai-tung. The brother, his astonishment turning into anger when they arrived, yelled at his sister, "Look at you! You are losing face for your family! I forbid you to return to Deer Field! I'll give you money and food and two choices: either return to Fon-yuen, or find yourself a decent temple such as the Temple of Clear Awareness in Tze-ben!"

The two young nuns decided to return to Fon-yuen. Chin-yun and Kind Clouds Sheh-fu, taking the brother's advice, headed for Tze-ben, a small town not far from Tai-tung. The Temple of Clear Awareness was a peaceful abode, and the master was an aged nun. Chin-yun and Kind Clouds Sheh-fu became friends with all the nuns there and joined their daily routine: work, pray, and study the scriptures of Buddhism.

Combining these scriptures with her own thinking, Chin-yun's wisdom expanded. But even with such wisdom, her peace of mind was constantly disturbed by an invisible rope around her neck—her mother's love.

"I feel like a fugitive, hiding from a search party," she said to Kind Clouds Sheh-fu. "Do you know that when you want to do something but run into opposing forces, the strongest force usually comes from your loved ones? And you cannot fight them. You can only wish that their opposition will change into a helping hand. But how can I change my mother's way of thinking? Must I hide from her forever?"

"Why don't you tell her where you are? Let her come. You may or may not change her way of thinking, but at least you won't need to hide from her any more," Kind Clouds Sheh-fu suggested.

Chin-yun thought it over and wrote a letter.

". . . please forgive me for running away, Mama, but please give me the freedom to become a nun. Don't come for me, for I will not come home . . . not yet. There is an old saying: a proud horse will not return to feed upon the field from which it had already fled. I am proud, and will not return to Fon-yuen until I become a success. . . ."

* * *

Once they returned to the Temple of Kind Clouds, the two young nuns talked to the others about their searching for the deity with their master and Chin-yun. Word traveled quickly to the ears of Mrs. Wong. When Chin-yun's letter arrived home, Mrs. Wong was just about to go out of the door.

"Chin-yun will come home with us wearing the clothes in my suitcase!" Mrs. Wong said to her brother-in-law after reading the letter.

They traveled by train to Tai-tung, found one of the very few taxis and arrived in Tze-ben. The wind was blowing fiercely, the weather becoming colder, as the taxi zigzagged up a mountain road. When the road became worse and the driver refused to go any farther, Mrs. Wong and her brother-in-law continued on foot to climb a narrow path with a steep drop on one side. It was extremely difficult for Mrs. Wong, who was afraid of heights.

"A rope bridge!" She screamed and stood frozen at the end of the road near the edge of a cliff. "I've never crossed a rope bridge in my life!"

The bridge was about three hundred feet long and two feet wide, constructed by tying thin boards together to connect two cliffs that were nearly a mile above a tumultuous river.

"Don't be afraid," Mr. Wong said, taking a step towards the bridge. "Do what I'm doing . . . hold your suitcase with one hand and use your other hand to hold on to the railing."

"But the railing is also made of rope!" Mrs. Wong hesitated. "And it has already rotted in many places!"

"The Temple of Clear Awareness is at the end of this bridge," Mr. Wong said with encouragement. "And Chin-yun is in that temple!"

Mrs. Wong forced herself to step on to the bridge, which was already screeching and shaking under the weight of her brother-in-law. Her knees soon buckled and she almost fell.

"My heart is willing to risk anything for my Chin-yun, but my body doesn't know how to move on this thing!" she said and began to cry.

"Well," Mr. Wong thought it over carefully, "you and I are like brother and sister. It'll be all right for me to carry you on my back."

Mrs. Wong agreed in embarrassment. Her brother-in-law gave his suitcase to her, squatted, and she leaned onto his back holding both suitcases. Carrying her, he began to cross the bridge. She closed her eyes but could feel the powerful wind tossing the bridge back and forth with them on it.

"Chin-yun, Mama is coming to you!" she called, trying to push aside her fear.

The bridge seemed to be many miles long. When they reached the other end, Mrs. Wong jumped off her brother-in-law's back and noticed that he was drenched in sweat.

They continued on the mountain road where they met a few woodsmen who showed them the direction of the temple. They hurried under a graying sky and reached the Temple of Clear Awareness when the first star appeared.

It was a modest temple with a very low roof. An aged nun greeted them and introduced herself as the master.

"We want to talk to Chin-yun Wong," Mrs. Wong said. "I'm her mother and I've come to bring her home."

The master bowed humbly but did not answer or move.

Mr. Wong stepped forward, "I am Chin-yun's uncle. We traveled a long way. Please ask Chin-yun to come out."

The master bowed again, then left for the inner room.

"We are born to suffer.
But all sufferings are merely a candle's teardrops
that will cease to fall when embraced by the wisdom of Buddha.
For example: illness, old-age, and death are teardrops,
but when realizing that all living beings must go
through the same circle, the tears will not fall too far."

— *Master Cheng Yen* —

In the inner room, Chin-yun was studying by candlelight. Turning a page, she looked away from the Sutras and glanced at the candle.

The light was flickering, the candle shedding tears. Staring at it, she noticed that as a tear rolled down, a thin membrane began to form and protect the tear from rolling farther.

She could no longer study. Her thoughts flew back to her childhood days. As a little girl, whenever she was hurt, her mother would call her softly, "My little Chin-yun, come to Mama, and Mama will comfort you."

In Taiwanese, the word "comfort" is a homonym for the word "skin."

Without looking away from the candle, Chin-yun said to Kind Clouds Sheh-fu, who was studying beside her, "A mother comforts her child like a protective skin, and the wisdom of Buddha comforts us the same way."

The candle continued to glimmer, and Chin-yun went deeper into her thoughts, sharing her thinking with Kind Clouds Sheh-fu. "We are born to suffer. But all sufferings are but the teardrops of a candle; they will cease to fall when embraced by the wisdom of Buddha."

Kind Clouds Sheh-fu thought, then nodded her head. "The wisdom of Buddha is a layer of protective skin."

Smiling, Chin-yun was pleased by her friend's quick mind. "The pain of childbirth is a teardrop for a woman, but the joy of becoming a mother is the protective skin that keeps the tear from falling further. Illness, old-age, and death are more teardrops, but when realizing that all living beings must go through the same circle, a protective skin is formed and the tears will not fall too far.

"For a person to be parted from his loved ones is another teardrop, and to lose his worldly possessions is another. He needs the wisdom to know that life is impermanent, that none of his loved ones can stay with him forever. And he must also understand that he does not own anything in this world, that all his possessions are his only for a fleeting moment. With such wisdom a protective skin is formed, and this person will no longer cry when losing anyone or anything. . . ."

She was interrupted by the master of the temple. "Your mother and uncle are here to bring you home!"

"A mother's love stays with her daughter throughout eternity,
but a gift that is merely a material thing does not have
to be in the daughter's possession.
And a daughter's love will remain with her mother endlessly,
although the daughter's physical form is no longer
at her mother's side."

— *Master Cheng Yen* —

Mrs. Wong and her brother-in-law did not recognize the young girl in a gray robe. But the girl brought her hands forward with palms touching, bowing deeply and silently.

"My Chin-yun!" Mrs. Wong let out a cry when she recognized her daughter. "How did you become so thin? Don't they feed you at all in this place? And what an awful robe you have on! Why, it's covered with patches, and you've never worn any patched things in your life! I'm so glad that I've brought a few pretty dresses for you! You must change before going home!"

Chin-yun remained silent. The temple was dimly lit with an oil lamp. Mrs. Wong could see that Chin-yun's face was bloodless and her lips trembling. "My poor child! You look malnourished and ill! On second thought, let's go home right now! You can come with me in that robe and change later!" With these words, Mrs. Wong took Chin-yun's hand.

"Yes, you must come with us this very moment!" Mr. Wong said, taking Chin-yun's other hand.

Chin-yun looked at the other nuns and the master in the distance. It was clear that none of them intended to interfere, not even Kind Clouds Sheh-fu. Sighing, she realized that it would be unwise to create a scene. "All right," she said as she was escorted out of the temple. "My body will go wherever you want but not my soul."

They walked under the night sky, finding their direction by moonlight. Mrs. Wong kept talking to Chin-yun, but the girl only answered with the shake or nod of her head. Thinking that her daughter was embarrassed by being caught, Mrs. Wong decided that the conversation could wait. They proceeded in silence and soon reached the rope bridge.

"You go first," Mr. Wong said to Chin-yun, eliminating her chance of running away.

Being carried on her brother-in-law's back and holding on to the suitcases, Mrs. Wong kept her eyes on Chin-yun. Without helping with the suitcases, Chin-yun moved carelessly, without holding on to the railing. In the middle of the bridge, she raised her hands to untie her hair, shook her head, and sent her hair flying in the night wind. A sudden fear chilled Mrs. Wong's heart: is my Chin-yun thinking of doing something foolish?

They crossed the bridge and were soon on the steep path that was only wide enough for two. Mr. Wong led the way. Chin-yun walked on the cliff side. Mrs. Wong looked over and saw the river below shimmering in the moonlight.

"Chin-yun, let us change places!" she said, casting aside her fear of heights, relieved that Chin-yun obeyed without arguing.

They reached Tai-tung but missed the last train and bus for Fon-yuen. They checked into a hotel, and Mrs. Wong insisted that she and Chin-yun share a room. Chin-yun removed her tattered robe and went immediately to bed. When she was not looking, Mrs. Wong took the robe and tossed it under the bed, thinking that she had tossed away Chin-yun's desire to become a nun.

Mrs. Wong joined Chin-yun in bed but forced herself to stay awake throughout the night. Every time Chin-yun turned, she thought that the girl was getting ready to run away again.

Morning finally came. In the dim light of dawn, Mrs. Wong saw Chin-yun lying on her back, staring at the ceiling.

Turning and meeting her mother's eyes, Chin-yun said, "I need three hundred dollars, and I must pay a quick visit to someone in Deer Field."

Mrs. Wong gave Chin-yun the money without asking any questions. When Chin-yun searched for her gray robe, she told her to choose one of the silk dresses from the suitcase.

Chin-yun did not argue. Nor did she look further for her robe. She looked away from the colorful dresses and took one that was pure white.

Mrs. Wong watched Chin-yun wash her face and comb her hair without looking into the mirror. It'll change, she thought, my

Chin-yun is a beautiful young girl; of course she will soon become interested in her appearance again.

Mr. Wong knocked on their door. After a quick breakfast, they went to Deer Field by taxi. Mrs. Wong followed Chin-yun into the small store, where the owner instantly recognized Chin-yun.

"It's good to see you again! We missed you and your friend!" the man said, and the next moment his eyes widened. "How beautiful you are in that nice dress!"

"May I buy my necklace back?" Chin-yun asked, putting the three hundred dollars on the counter.

"Ah, the toy necklace for my little girl. But I forgot to give it to her. Where did I put it?" Staring at Chin-yun, the man tried to remember.

Chin-yun pointed at the nearest drawer, "When you bought it, you tossed it in there."

The man opened the drawer. He had tossed many more things into the drawer. Digging into a stack of bills and other things, he finally found the necklace and threw it onto the counter. "Are you sure you want to buy back this useless thing?"

Chin-yun took the necklace, turned and quickly fastened it around her mother's neck. She then walked around to face her mother. There was a sad smile on her face and many unspoken words on her parted lips. Her eyes were gleaming with tears, and behind the unshed tears was a silent message: Mama, I'm giving you back the gift of love from you and Baba. Your love will always be mine, although I will no longer wear the diamond around my neck. And my love will always be yours, even when you do not have me by your side.

However, at that moment Mrs. Wong did not receive the message.

They rushed to the bus station in Tai-tung, and Mr. Wong purchased three tickets. The suitcases were soon checked in. Chin-yun was quiet while they waited in line. The bus came, and they moved towards the door, with Chin-yun in between Mrs. Wong and Mr. Wong. When they reached the bus, Mr. Wong boarded first, then turned to give Chin-yun a hand. At that instant Chin-yun suddenly switched places with her mother—Mrs. Wong boarded the bus, but Chin-yun stepped aside and disappeared into the crowd.

The other passengers pushed hard. Mrs. Wong and her brother-in-law yelled and struggled but could not move in reverse. The crowd forced them to move on. There was no back door for them to get off. As soon as they took their reserved seats, the aisle was filled with people and carry-on luggage. They continued to scream and try but still could not leave their seats. The only thing that they could do was look out the window and search for Chin-yun.

The station was swarming with people. They did not find Chin-yun until the bus started to move. They saw her stepping forward from behind the crowd, revealing herself, and all the pent up emotions broke like a dam as she stood waving, her tears streaming down her face and onto the white dress.

"Good-bye, Mama! Good-bye, Uncle!" Chin-yun mouthed these words as she continued to cry and wave.

"Chin-yun! My Chin-yun! My child! My baby! Come back! Please!" Mrs. Wong wailed, waving frantically.

The bus turned. Chin-yun was out of sight. Mrs. Wong felt a sudden pain in her heart. Caressing her chest, her trembling fingers touched the diamond hanging from her neck.

She bowed her head, stared at the diamond, visualized the small store in Deer Field, and remembered Chin-yun's expression when returning the necklace. Suddenly, Chin-yun's message reached her heart: a mother's love stays with her daughter throughout eternity, but a gift that is merely a material thing does not have to be in the daughter's possession. And a daughter's love will remain with her mother endlessly, although the daughter's physical form is no longer at her mother's side.

The pain in Mrs. Wong's heart began to ease. After a while, she stopped crying. Unknowingly, her lips curved up to form a faint smile.

*"A proud horse will not return to feed
upon the field from which it had already fled,
and I will not return to my home town
without first becoming a success."*

— *Master Cheng Yen* —

Once back in Fon-yuen, Mrs. Wong asked her brother-in-law to help take care of the theaters. To her surprise, the business continued to bloom, and at home things also went smoothly with the help of her other children.

"I should have set Chin-yun free a long time ago!" Mrs. Wong sighed. "It was wrong of me to hold on to her!"

Mrs. Wong wrote to Chin-yun, and her every letter was answered with love and concern. Her younger children also communicated with their elder sister, and Chin-yun's letters to them were compassionate and encouraging, just like she had always been to them. Everyone missed Chin-yun, but they were no longer dreaming of having her back as a permanent member of the family.

In the summer of 1962, while alone at home, Mrs. Wong heard a soft knocking on the door.

Answering it, she saw a young nun in a clean gray robe. The nun's head was shaved, giving her the general appearance of all nuns.

"What can I do for you, my honorable Sheh-fu?" Mrs. Wong brought her hands up with palms touching and bowed to the nun.

Smiling and bowing back, the nun said calmly, "Mama, it's me."

Having learned to accept the fact that her most treasured daughter had become a nun, Mrs. Wong still could not hold back the sudden tears as she reached a trembling hand towards Chin-yun's head. "My child! You shaved off your beautiful hair! So you've become a real nun!"

Chin-yun stood patiently as her mother caressed her, then answered softly, "No, Mama, I have not yet become an ordained nun. I shaved off my hair by my own hands. I still need to find a master who is qualified and willing to take me as a disciple. I can't become a nun without a formal initiation. I'm here to let you know that I'll be moving again."

"Moving again? Why? And where to?" Mrs. Wong asked, trying her best to keep herself from sounding like a pleading mother: Chin-yun, won't you please move back home?

"I'm moving without any particular reason. It's just that I don't feel I belong to the Temple of Clear Awareness, although the master and everyone have been very kind to me. I don't know exactly where I'll be going, but Kind Clouds Sheh-fu will be going with me. We may try a few places first, then go to Hwalien, the city on the eastern shore. I will not settle until I find a temple where the master and I share the same belief in Buddhism."

Chin-yun stayed in her home for the next two days. During that time, she did not go out of the house because she had not forgotten her vow: she would not really return to her home town without first becoming a success. On the third day, she rose at dawn, said good-bye to her family, and bowed to her mother at the door.

"Don't worry, Mama. I'll write to you as soon as I have a return address," Chin-yun said before walking away.

"Take care of yourself, my precious child!" Mrs. Wong said, forcing back her tears. She watched the young nun in a gray robe disappearing at the corner of the street, then added softly, "Take care of yourself, my honorable Sheh-fu!"

CHAPTER NINETEEN

*"Maybe there is no miracle under heaven.
Maybe the so-called miraculous events are merely
the way things were, still are, and always will be."*

— Master Cheng Yen —

OUTSIDE THE WINDOW, neon lights sparkled against a dark sky, reflecting stories of city life. Mrs. Wong glanced out the window and said with a peaceful smile, "In 1962, as Taiwan prospered into an island of lights, my Chin-yun remained in the mountainous areas where candles were still being used to brighten the night. She worked hard to acquire the knowledge needed for her mission in life and continued to travel from temple to temple in search of a place where the master's belief would be compatible with hers.

"We communicated frequently and became no longer mother and daughter but best friends. Reading her letters, learning her current situation and future plans, I felt that I was going with her from one place to another." Counting on her fingers, Mrs. Wong tried to figure out the sequence of events. "I'm old and can't remember things in their exact order. Some of the things that I'm about to tell you might not have taken place on the precise month and year as I say, but all of them happened, and each of them was important."

* * *

Throughout the autumn of 1962, Chin-yun and Kind Clouds Sheh-fu continued to journey through the eastern part of Taiwan. For a time they were in a town called Yu-li, in a temple named Jade Spring. But then Chin-yun decided to resume searching, and once again they were on the road.

In December they arrived in Hwalien by train. Raindrops fell softly, shrouding the city like a wet net. Standing at the train station and watching people rushing in every direction, they felt lost.

"Where can we go?" Kind Clouds Sheh-fu asked. "We know nothing about Hwalien, and here we don't even have one friend."

"Remember we've heard about a place called the Temple of Eastern Purity?" Chin-yun said. "We can go there and maybe the master will take us in."

A pedicab appeared in the misty rain. "Do you know the Temple of Eastern Purity?" Chin-yun asked.

"Of course," the driver answered. "It's quite far from here. It'll cost you five dollars."

Chin-yun and Kind Clouds Sheh-fu did not have much more than that. But they agreed to pay and got on the pedicab. The rain began to come down in torrents as the driver struggled up a steep hill. Chin-yun and Kind Clouds Sheh-fu looked at each other, feeling unkind to just sit and watch the man labor. They got off the pedicab and pushed it uphill while the driver remained on his seat.

They reached the top of the hill and saw, through the pouring rain, a temple with an arched roof. They were soon close enough to see faces staring from behind the windows and hear voices saying, "Two dumb nuns pushing a pedicab in the rain and the driver is sitting there smiling!"

They emptied their pockets to pay the driver and entered the temple dripping wet and feeling like fools in front of the neatly dressed people.

"You may not be too wise, but you are certainly kind. And I like kind-hearted young people; they are hard to find these days," an old lady said, as she approached them with dry towels. "I am Mrs. Wan, and my son is a police officer in Tai-tung. I'm staying here temporarily, praying, studying scriptures and relaxing. I know the master well. If you wish to stay, I'll talk to her."

Chin-yun and Kind Clouds Sheh-fu took the towels and began to dry themselves, seeing on the gentle face of Mrs. Wan the kindness of a grandmother.

"Where are you coming from and where are you going to?" Mrs. Wan asked with concern.

It would be too long a story to tell. "We've come from afar," Chin-yun answered vaguely, groping for words until a sudden idea came to her mind, "Maybe we will go to Taroko, to see the Gorge of Hwalien."

"Ah!" Mrs. Wan was excited, "You must let me introduce you to Mr. Chung-ming Hsu, a gentleman about my age, wealthy and generous and a devoted Buddhist who has already financed the building of several temples and is going to build many more. He will be here tomorrow, taking a group of people to the Gorge on a chartered bus. He is thinking about building a temple near the Gorge, and wants the architects to survey the site he is considering."

Through Mrs. Wan's introduction, Chin-yun and Kind Clouds Sheh-fu met the master of the Temple of Eastern Purity and received permission to stay for as long as they wished. The next morning they went to the Gorge with Mrs. Wan and Mr. Hsu, and the seventy-year-old gentleman showed a grandfatherly tenderness towards them. "Whenever the two of you need help, please contact me," he said, giving them his cards.

The trip lasted a whole day, and, by the time they returned to the temple, Kind Clouds Sheh-fu, who had been chilled in the rain and exhausted from pushing a pedicab, became ill with a high fever. Mrs. Wan sent for the doctor, paid the man, then took care of her for the next week until the fever started to go down.

During this time, Chin-yun realized that she did not belong to any of the temples that she had seen, nor the temples that she might see in the future, because she disagreed with every master she had met, and the possibility of meeting a master sharing her belief was rather slim. For instance, to Chin-yun, burning paper money for the dead was ridiculous, and asking Buddha to perform miracles was irrational. She believed that nuns and monks should work hard to earn their keep instead of living on the donations of followers. She could not become a novice nun and obey the master's orders while waiting painfully for the slow promotion to eventually bring her the power to do things her way. What she truly wanted was a temple of her own and a group of followers to carry out her ideas, but it was beyond her reach at this moment; therefore, she had no choice but to move from one temple to another.

When Kind Clouds Sheh-fu was strong enough to travel, Chin-yun approached her apologetically, "My friend, I know you are still weak. But we must leave the Temple of Eastern Purity and start searching again."

Without uttering a word, Kind Clouds Sheh-fu started to pack.

Chin-yun told Mrs. Wan the true reason for their leaving, said good-bye, and received a recommendation letter to the master of a temple in Tai-tung, named Lotus House.

Chin-yun and Kind Clouds Sheh-fu taught in the Lotus House as a team. Their subject matter was based on the scriptures of the Guardian of Earth, their teaching method created by Chin-yun: they simplified the complicated scriptures and used the current events to exemplify the ancient happenings. Most of the listeners found their teaching refreshing, but a few criticized and accused them of being disloyal to the original scriptures. As soon as the session was over, Chin-yun saw the necessity of moving on and started to gather her things.

"Where are we going this time?" Kind Clouds Sheh-fu asked while tossing her meager belongings into a bag.

"Let's go back to Hwalien and pay a visit to Mr. Chung-ming Hsu," Chin-yun said. "He has financed the building of many temples, maybe one of them is unoccupied . . . would you like that?"

"I would like it only if you would," Kind Clouds Sheh-fu said with devotion. "It would be great if we could find a vacant temple where you can be the master and I your number one disciple."

Mr. Hsu received them kindly in his fabulous home, filled with family members and servants. He listened to Chin-yun and said, "There is a vacant temple in the village of Shu-lin, called the Temple of Prevailing Light, only recently constructed by me and a few others for the Guardian of Earth. But the two of you can't stay there . . . there are no living quarters. However, you may take a look."

The next day they arrived at the village of Shu-lin and walked towards the Temple of Prevailing Light.

"I know this place! I've been here before!" Chin-yun said, staring at the small temple with three doors.

"It's impossible, my child," Mr. Hsu laughed. "The temple is brand new. As a matter of fact, it has just had its opening ceremony."

"But I'm telling the truth!" Chin-yun said stubbornly. "I've been here more than once! I know exactly what it looks like inside!" Standing outside the closed temple doors, she began to describe the interior in detail.

Mr. Hsu's jaws dropped and his eyes widened with surprise. "You were absolutely right!" he said, tilting his head to one side and blinking in disbelief. "But how did you do that?"

"I have no idea!" Chin-yun said.

Mr. Hsu led them into the temple. Everything fit Chin-yun's description. The next moment Chin-yun's voice trembled, "I was here when I was only fifteen years old! It was in my dreams! I was in this temple three nights in a row . . . when my mother was sick and I was praying for her recovery!"

She recounted her dreams to Mr. Hsu and Kind Clouds Sheh-fu: the appearing of the Goddess of Mercy in a white robe, the presenting of the medicine in a glowing bottle, and then the magical recovery of her mother.

"This is incredible! And I thought you did not believe in miracles!" Mr. Hsu said, shaking his head.

"Maybe there is no miracle under heaven. Maybe the so-called miraculous events are merely the way things were, still are, and always will be. And my finding this temple made me realize that my search is over," Chin-yun said with tears streaming down her face and at the same time smiling broadly. "There is no more traveling. This is where I belong!"

*"When it is our Karma to part,
there is no use fighting against it."*

— *Master Cheng Yen* —

As the night grew deeper, Mrs. Wong continued to talk, her voice now hoarse:

"Chin-yun found the place of her dreams, but could not move in because there were no living quarters. She and Kind Clouds Sheh-fu continued to stay in Mr. Hsu's house, and he informally adopted them as granddaughters. They went to the Temple of Prevailing Light every day, where they taught the nearby villagers the scriptures of Buddha, just as they had done in the Lotus House. Once again Chin-yun's teaching method received objections from a few but was appreciated by the majority. She soon gained a reputation as a fine teacher and was asked to go to many temples to teach.

"Kind Clouds Sheh-fu's health continued to decline, and she eventually had to stop teaching. At the same time, being treated like royalty in Mr. Hsu's house caused Chin-yun to feel guilty. She wanted them to move out of there and earn their own living, but her friend was unable to do so.

"Kind Clouds Sheh-fu knew that she could no longer struggle beside Chin-yun. She decided to go back to Fon-yuen, to the Temple of Kind Clouds where she would be the master and life would be easier.

"Chin-yun was sad to part with her friend. They had traveled together for a long time and shared joyful days as well as sorrowful moments. But they both knew that all people on earth only meet by Karma, that once it is their Karma to part, there is no use fighting against it.

"After Kind Clouds Sheh-fu had left, Chin-yun continued to stay in Mr. Hsu's house because she was not an ordained nun, and it would be improper for a young girl to live alone. Chin-yun told Mr. Hsu that she would try her best to become ordained, and as soon as the initiation had taken place, she would move out of his house."

"When a person is waiting to see
what Karma has in store for him,
he cannot stay idle but must continue to work hard."

— *Master Cheng Yen* —

Mrs. Wong went on, "Throughout the winter of 1962, the seventy-year-old man and the twenty-five-year-old girl treasured their days together, like a grandfather and a granddaughter enjoying each other's company with the knowledge that their togetherness would not last longer than the rays of a setting sun."

When spring of 1963 was in the air, Chin-yun went to Mr. Hsu with excitement glowing in her eyes, "There will be an initiation ceremony in the Temple of Lin-chi in Taipei! I'll go and ask them to initiate me! When I come back to Hwalien, I'll be an ordained nun!"

Mr. Hsu looked at her sadly, nodding with understanding, "And then you'll move away from me."

"Yes," Chin-yun said, her eyes misty but her voice firm. "I can't live forever under your roof."

"But where can you live?" Mrs. Hsu asked worriedly, "There are no living quarters in the Temple of Prevailing Light."

"I have it all planned," Chin-yun said with a smile. "In the back of the temple there is a very small lot, but large enough for a one-room dwelling. Will you please build me a hut? I want it to be as frugal as possible, because a good nun's life has to be extremely simple."

"I'll talk to the builders today and start building it tomorrow," Mr. Hsu said.

Chin-yun stated once again that her future home had to be modest, that if it was not built according to her wish she would build another shack with her own hands. Mr. Hsu promised reluctantly, and Chin-yun left for Taipei.

She arrived at the Temple of Lin-chi on the day of the initiation and told the nun in charge that she wished to be initiated.

"Who is your master?" the nun asked.

"I don't have a master," Chin-yun answered.

"You can't be initiated without a master!"

"Why not?"

"It's the rule," the nun said in regret, then went on to explain, "As a rule, you must be a novice nun in a temple and serve at least two years under the instruction of a master. When the master thinks that you are qualified for initiation, she or he will arrange it for you."

Chin-yun talked more to the nun but still could not bend the rule. She was disappointed and decided to go back to Hwalien to wait and see what Karma did have in store for her. However, while waiting, she could not stay idle.

"There are some scriptures that are unavailable in Hwalien," she said to the nun in charge. "Do you know where in Taipei I can find them?"

"I can take you to the Temple of Informing Sun," the nun, eager to help, answered. "They have a well-stocked bookstore."

Chin-yun arrived at the Temple of Informing Sun accompanied by the helpful nun, who suggested that, before buying books, they ought to pay respect to the master in charge—Master Yin-shuen.

Chin-yun had read much about Master Yin-shuen but never dared to dream of meeting him. He was born in 1906, in the south of the Chinese mainland. After teaching in an elementary school for eight years, he had become a monk and spent the next twenty years studying Buddhism. When mainland China was taken over by the Communist party, he had moved first to Hong Kong and then Taiwan. He had written many books, and one of them had won him an honorary doctoral degree from a university in Japan.

Master Yin-shuen, a round-faced man of fifty-seven, listened patiently when the nun introduced Chin-yun. Hearing that she had come from Hwalien, he asked casually, "Did you come to Taipei to be initiated?"

Chin-yun bowed her head, "I would like to be, but can't . . . I don't have a master."

She looked up at the Master who appeared to be extremely gentle and wise and suddenly glimpsed a thread of hope. She gathered her courage and asked, "Master Yin-shuen, will you be my master?"

Master Yin-shuen laughed, "In my entire life, I have taken only four disciples and have absolutely no intention of taking a fifth!"

When he stopped laughing, Master Yin-shuen studied Chin-yun's eager young face, then added hesitantly, as if to convince himself, "Besides, a master has to know his novice monks and nuns for at least two years before their initiation."

He glanced at the wall clock, "There is only one hour before the next initiation."

Chin-yun did not speak, but continued to look at Master Yin-shuen pleadingly.

The master turned and was about to walk away. The next moment, as if pulled by an invisible hand, he turned again. Facing Chin-yun and examining her closely, he suddenly smiled and nodded his head.

"A strong voice in my heart is telling me that it is my Karma to be your master and your Karma to be my disciple," he said, looking at Chin-yun deeply. Then he took another look at the clock and raised his voice, "We better hurry! Don't you know that we have less than an hour to reach the Temple of Lin-chi?"

Using all her willpower to hold back a joyful cry, Chin-yun kneeled quickly. She kowtowed three times, looked up at Master Yin-shuen, and said in a voice trembling with gratitude, "Thank you, my Master. I will strive the rest of my days to be a good nun and never let you down!"

Nodding his approval, Master Yin-shuen helped Chin-yun up and said slowly, "In order to be a good nun, you must live the rest of your days for only two reasons: to serve all living beings and to enlighten them with Buddhism."

"To serve all living beings and to enlighten them with Buddhism," Chin-yun repeated after her Master as she stood facing him with her eyes meeting his. "My Honorable Master, I, Chin-yun Wong, will remember your words every day for as long as I shall live."

"Your name, Chin-yun Wong, will be forgotten forever from the moment you are initiated. I will give you a new name . . . ," Master Yin-shuen paused to think.

"Ah!" he said when found the exact words that he was looking for, "Your new name will be Cheng Yen—'to achieve strict commandments and morality.'"

With an encouraging smile, Master Yin-shuen added, "And if you work very hard to serve all living beings and enlighten them with Buddhism, maybe someday your name will be changed from Cheng Yen Sheh-fu to Master Cheng Yen."

"A person's wealth is not judged by
the monetary things around his physical form
but the spiritual elements within his heart."

— *Master Cheng Yen* —

Outside the window, the night city was a mosaic of bright colors from the neon lights flashing from high above, the tail lights of cars whirling along the ribbons of roads, and the lighted windows of apartments filling the empty spaces in between.

Mrs. Wong continued, "Cheng Yen Sheh-fu stayed in the Temple of Lin-chi for the next thirty-two days, learning the basic rules for ordained nuns. She then returned to Hwalien, moved out of Mr. Hsu's house, and into a spartan hut.

"I went to Hwalien for a visit, and she walked in the blazing sun all the way to the train station to meet me because she did not have three dollars for the bus fare. Her feet were blistered and she was limping when I saw her. We returned to her hut by bus, and my heart ached all the more when I saw the place of poverty that she was now living in.

"Reading my mind, Cheng Yen Sheh-fu told me that, although without money, she felt rich—that a person's wealth is not judged by the monetary things around his physical form but the spiritual elements within his heart.

"I went back to visit her frequently, and on the third visit I discovered that she was no longer living alone . . . she had started to take in disciples. Tze Sheh-fu was her first disciple. By the autumn of 1964, her disciples increased to five, and the six of them continued to stay in the same place.

"In 1967, they needed a larger and quieter place, and that was the first time that my daughter asked for my help. I gave her some money to buy a piece of land; I was so pleased by an opportunity to help her. I helped her several times more . . . which is now history and common knowledge to people in Taiwan and all over the world."

Mrs. Wong coughed, drank some tea, then dabbed at her lips with a white handkerchief. She put the handkerchief back into her black purse and prepared to leave.

Standing, she smiled lovingly just before going towards the door, "You know, sometimes I can still see her as my dearest, loveliest, and most precious baby."

Pausing at the door, she returned my farewell bow and brought her hands up with palms touching. Her voice was strong and her head held high when she said slowly, "I am so proud that after all her hardships my dear, lovely, precious baby has millions of followers and is known to the world as Master Cheng Yen!"

PART FOUR

GONG OF LOVE

The author and her husband Bai Shang at the Gong of Love

The author at the Gong of Love with the Tzu-chi members
from various parts of the world

CHAPTER TWENTY

*"With the sounding of the gong,
we will send our love and mercy to wherever help is needed
regardless of the differences in race, religion, or nationality."*

— Master Cheng Yen —

A TROPICAL SUN SHONE BRIGHTLY, bringing the temperature to 72 degrees Fahrenheit. People crowded the park in Taipei, filling every corner with a festive air. We found the Tzu-chi members immediately—the dark blue suits of men and navy dresses of women caught our eye like a peaceful sea. "Shang! Ching!" a woman's voice rose from the center of the sea. "I'm so glad you made it back to Taipei just in time!"

It was Mrs. Ming Der Wang. We hurried towards her, and the next moment our arms were grabbed by her husband who, as usual, had been only inches from her. Mr. Wang hastened us to a lady with a basket filled with silk flowers. He pinned a flower on Shang's lapel, then another on mine. We noticed the same flowers on the lapels of every Tzu-chi member. "Please come with us to the platform," Mr. Wang said, leading the way.

Standing on the platform and among the Tzu-chi members, we participated in the flag-raising ceremony. After that we were fascinated by the dragon dance, which I had not seen for several decades and was a treat for Shang. A lovely young lady began to perform, singing a song. She had to be very popular because the audience in the front rows screamed and tried to touch the hem of her skirt. When she finished, the auction began.

The park was a field of booths. Long lines formed quickly in front of the stands that sold fried food; the peddlers advertised with the aroma of their products. Girls and women assembled at the tables covered with jewelry. Boys and men met at the stalls displaying model cars. Nylon jackets were piled on several booths, cotton quilts on several more. Shang and I stopped at a kite booth, watched the man making them, and heard his wife talking to their customers, "My husband and I are not rich. We took all the money out of our savings account to buy materials to make these kites. Like all the other peddlers, the money we make will go to the Tzu-chi Foundation." She handed a kite to a lady with a child, "Thanks for buying it. Your money will travel to wherever people are sick or hungry."

She was interrupted by the sounding of a gong. The next moment we heard footsteps and saw people running towards the direction of the sound. We followed the crowd and soon reached a low stage. A giant brass gong was suspended from a thick wooden post adorned with a scarlet bow. Forming a multi-layer semicircle around this structure were men, women, and children. A mallet, with its striking end wrapped in red, was held in the hands of a gentleman in a dark blue suit. Raising it high, he banged it against the gong, creating a mighty sound that vibrated throughout the park, its echo riding the air.

"One!" the crowd shouted in unison, overpowering a band playing nearby. At each strike, the counting rose in volume as the congregation became more and more excited.

Mrs. Wang appeared from behind us and explained with a smile, "With every blow, that man is donating fifty thousand Taiwan dollars to the Tzu-chi Foundation."

I counted in my mind: the amount was equivalent to about two thousand dollars in U.S. currency. After the gentleman banged the gong four times, the mallet was passed on to another gentleman who then proceeded to hit the gong ten times, donating 20,000 American dollars. As Shang and I stood watching, a white-haired lady approached the platform and took over; when she finally walked away from the gong, the Foundation had gained another large sum for its charity work. The mallet was passed from hand to hand, the sound of the gong continued to fill the park, and eventually Mr. Wang began to bang on the gong unhurriedly.

". . . eleven, twelve . . ." the crowd counted on. ". . . nineteen, twenty!" The counting turned into screams toward the end.

I turned to look at Mrs. Wang. Her expression was not that of a woman who had just watched her man give away forty thousand U.S. dollars, but a proud wife who had witnessed her husband do a good deed. She said, "The Gong of Love's first clamor rose from Taiwan on December 25, 1991, when people in China suffered from a severe flood. Master Cheng Yen thought of collecting money this way then, and now, as another flood has hit China, she told us to strike the gong again."

The gong had never stopped sounding. There was a line of men and women waiting to take over the mallet. I noticed the same white-haired lady, who had already banged the gong a while ago, was once again standing in line. I mentioned this to Mrs. Wang and she said, "Disasters can hit the same person more than once. Why can't a person repeatedly help the unfortunate ones?" She then closed her eyes to listen to the sounding of the gong. "It's a beautiful sound, repeating the words of Master Cheng Yen: 'All lives deserve to be loved and respected, and all living beings ought to be spared from suffering. With the sounding of the gong, we will send our love and mercy to wherever help is needed regardless of the differences in race, religion, or nationality.'"

Mr. Wang joined us, placed his large hands on his wife's delicate shoulders, and whispered with a sigh, "However, I wish the Gong of Love would remain silent in the years to come . . . which would mean that the suffering in the world has come to an end!"

*"Being old and lonely is a very painful part of our journey in life.
Therefore we should be loving and merciful to the aged
who are forsaken."*

— *Master Cheng Yen* —

We were invited to share the bus chartered by the Tzu-chi Foundation to ride to the auctions in two other parks. The Wang couple introduced us to several other passengers on the bus who were not residents of Taiwan but overseas Chinese residing in various continents of the world. Shang and I sat in different sections of the bus and began to talk to these members as the bus wound its way through the streets of Taipei, heading across town to the next park.

"My family and I live in Canada," a middle-aged gentleman said. "About eight years ago, I read a book written by Master Cheng Yen and became fascinated by her teaching. I introduced the book to my wife, and she went searching for the Master's cassette and video tapes. After listening to the cassettes and watching the tapes, we decided to come back to Taiwan to pay her a visit, and after meeting her once, we could not help but return to her again and again.

"The Tzu-chi Foundation has a large branch office in Vancouver, British Columbia. There are hundreds of members, carrying out Master Cheng Yen's teaching. The members are increasing in number and spreading into every province of Canada. In Vancouver, we have been busy with a variety of events, the most recent being the visiting of nursing homes. . . ."

He went on. Through Master Cheng Yen's teaching, the Tzu-chi members realized that being old and lonely was a very painful part of their journey in life and that they should be loving and merciful to the aged who were forsaken. They went to the nursing homes in various places to visit old men and women remembered by no one. They also formed a group of forty children and teenagers who were either born in Canada or immigrated there while still babies. Wearing green vests and led by their parents, these youngsters, who could speak perfect English, had been visiting nursing homes on weekends.

During the visiting hours, laughter had parted the sealed lips and revealed the toothless mouths, and the light of life had brightened those dull and lifeless eyes. Witnessing that, the nursing home administrators granted the Tzu-chi members permission to take the residents out whenever the weather was nice and warm. The older Tzu-chi members drove a chartered bus, and the younger members helped the nursing home residents, some of them in wheelchairs, to board. They visited lakes and parks, and sometimes the shopping malls. Wherever they went, their procession—the old walking with the help of the young, and the wheelchairs being pushed by children and teenagers—always caught the attention of all that passed by. Pictures of these outings were taken by the Tzu-chi members and given out, placed on bedside tables. During the week, the old would gaze at these pictures, smiling as they relived the joyful time.

"Mama and Baba," the younger Tzu-chi members had often said to the older ones at home, "can we adopt a grandma and a grandpa? Orphans are often adopted, why can't the same be done for the aged ones?"

"Loving and merciful,
a person is able to give compassion to all living beings
who are suffering because of their bad Karma.
And while giving, a person is helping himself
by creating good Karma."

— *Master Cheng Yen* —

The lady from Chicago was in her early forties. When the man from Vancouver moved to a different seat, she took the seat and started to talk: "Master Cheng Yen's writings can be seen in Chicago and all the other major cities in the U.S.A.; her cassette and video tapes are available everywhere. My husband and I share her books and tapes with our children, and the whole family comes to Taiwan to visit the Master at least once every year. We have donated many things for the auction, and all of us have banged the Gong of Love. When in Chicago we were always busy turning the Master's words into actions, among them our frequent visits to the nursing homes.

"It was raining on a November day. As usual, the Chicago wind was strong, bringing the temperature down. There were a dozen of us, studying a map as we looked for another nursing home."

They had gone through the north of Chinatown and circled the area several times before finding the place. They had gone to the fifth floor of the nursing home, talked to the administrator, and learned that most of the residents were not only aged but also sick, and their families seldom remembered them.

They had also learned that there were several Chinese residents, both men and women, who had come to the United States many decades ago from the villages alongside the Pearl River when they were not much older than children. Digging the ground for the railroad company, cooking and washing clothes for the white men and women, they had taken root in the new land. When they reached marriageable age, the men had either sent for brides from their hometown or married the first Chinese girls they could find, and the women had married whomever was chosen by their parents. As soon as their children were old enough to understand, they had hammered these words into every child's mind: you will go to the white-man's school, graduate from a university, and become either a doctor, a lawyer, or a professor! The second-generation Chinese had followed their parents' instructions, but once they had reached a professional level, some of them had begun to feel ashamed of their parents, who still maintained their old peasant ways; the old had no place in the high society where the young now functioned. Some of the young had married outside their race. Persuaded by their spouses, they had decided it would be better for all concerned if the old were placed in a nursing home.

The Tzu-chi members had faced the aged Chinese of an older generation, looked into their eyes, and detected fear, anger, sorrow, and helplessness. They seemed to be asking with their empty gaze: where are you, my child? I fed you with my sweat and blood together with love; why do you repay me with desertion and a cold heart?

The lady in the bus said with downcast eyes and a hoarse voice, "Facing them, we thought of the words of Master Cheng Yen: 'All living beings suffer because of their bad Karma. Loving and merciful, a person should be able to give compassion to the suffering. And while giving, a person is helping himself by creating good Karma.'

"We wondered what these old men and old women did in another lifetime to cause such suffering. And we couldn't help thinking that, decades ago, when these old folks were strong and their children innocent, if they had taught the children love and mercy besides the importance of monetary things, perhaps they would not be left in this nursing home and forgotten." The lady raised a hand to show me her naked fingers, then went on. "I arrived in Taiwan wearing diamonds, but now they are somewhere on a table waiting to be auctioned off. I used to save all my diamonds for my children, but I changed my mind since visiting that nursing home. I still love my children but will not count on their putting up with me in my old age. My old age may be good or bad, and it is beyond my control. What I *can* control is this moment, when I am still strong enough to help myself by doing good deeds and creating good Karma."

CHAPTER TWENTY-ONE

*"The most rewarding thing in life is being able to forgive those
who have wronged us and to give our love and mercy
to those who are but strangers.
And such reward is to be carried by us to our next lifetimes
through our Karma."*

— *Master Cheng Yen* —

O UR BUS WAS GOING THROUGH an old section of town when it was
forced to slow down. Pedestrians crowded the street,
ignoring the driver's continuous blowing of the horn.
Looking out the window, I saw swarms of people gathered around
the many make-shift stalls piled with the vendors' wares. Behind
them, more people assembled under a wide walkway that bordered
a vast courtyard leading to a temple. The multi-layered roofs were
adorned with carvings of gargoyles, the huge posts decorated with
engravings of dragons. Smoke shrouded the entire building from
the incense burning in massive brass urns decorated with a variety
of figures and Chinese characters.

"This is the Temple of Mount Dragon," my new neighbor, a
white-haired gentleman, said. "It is one of the oldest among the
four thousand and two Buddhist temples in Taiwan, and also the
busiest."

I peered through the smoke and saw tables filled with candles, incense sticks, steamed buns, bowls of rice, a variety of fruit, and huge bouquets of flowers.

"I was born in Taiwan and lived here until I was twenty-six," my neighbor said. "My grandmother used to take me to this temple. She told me that the spirit of my father would come and eat the food laid out. She also said that by offering candles, incense, and flowers to Buddha, I'll receive good luck in return."

He shook his head and smiled sadly. "I believed every word until I entered medical school. Unable to share her belief after that, I found myself arguing with her often. I never thought for one moment that her belief could harm anyone, although it seemed foolish to me. I shouldn't criticize my grandmother's belief, since she is now long dead.

"Look at those people out there!" he said, pointing out the window at a fashionably dressed young girl. Standing before the urn, she held a bundle of incense sticks in front of her and shook them back and forth as she moved her upper body in the same rhythm. "She probably thinks that once she inhales the smoke, Buddha will find her a rich and handsome husband."

He then pointed at a young man in gray pants and a red jacket kowtowing in front of an altar. "I presume that he is either talking to one of the deceased members of his family or asking Buddha to grant him success in whatever he is about to do."

He pointed further, and I saw a group of people facing one of the urns, throwing things into it and causing the flame to rise high. He said, "They are burning paper money, paper houses and furniture, paper cars and pedicabs and servants—all gifts to the departed. They believe that the dead will receive these things and find use for them in the other world."

He continued to point with a shaking hand. "And look over there, where people are throwing joss sticks to find out their fortune. That is what the Temple of Mount Dragon is famous for!

"A number is written on each stick. Bringing the number to one of the monks, one will receive a small piece of paper containing a short poem which can be deciphered in various ways."

The man withdrew his trembling hand. Glancing over, I saw him clenching his knees, his knuckles white. Looking at his face, I detected anger in his tight lips and sorrow in his misty eyes. He struggled to take control of his emotion and was finally able to resume talking.

"During my year of interning, I fell in love with a nursing student. I was twenty-five and she was nineteen. We wanted to get married. But because my father was dead, my grandmother, the oldest in the family, had the final say. My grandmother gathered me, my mother, all my uncles and aunts, and we came to the Temple of Mount Dragon. She kneeled. We all kneeled behind her.

"'Great Buddha in heaven, please tell us if my grandson should marry that girl,' she said, then shook the bamboo container that held a bunch of sticks.

"Only one of the sticks fell out. My grandmother double-checked with Buddha by tossing two small pieces of stones on the ground. Each stone had an up-side and a down-side. When one stone landed up and the other down, my grandmother knew that Buddha had confirmed the message carried on the stick.

"We went to a monk, told him the number written on the stick. The monk's face was dark with sympathy when he handed us a piece of paper.

"'Joss sticks are divided into three categories: good-good, good-bad, and bad-bad.' he said. 'Your stick says bad-bad!'

"Neither my grandmother nor anyone in my family could untangle the meaning of the poem. But it didn't matter. They all agreed that Buddha had spoken—I must not marry my girl!

"My girl and I tried to fight tradition but eventually surrendered. With a broken heart I went to the United States to be a resident doctor and finally married there. Now I am sixty-three and a grandfather. My marriage is not bad, but I have not forgotten my first love. I heard that she had stayed in Taiwan to finish nursing school, then went to Canada and married there to someone also from Taiwan. She is fifty-seven years old now. I often wonder if she thinks of me now and then, like I do her, and if she still remembers the joss stick that parted us."

The bus was moving again. The white-haired man stared out the window and sighed deeply. He seemed relieved to see the Temple of Mount Dragon disappearing. I could not hold back a question, "At one time you were a victim of Buddhism. But now you are wearing the dark blue suit of a Tzu-chi member. What enabled you to forgive Buddhism for parting you and your girl?"

The man looked at me with a smile. "It all started in May of last year, when Los Angeles was burning in a fire started by a few men angered by the brutal beating of Mr. King.

"I was working late that day. Soon after leaving my clinic, I discovered that the gas gauge in my car was pointing towards empty. I hesitated, because the station where I usually refilled my car was located very close to the burning area. I decided to take a chance, thinking that running out of gas would be disastrous on a night like this.

"I stopped at the self-service station, got out of my car, then saw a group of teenage blacks charging out of the office that they had taken over. There were over a dozen of them, most of them holding iron bars, and they surrounded me so quickly that I did not have a chance to get back into my car.

"'What are you? Korean? Japanese? Chinese?' the tallest of them asked, glaring at me.

"Since to be any of the three nationalities was equally dangerous in L.A. on that night, I decided to tell the truth, 'I am Chinese.'

"'Are you from Taiwan?' the same person asked again. The question surprised me because to most of the people in America, a Chinese has to come from mainland China.

"'Yes, I'm from Taipei, Taiwan,' I answered.

"The next moment their expression changed. The hatred, so deeply carved onto their young faces, was replaced by friendly smiles. The iron bars in their hands were lowered.

"'I see that you are a Tzu-chi member, too!' One of them looked at the dark blue pants and a white shirt I just happened to wear on that day. 'In that case, you are a friend!'

"I opened my mouth to ask what a Tzu-chi member was, then decided against it, but nodded my head instead. I proceeded to fill my car as the group stood next to me in a protective line. Several other cars pulled up with their engines running and the black drivers scrutinizing me, but my protectors waved them away. My heart was beating in my throat and my hands were shaking, but I managed to hear my protectors talking:

"'You Tzu-chi members are very good to us. There are scholar-ships in our schools, established by your society. You came to our section of town, gave us clothes and toys that were brand new. Our baby brothers and sisters even got new bikes from you. When we were leaving home tonight, they reminded us that we must not hurt any Chinese from Taiwan!'

"The next day I began to ask around: what is this Tzu-chi Foundation? Upon hearing that it was created by a Buddhist master, I flinched. And then I was amused by a sudden realization: a joss stick in a Buddhist temple took my first love from me, and now a Buddhist organization saved my life!

"As I learned more about the Foundation, all my resentment towards Buddhism disappeared. I searched for books by Master Cheng Yen, read and reread them, gained enormous respect for her, and acquired an understanding about true Buddhism. What affected me the most was the Master's view on forgiveness and giving: the most rewarding thing in life is being able to forgive those who have wronged us and give our love and mercy to those who are but strangers. And such reward is to be carried by us to our next lifetimes through our Karma.

"I became a devoted Buddhist and joined the Tzu-chi Foundation. When the Buddhist Tzu-chi Free Clinic in Alhambra opened its door to the public, I became a volunteer doctor. I'll retire in two years, and after that I'll become a fulltime doctor there."

"When helping people,
a person must put his heart and soul into what he is doing
and never expect anything in return . . .
not even a simple 'thank you.'"

— *Master Cheng Yen* —

The middle-aged lady had a lovely oval face. She sat on the seat next to mine and began to speak, telling me that she was from California. "In southern California, it was dry and hot in October, 1993. Strong wind came from Santa Ana, scorching everything. As the wind continued to blow, the trees died, and even the cactuses turned into brown sticks."

A forest fire soon started, spreading like the hands of a long-armed monster, destroying homes and grabbing those too slow to run. Firemen sped towards the blazing area, but within a short time the three hundred miles of forest between Los Angeles and San Diego were aflame, burning in twenty-five different places that extended through six counties. When the inferno was finally under control, four hundred and fifty-some homes had been demolished, and seventy thousand acres of land consumed. After the fire, California was declared a disaster area, and the scene of the holocaust appeared on televisions everywhere, including Taiwan. Master Cheng Yen was in Hwalien at the time. Seeing onscreen those who had lost their homes, standing on the charred ground, she called the Tzu-chi Foundation in California.

The next morning the Tzu-chi members arrived at the location carrying checkbooks and ready to hand out three hundred U.S. dollars to each family. But instead of accepting the checks, most people looked at the members suspiciously and asked, "What do you expect us to do in exchange for the money?"

The Tzu-chi members reassured them that they did not have to do anything but had a hard time persuading most of them. They studied the checks carefully and seemed to doubt that they could actually be cashed. And then they became more worried when the Tzu-chi members asked them to sign forms needed for the records, and a few even said jokingly, "You Chinese are tricky! We don't want to sign ourselves into white slavery!" The Tzu-chi members finally convinced them and gave out hundreds of checks in four different locations, but among those who accepted the money, only a few truly and sincerely thanked the Foundation.

The lady next to me sighed deeply, "With or without being thanked, we felt greatly rewarded. And we did not just give each needy family a check and forget about them. We did a follow-up on each person and returned to the ones that could not get back on their feet without further help. We did all this carrying in our minds the words of Master Cheng Yen: 'When helping people, a person must put his heart and soul into what he does and never expect anything in return . . . not even a simple "thank you".'"

CHAPTER TWENTY-TWO

"Life is not over when your remaining days are gone.
Except for those who deserve the state of Nirvana,
all of us will be reborn.
In the endless circle of rebirth,
Karma is the only thing that a person can take with him.
Karma, created by a person's behavior, determines everything:
observing a person's current life, we can tell his behavior
in a previous life, and watching his current behavior,
we can predict his future life."

— *Master Cheng Yen* —

WE ARRIVED IN A PARK located in San-chung on the outskirts of Taipei. After the dragon dance and a series of performances, the auction began and the Gong of Love was being banged. It was near noon; the sun glared down from a cloudless sky. Shang and I joined a circle formed by the Tzu-chi men and women in the shade of a tall bamboo grove, and they began to speak English for Shang's benefit.

"I'm in my fifties now. When in my forties, I was far from a good person," a man started with a sigh. He had a high forehead, his eyes deep and his nose high-ridged. Above his thin lips, his mustache was neatly trimmed. At one time he must have been a handsome young man and was still good looking. "When in my mid-twenties, I went to France as an exchange student. During the next twenty years I received my degrees, worked hard in Paris, then started my own business, earned a lot of money and bought a big house in the country. I felt that my days were limited, and I had to grab the fleeting moments to reward myself. I also felt that, since my wife had stayed home to raise the children and never participated in my struggle, I owed her nothing. I bought myself an expensive sports car, gave her an old station wagon . . . just one example of how I treated her. I kept reminding her that she was lucky to be my wife, that she should show her gratitude and keep any complaints to herself.

"And then I became fascinated by young girls. I seldom came home and was always involved in an affair. My wife soon knew and was deeply hurt. We quarreled, fought, and the children were frightened.

"It was the Mid-Autumn Festival. My wife and I were invited to a gathering of overseas Chinese. After a pot-luck meal, the hostess began to show a video tape of Master Cheng Yen. With a drink in my hand, I looked away from the screen, searching for an excuse to leave early. As usual, my wife and I had arrived in separate cars.

"'. . . And life is not over when your remaining days are gone. Except for those who deserve the state of Nirvana, all of us will be reborn. In the endless circle of rebirth, Karma is the only thing that a person can take with him. Not money, nor fame. . . .'

"I heard those words, glanced at the screen casually, and could not look away from the nun in a gray robe. Her face was so kind, and yet her eyes had the power to penetrate my soul. I felt that she had seen all the evil things that I had done and was now talking to me alone.

"'. . . By observing a person's current life, we can tell his behavior in a previous life. And by watching his current behavior, we can predict his future life . . . ,' Master Cheng Yen continued.

"I dropped the glass I was holding. Her words hit me like someone had struck me on the head with a hammer. Cold sweat poured down my back. I said to myself that I must have done something good in my previous life to be successful in this life, but with my current conduct what kind of life would I have upon rebirth?

"When that night was over, I changed into a different man. I quit drinking and smoking, and I tossed away the book that contained the phone numbers of all my girlfriends. I sold my sports car and the old wagon and bought a new car for the family. I began to go home directly from work and take the family out on weekends. I also treated my employees better than before.

"I was able to concentrate on my work, and my business prospered more. My wife could not understand the change in me, but she was delighted and forgave me for what I had done. My children, who had been afraid of me, were close to me again. And the most wonderful thing was that I began to like myself. I had always known that I was wrong, but had made excuses for my behavior. It is great that I don't have to justify my actions any more."

"The length of a person's life is measured
by the useful things that he has done.

"Time is a diamond to a wise person, but dirt to a fool.

"A person has to gather his wisdom to find life's true meaning,
and use his willpower to become the master
of his limited time on earth.

"Life can start anew at any moment of any day."

— Master Cheng Yen —

A woman in her forties cleared her throat and began to talk. Her clothes were simple but of high quality. She appeared humble and kind, and yet carried herself with an elegant air. "My husband and I emigrated to England a few years back, bought a house in a nice neighborhood, and sent the children to an expensive school. My husband started a business and soon became very successful. I had a maid who came every day to cook and clean, and keeping myself from boredom became my major problem.

"A friend of mine introduced me to a mahjongg club, where square tables filled a room, and behind the room was a kitchen, a bathroom, and two bedrooms for the tired players to rest. I began to play every day. The game could start at any time, frequently lasting for ten hours or more. While mixing the tiles, the ladies compared the rings on their fingers and bragged about their husbands' success. While one player was debating which tile to discard, the rest of us talked, gossiping, putting down those we all knew but were not at the club at this moment. As we played, the stakes went higher and higher, and my household budget was soon affected by it. When I won, my maid would receive a tip, and my family would eat shrimp and lobster. When I lost, the maid was not paid, and my family would have plain rice and a dish of vegetables.

"The maid threatened to quit, and my family stopped counting on my feeding them—the children were filling themselves with potato chips and candy bars and my husband seldom came home for dinner.

"In order to win back the lost money, I stayed in the club longer and longer. When I finally came home, I slept through all hours and didn't even rise to give orders to the maid, who eventually did quit. I couldn't find another maid. The house was in chaos, the laundry was never done, and the meals were heated canned goods.

"My children started to spend more and more time away from home—to watch movies, play video machines, sleep at their friends' houses. My husband and I hardly ever talked to each other except to fight, and he, too, began to spend very little time at home.

"One morning two years ago, I looked into the mirror and saw bags and dark shadows under my eyes, and decided that perhaps a new hairdo would solve my problems. I went to a beauty salon operated by a Chinese, and while sitting under the dryer, I picked up a book from the magazine rack.

"Leafing through it, I saw a line: 'The length of a person's life is measured by the useful things that he has done.'

"I closed my eyes, searched for the useful thing that I had done but could find none. 'So I've never lived!' I shouted from under the dryer with my eyes wide open, causing the ladies on either sides to turn their heads.

"I read another line: 'Time is a diamond to a wise person, but dirt to a fool.'

"Staring at that line, I realized that I'd been wasting my time like dirt, and therefore I'd been a fool.

"'A person has to gather his wisdom to find life's true meaning, and use his willpower to become the master of his limited time on earth,' the following line read.

"My hands began to shake as I thought: gambling is now the master of my time, and my life is controlled by the mahjongg tiles!

"I steadied myself and read on, and another line caught my eye: 'Life can start anew at any moment of any day!'

"I didn't even wait for my hair to dry. I ran out of the beauty salon with wet hair, reached home, and started to clean house. Later on, I surprised my children by picking them up at school. And I will never forget my husband's face when he returned home that night to a neat house filled with the aroma of food!

"It wasn't easy to quit gambling. My mahjongg partners kept calling, and when I refused to go, they asked if my husband's business was failing and I was no longer able to afford the game. It took a lot of will power to force myself to say good-bye to them politely, because I really wanted to scream: Why don't you wake up and find better use for your limited time?

"I paid the beauty shop another visit and found out where the owner had purchased the book. I did not know until then that the book was written by Master Cheng Yen, a Buddhist master in Hwalien.

"I ordered all the books written by either Master Cheng Yen or her followers. In the beginning, I had problems understanding Buddhism, because I had never before read anything about it. Gradually, I grasped the meaning, and shared what I had learned with my husband and children.

"Last summer we came back to Taiwan and visited the Master, and soon after that my husband and I accepted Buddhism and joined the Tzu-chi Foundation. Ever since then, my life in the foreign land has not been lonely or empty but fulfilled and busy. The Master told the Foundation members that they must take care of their homes and families before going out to do other things; therefore, I have not been ignoring my husband and children. My children stay home every night now and their grades have improved, and my husband and I have become very close. On weekends we go out as a family to carry out the Tzu-chi Foundation's mission, and now we are all in Taiwan to bang the Gong of Love."

"Ti-tsang, the Guardian of Earth, will keep returning to hell
until all souls are redeemed from agony.
And a loving and merciful person will share the suffering
of all living beings until they are delivered from pain."

— *Master Cheng Yen* —

"It is said that where there is sun, there are Chinese, and where there are Chinese, there are Tzu-chi members. Each member is an eye and a hand for Master Cheng Yen, searching for those in need of love and mercy and then giving them out," the tall and slender young man said in a deep voice. "I live in Hwalien, Taiwan. But like all Tzu-chi members, I travel far to deliver love and mercy."

After a brief pause, he continued, "It was in early autumn that the government of Nepal sent out a plea to all foreign nations. The Master called us to meet in the Tzu-chi Hall of Taipei. After a careful discussion she decided to send a small group to Nepal for the purpose of studying the situation.

"I had always thought of Nepal, Buddha's homeland, as a mysterious land of beauty. I could see, in my mind's eye, temples standing in misty mountains and half-hidden behind clouds. I also imagined people wearing long silk garments, smiling and bowing humbly with their palms touching.

"Upon arriving in Nepal, we were guided to a village site where homes for over a thousand families had once stood. What we saw were endless gray sand and white rocks and occasionally a few dead trees. The temples were more solidly built on high ground, and the flood had not damaged them as it had the homes. Most of the people had nothing to wear but rags that barely covered their bodies, now merely skin and bones.

"In the south-central and eastern area of Nepal, the river had overflowed and the dam broke. The rushing wall of water slammed into the villages, destroying bridges, uprooting trees, sweeping away schools and homes. Thirty-three counties were under water, thousands of human lives lost; nearly eight hundred people vanished without a trace, twenty-five thousand cattle and other farm animals perished, and four hundred thousand individuals were left homeless.

"We had brought with us, along with a variety of other items, sheets of blue plastic. The sheets were given out and quickly became people's garments and bedding. Some of the homeless stretched the sheets from tree to tree and formed tents that created a home for the entire family. We also gave out canned goods. The food was quickly eaten; the empty cans became their only cooking and eating utensils. We wished that we had brought a lot more, for to see the looks of expectation on their faces, especially those of the children, when the food was gone, was most difficult.

"Children of Nepal were a heartbreaking sight. Most of them were naked, and more than half of them had hook-worms. Their arms and legs were thin sticks; their ribs seemed to be piercing through their skin, their abdomens swollen like balloons.

"I was in a half-crumbled shelter where many flood victims had gathered. The families who had lost their homes huddled together, but in the darkest and wettest corner, a child squatted alone. He was so skinny, his face the face of a skeleton except for his large, bright eyes. He stared at us and seemed unable to decide whether to come forward or run away.

"I was told that he was the lone survivor of a large family. He had watched his parents and siblings being carried away by the flood. He now went out of the shelter each morning to comb the streets for edibles and beg for food, but was usually still crying from hunger when he returned to the shelter at night. I was also told that children like him could be found all over Nepal.

"The Tzu-chi Foundation members will soon go to Nepal again, to build eighteen hundred homes for the victims plus help them in many other ways. Until the people in Nepal are no longer hungry and cold, all of us will share their torment. We are doing this because of Master Cheng Yen's teaching: 'Ti-tsang, the Guardian of Earth, will keep returning to hell until all souls are redeemed from agony. And a loving and merciful person will share the suffering of all living beings until they are delivered from pain.'"

CHAPTER TWENTY-THREE

"There will be no violence on earth
only when all butchers have lain down their killing knives."

— *Master Cheng Yen* —

With the Gong of Love echoing in our ears, Shang and I left Taiwan and were soon thirty-seven thousand feet above the Pacific Ocean, flying towards California.

"Please pull down the shades over your windows," a stewardess announced over the speaker. "We'll be showing a movie in just a few minutes."

A few minutes later, on three screens located in different areas of the darkened cabin, a picture began. A man and a woman were arguing. That was followed by car chases, bullets flying, and blood splashing.

With our minds still filled with the peaceful images of Master Cheng Yen and her followers, neither Shang nor I could accept the scenes of violence. Opening my carry-on bag, I found a stack of cassette tapes given to us by the Tzu-chi members. There were songs and instrumental music, but mostly Master Cheng Yen's speeches. I took out a tape. Shang and I shared a set of earphones plugged into our portable recorder. Since Shang could understand only some of what was said, I translated quickly as Master Cheng Yen's unhurried voice reached our ears.

"I used to look up at the sky and watch the airplanes flying by. I was only a little girl then, living in Clear Water and going to elementary school.

"The airplanes were not carrying travelers, but soldiers. They dropped bombs over Taiwan, leveling our homes, destroying our farmland and killing thousands of us.

"There was a temple in Clear Water, with the statues of Kwan-yin, the Goddess of Mercy, inside. Hearing the air raid and starting to run, people always cried, 'Goddess of Mercy, please protect us!'

"I'll never forget that day when the airplanes appeared in the sky at lunch time. Running in a hurry, many housewives still held on tightly to their butcher knives. The bombs were dropped, shaking everything in the shelter, causing the dirt to fall from the ceiling.

"'Goddess of Mercy, please don't let us be killed!' people around me cried louder.

"There was an old man in the shelter, wearing solid black. He shook his head and said, 'How can the Goddess of Mercy protect you? It's your Karma that caused this to happen! Can't you see that your wrongdoings have saddened the Goddess of Mercy? She is crying harder than you; she has no more tears left and is shedding blood! Don't you know that the only ones who can save you are yourselves? According to the teachings of Buddha, there will be no violence on earth only when all butchers have lain down their killing knives!'

"I stared at that old man in black and remembered his every word, not knowing that it was at that very moment Buddhism entered my heart. Yes, it was almost five decades ago, when I was a child in Clear Water, hiding in a bomb shelter and listening to the airplanes soaring overhead!"

The tape stopped. What we had heard, we discussed for some time. Then Shang turned the cassette to a new side as the airplane continued to fly closer to the U.S.A.

"It is human nature to take things for granted
and think that they will last forever.
But life is short and all things are fleeting,
and we must treasure the moments when there is peace
and we are with our loved ones."

— *Master Cheng Yen* —

We arrived in San Francisco, claimed our luggage, then stood in line to go through customs. The young couple in front of us reached the officer in charge and were told to open all of their suitcases.

"I can see that you've brought back plenty of things from Hong Kong," the officer said to the young wife, counting the contents of one of her suitcases, "Silk dresses, leather shoes . . . plus the Rolex watch and all that jewelry."

The couple had to pay a high tariff. The husband blamed the wife.

"You did your share of shopping too!" she shouted back.

They were still arguing while we were all in a coffee shop waiting for the next flight. We couldn't help overhearing that they had been on their honeymoon but now regretted that they had married each other.

"It's a shame that they are arguing about what has already taken place," Shang said. "While in anger, they are letting the precious moments slip away."

And I said, "How I wish that you and I were as young as they! It's too bad that the young usually take their youth for granted."

Fast-beat music filled the coffee shop but couldn't drown out the young couple's angry words. Shang placed our portable cassette player on the table and pushed the button. The next moment Master Cheng Yen's calm voice reached our ears and drove away all unpleasant sound.

"It is human nature to take things for granted. As soon as the war was over, people would forget the bombs and think that the peaceful days would last forever.

"But I never felt that way. I simply could not forget the bombs that had killed so many of my friends and their families. Although still only a child, I was already afraid that another war would take place at any day. I treasured my loved ones, and loved them with all my heart.

"Among all that I loved, I was closest to my father, who was my biological uncle but had legally adopted me. He was a fat man. During those days, fat was considered healthy, and everyone predicted that he would live to be at least ninety.

"It was another ordinary day; my father and I were working together in one of our theaters. He complained of a headache, and we called our family doctor, who gave him a shot to treat the high blood pressure, then walked away without paying much attention to the patient. I took my father home on a pedicab. As he stayed unconscious in bed, I went to the open courtyard, kneeled in the glaring sun and began to pray. I had not yet acquired the knowledge of true Buddhism at the time, nor had I learned that when a person prays, he should pray to no one but himself. I prayed to the Goddess of Mercy: Please make my Baba well!

"I prayed for a long time, but in spite of all the prayers, my father died the next day.

"It was long after the death of my father that I finally remembered the old man dressed in black in the bomb shelter—my father and I were destined to part, and not even the Goddess of Mercy could change our Karma."

A voice came out of the airport speaker announcing that the flight to Chicago was ready for boarding. Shang pressed the off button on the cassette player, and we started towards the gate; the sound of the young couple arguing was left behind.

"Buddhism is a positive and active way of living, and
we Buddhists will continue with our good deeds to help
the suffering masses, and bring joy to those living in sorrow."

— Master Cheng Yen —

During our flight to Chicago, Shang turned on the cassette player once more.

"As a young girl in need of religion, I had reached towards Christianity," Master Cheng Yen said. "At the time, there was a Christian minister in Chang-hwa, who was also a physician working in a hospital. It was said that he had removed a part of his own skin and the skin of his wife, to transplant it onto the burned body of a child. He was a foreigner and a white man, but I admired him for what he had done.

"Knowing that I was studying Christianity, several Christians offered me the Bible and many booklets. I read them carefully but found them lacking many things. And then I read the scriptures on Buddhism and felt an instant fulfillment: in Buddhism, there is logical explanation, scientific proof, and philosophical reasoning.

"I stopped searching but was not totally satisfied with Buddhism. In the eyes of many, Buddhism is a passive religion and an escape from reality. Buddhism is also viewed as the superstitious belief of the ignorant poor, who lived in backward nations and belonged to the lower class of society.

"And that was when I decided to bring Buddhism back to its original form, as Buddha had wanted it to be twenty-five hundred years previously. I promised myself that my followers and I would prove to the world that Buddhism is a positive and active way of living and that we Buddhists would continue with our good deeds to help the suffering masses and bring joy to those living in sorrow."

Shang and I continued to play the tape over and over again until we were preparing to land in Chicago.

"A baby's growth is nourished by milk,
and a Buddhist's growth is nourished by courage and patience."

— Master Cheng Yen —

We boarded a commuter plane to complete the last leg of our journey home. It could seat only eighteen people, among them a young mother holding an infant child.

During take-off, the child cried frantically, and his mother crooned patiently, "Don't cry, my baby. Don't cry, my love. . . ."

Single seats lined each side of the plane with a narrow aisle running its length. Shang and I had to huddle closely to share the earphones. Master Cheng Yen's voice continued:

"A baby has to grow day by day to become an adult, and a Buddhist must do the same. All Buddhas and Bodhisattvas were but ordinary humans at one time; it was through a slow process of growth that they eventually reached enlightenment.

"A baby's growth is nourished by milk, and a Buddhist's growth is nourished by courage and patience."

It was a short flight. Shang and I soon had to put the cassette player away. Glancing out the window, we saw the high buildings vanishing, and the sparsely populated upper peninsula of Michigan appearing. Most of the area was white with snow, and Lake Michigan was a solid piece of sparkling ice.

I was exhausted. Knowing that we were once again far from the busy world, with our lovely little nest waiting in a quiet town, I suddenly became unbearably homesick.

"We are almost home," I said. "Once there, the first thing I'll do is to hug our cats and dog. How about you?"

"The same," Shang said. "And then I'll rest well and wait for a new day to begin. We'll rise at dawn and start working on the book."

As soon as he mentioned the book, all my weariness was gone. I sat up straight and said, "Yes, we'll start working on the book the first thing in the morning. We'll put our very best effort into writing about the master of love and mercy."

All of a sudden, Master Cheng Yen's face appeared clearly in my mind, and my heart was filled with the echoes of her voice. At the same time in my memory's eye, I could see the Pure Abode of Still Thoughts gleaming white, the Tzu-chi Halls of Taipei and Tai-chung with their shining doors open wide. The next moment a parade of images emerged out of recollection—the images of the honorable Sheh-fus and so many Tzu-chi members.

"Shang," I said, "on the way back we traveled twelve thousand miles listening to Master Cheng Yen's voice, and by doing so, we carried her teachings all the way from Taiwan to Michigan."

Shang nodded, "We also carried the friendship of so many people, together with a certain amount of the wisdom of Buddha."

I smiled, and my voice became stronger with confidence, "Carrying such powerful forces, we'll be able to write a book to serve people and enlighten them with Buddhism through the teachings of Master Cheng Yen!"

EPILOGUE

"There is always parting, but there will always be reunion."

— Master Cheng Yen —

SEVERAL MONTHS HAD PASSED, and Shang and I were once again in Taiwan to find answers to a few questions that had occurred to us during the writing of the book.

It was early spring. The entire island was a flower garden blooming with azaleas in red, white, and pink. In Hwalien, the high mountains were shrouded by low flying clouds, and the valleys lay peacefully in soft sunlight. There had been a storm, and the sky was clear like blue crystal.

Shang and I quickened our steps along the path under a canopy of green leaves. A white structure soon appeared, with the familiar sparkling posts and glistening roof.

The next moment two figures emerged in front of the abode, their gray robes flowing, their wide sleeves flapping in the wind.

"Shuen Sheh-fu! Ming Sheh-fu!" I called, racing forward.

With each step, their faces became clearer. Shuen Sheh-fu's intelligent eyes gleamed like they always did in my memory, and Ming Sheh-fu's enchanting smile was unchanged from the image left carved on my brain.

"Welcome back," Shuen Sheh-fu said calmly, bringing her hands forward with palms touching.

"It's good to see you again," Ming Sheh-fu whispered, nodding gracefully.

Serene and composed, they reminded me of an ocean where the waves of emotion were hidden unnoticed in its bosom. I grabbed hold of myself and tried my best to take control of my sentiment.

"The Master will be glad to see you," Shuen Sheh-fu said, leading the way.

My heart began to drum as I climbed the steps and entered the room. I had been in this room but once, and yet I knew it so well because it had frequently surfaced in my conscious thoughts and unconscious dreams—the rattan chairs covered with thin cushions, the low tables topped with simple flower arrangements, the six desks crowded with computers and typewriters, and the young girls with long queues working behind them. I caught a glimpse of all this from the corner of my eye as I stared straightforward at a single chair behind a glass-topped table.

Master Cheng Yen rose slowly from the chair. She looked so much healthier than she did in my thoughts and dreams. Her face was a little fuller, her eyes much brighter, her cheeks and lips no longer bloodless but with the natural color of pink coral. She had been sick when I saw her the last time, suffering from a severe cold and taking intravenous shots. It was gray winter then but splendid spring now, and her appearance had changed just like the weather.

"I'm delighted to see that you've returned to Taiwan," she said, touching her palms and nodding without taking her eyes from mine.

In the past three months, she and I had lived with twelve thousand miles between us, and within these miles rested high mountains and a wide sea. And yet nothing had truly kept me from her. At this very moment, I felt that we were no longer strangers like we had been before. The gap had narrowed and the closeness increased, and the alteration had taken place without the exchange of a letter or a phone call.

"I wish I could say that I've returned to stay forever," I murmured as I waited for her to sit, then sat next to her.

"I have something for you," she said in the soft, clear voice that had reverberated in my mind. She slowly opened her clenched left fist.

A small gold ring lay in the center of her palm, a narrow band sending out a humble spark. I leaned forward and looked closer, recognized the wedding ring given to me by Shang twenty years earlier.

"But . . . ," I could utter only one word.

"You gave it away for the auction," the Master said, bringing the ring closer to my eyes, "and I bought it."

The next moment she took my left hand and began to slide the ring onto my finger, saying gently, "This ring has too much meaning for you. You must never take it off again."

Tears poured out of my eyes. I could not trust my voice to speak, although words filled my heart: Master Cheng Yen, the ring is a part of me. I left it in Taiwan with the hope that whoever bought it would visit you and bring me with her. I didn't know that a part of me has been with you all this time! No wonder I feel so much closer to you now than I did before!

I swallowed hard but could not hold back a choking sob. I blinked and felt hot tears pouring down my cold cheeks and then gushing over my trembling lips. I sank my teeth into my lip, trying to regain control. Considering tears a sign of weakness, I seldom cried. I was ashamed of the outburst now, although I knew that my tears at this moment were caused by the Master's gesture of ultimate love.

"I know how much this ring means to you, because I read one of your books written in Chinese," the Master's tender words reached my ears over my continued sobs.

I stared at the Master. I had never thought that she, who must read so many important things, would take time to read my insignificant book.

For the next three hours we never stopped talking. Finally, our voices faded into silence.

"No more words are needed now," the Master said, shaking her head.

"No," I said with a deep sigh. "Words are nothing but words."

After a long interval, she whispered, "I don't know why the members of the Concerned Group asked you to come to me for this book."

"Nor do I," I said.

And then, looking steadily into her eyes, I asked slowly, "Was it really *they* who made certain that I would come to you?"

Gazing back at me unwaveringly, she smiled, "I don't know!"

Our eyes locked. We remained silent for a long time. I continued to feel that our hearts were busy communicating. I also had a strong feeling that my soul knew much more than I—did my soul remember something that happened in another lifetime, when the universe was at its dawn and the world was much younger than it is now?

The Master reached towards the side table and picked up a package.

"My blessings will accompany you to that faraway land," she said, putting a string of prayer beads on my wrist. On the largest green bead was a miniature picture of her.

She then picked up another item from the table, a macrame pendant of silver gray. The shining threads were interwoven into the shape of a lotus, and in the middle was a pocket containing two coins. "May it bring you peace, happiness, good health, and prosperity," she said, draping the pendant around my neck.

She gave the same things to Shang, and then the time began to fly, and Shang and I had to go and catch our plane.

The Master walked us to the door, took both of my hands in hers and said softly, "There is always parting, but there will always be reunion . . . when will you be back?"

"I . . . ," I lost my voice, then recaptured it, "A part of me will always come back to you and to this place . . . now and then."

She smiled, shaking her head, "It'll be much better to come back as a whole and stay for a long time."

I held on to her hands tightly, "I'll be back when *Master of Love and Mercy* is published . . . I'll bring the first copy to you for your approval."

A faint smile appeared on the Master's face as she nodded her head confidently, "Good. I'll be here to welcome you home."

Whispering good-bye, I looked into her eyes and a question appeared in my mind: was it her Karma to become the Master of Love and Mercy and my Karma to report her life's story to the world?

You may call or write directly to
The Buddhist Compassion Relief
Tzu-Chi Foundation

Main Office: 21 Kanglo Village, Shinchen Hsien,
Hualien County, Taiwan
Tel: 038 266779-80 Fax: 038 267776

United States Branch Office: Hall of Still Thoughts,
206 E. Palm Ave., Monrovia, CA 91016
Tel: 818 305-1188 Fax: 818 305-1185

You may address the author c/o the Publisher,

Blue Dolphin Publishing, Inc.
P.O. Box 1920, Nevada City, CA 95959
Tel: 916 265-6925 Fax: 916 265-0787